D1475336

ISRAEL AND PALESTINE

ISRAEL
AND
PALESTINE

Assault on the Law
of Nations

· · · · ·

Julius Stone

THE JOHNS HOPKINS UNIVERSITY PRESS
Baltimore and London

The Johns Hopkins University Press
Baltimore, Maryland 21218
The Johns Hopkins Press Ltd., London

Originally published, 1981
Second printing, 1982

Library of Congress Cataloging in Publication Data

Stone, Julius, 1907-
Israel and Palestine.

Includes bibliographical references and index.
1. Palestine—International status.
2. Israel—International status.
3. United Nations—Israel. I. Title
JX4084.I8S76   341.2'9'095694   80-8875
ISBN 0-8018-2535-0

To our daughter

ELEANOR FRANCES SEBEL

M.B., B.S., M.R.A.N.Z.C.P.

in tribute to her own high
dedications

Contents

· · · · ·

PREFACE AND ACKNOWLEDGMENTS   xi

LIST OF ABBREVIATIONS   xvi

INTRODUCTION   1

1. JEWISH AND ARAB SELF-DETERMINATION RIGHTS: THE
TIME-FRAME   9

Parallel Liberations: "Arab Asia" and Jewish Palestine   9

The Kingdom of Transjordan (Jordan) as a Palestinian Arab State   22

Displaced Palestinian Arabs and Jews Displaced from Arab
Countries: Principles of Redress   25

2. GENERAL ASSEMBLY RESOLUTIONS AND INTERNATIONAL
LAW   27

Resolutions as Lawmaking?   27

Standing of Resolutions: Simplistic Assumptions   29

Standing of Resolutions: Actual Legal Complexities   32

Taints in General Assembly Process as Lawmaking   33

Legal Perversions in General Assembly Resolution 3236   41

3. TERRITORIAL RIGHTS IN PALESTINE UNDER INTERNATIONAL
LAW   45

Israel's Rights from Lawful Self-Defense   45

Aggression by Attacks by Armed Bands   48

Ex iniuria non oritur ius and Territory   51

Contents

Arab States' Resistance to *ex iniuria non oritur ius*   53

Observations on Certain Methods of Argument   56

4. ABORTIVE PARTITION PROPOSALS   59

Legal Standing and Effect of Resolution 181(II)   59

Abortion by Arab Rejection and Aggression   63

5. INTERNATIONAL LAW AND ISRAEL-ARAB RELATIONS SINCE
1948   67

The "Right of Return"   67

Self-Determination Principle   69

Is Self-Determination Prescribed by International Law?   72

Intertemporal Law and Self-Determination   74

6. GENERAL ASSEMBLY: DISMANTLER OF SOVEREIGNTIES?   76

Selective Self-Determination as Pretext   76

Is Force Lawful against Sovereign States in Self-Determination
Struggles?   80

Force and Self-Determination: Context   81

The 1974 Definition of Aggression: Peoples and States as Agents
and Targets   86

The 1974 Definition: Defeat of Proposals to Legalize Force   87

The 1974 Definition: Limits on Self-Determination Rights   91

Problematics of Self-Determination   93

7. SOVEREIGNTY IN JERUSALEM: THE INTERNATIONAL
CONCERN   98

Corpus Separatum Claims against Jerusalem   98

Legal Evaluation of Claims   101

Holy Places: The Functional Concern   108

Post-1967 Resolutions and "The Status of Jerusalem"   110

Bases of Sovereignty under International Law   115

8. CONCLUSIONS: ASSAULT ON ISRAEL AND INTERNATIONAL
LAW   124

APPENDIXES:

MAPS   135

DOCUMENTS   145

DISCOURSE 1. Limited Bearing on International Law Issues of the *Elon
Moreh* Case   167

DISCOURSE 2. Jewish Settlements in Judea and Samaria (the West
Bank) and Geneva Convention, IV, Article 49(6) Relative to the
Protection of Civilian Persons in Time of War   177

NOTES   183

INDEX   211

Preface and Acknowledgments

· · · · ·

After three decades of tension and hostility between Egypt and other Arab states, and the State of Israel, the Treaty of Peace between the State of Israel and the Arab Republic of Egypt of March 26, 1979, against the background of the Framework for Peace in the Middle East agreed at Camp David of September 17, 1978, is an unmistakable milestone. That the further journey forward is slow and painful, and the full attainment of its goal still in doubt, are realities no less apparent. Those instruments are still affected by ambiguities, for example, on the meaning of "autonomy" for the Palestinians of the West Bank (Judea and Samaria) and Gaza, and as to the final disposition of territorial sovereignty in those areas. It was to be expected, therefore, that such issues would present obstacles on the road, even if the governments seeking to travel it were not each of them afflicted by uncertainties as to its political and economic power bases at home, and as to the impact of traumatic changes in the international environment, like recent events in Iran and Afghanistan.

Sometimes, as with the paper waved by Neville Chamberlain after Munich, ambiguity of an instrument is a trap set by guile, or a timorous betrayal for the unwary. Sometimes, though more rarely, ambiguity is a mark of limited imagination and limited skill in negotiators. Sometimes, however, ambiguity is not thus dysfunctional to the negotiatory and pacificatory process. For, on issues where the parties' positions are beset by passionate commitments, or by dire threats to their very existence as states, ambiguity—whether by indeterminacy or double-speaking or self-contradiction or even mere silence—may be a way of building as yet unresolvable conflicts into a genuine overall plan of rapprochement.

In this kind of situation ambiguity serves the critical purpose of providing, for parties deeply at variance on basic issues, a framework that can accommodate at present the specific matters on which they can agree, as well as (for the future) the movement of their positions from time to time on the critical matters on which they now differ. Ambiguity of this kind is dynamic. It moves in time between the poles of rapprochement and estrangement, of love and hate. If flux of time with its changing context and circumstance produces specific rapprochements on specific matters within the range of variance, the ambiguity moves the parties near to poles of love, binding them increasingly in a common meaning. If, conversely, the shift in time is toward estrangement, the ambiguity (verbal shell of concealed conflict that it is) presents to each side an armory of weapons for political warfare. The more the ambiguities, the greater the issues on which they bear, the more intensely will their use in political warfare exacerbate the conflict, moving the ambiguity to the pole of hate. It is, above all, this dynamic of the function of ambiguity that makes the term "peace process," rather than peace settlement, appropriate for the relations of Egypt and Israel in the present stage after the Treaty of Peace of March 26, 1979.

This volume is not directed to speculating about the chances of final success in the Arab-Israel peace process, much less to recommending what course it must take if it is to succeed. The design of this volume is the more modest one of establishing the matrix of international law, as hitherto understood, within which and from which adjustment by negotiation must necessarily proceed. I am aware that many people are skeptical, or even cynical about the role of law and lawyers in the settlement of conflicts, both within states, and especially between states. Yet even then these perspectives cannot be dispensed with. Without them we cannot distinguish between issues that are settled at a particular stage and issues that still have to be settled, between areas where the parties may move with impunity and confidence, and areas that demand the utmost caution and constant testing, as it were, in an endless minefield. There is also the positive side to this. For the parties concerned may have powerful reasons for rapprochement, as Egypt and Israel seem to have in the present constellations of power in the Middle East. In such circumstances, careful discrimination between areas of clear ground, where sacrifices of clearly vested legal rights are not being demanded, and hazardous areas where such sacrifices are demanded calling for a degree of accommodation or reciprocation, may provide some essential guideposts in the process towards peace. The matrix of law is thus important even where the legal issues at stake are simple and trivial, and not enmeshed in a web of pseudolegalities spun by the industry of political warfare. This work will show, however, that when the web is brushed away, the issues are complex and momentous, not merely for the parties, but for the whole international legal order.

No one writing in this area can now fail to be indebted to the massive three-volume collection of official documents and other source material, under the title *The Arab-Israel Conflict* (1974), edited by John Norton Moore, sponsored by the American Society of International Law, and published by Princeton University Press. I am particularly indebted for the convenience of the documentary collection in the 1196 pages of the third volume; but the first two volumes, with their balance and comprehensiveness of materials, have also been of great service. I am also indebted to Martin Gilbert, the author of *The Arab-Israel Conflict: Its History in Maps,* second impression, 1975, and to the publishers Weidenfeld and Nicolson, for kind permission to reproduce a number of the maps in that work which appear on pp. 136-43 hereafter.

As with many previous books, I continue to be indebted to my wife, Reca Stone, L.D.S., B.Sc., and to my research assistant, Zena Sachs, LL.B., for inexhaustible patience and enthusiasm in the process of editing and converting early drafts of complicated and obscure manuscript into the form in which it is here presented.

ISRAEL AND PALESTINE

List of Abbreviations

· · · · ·

Am. J. Int. L.	American Journal of International Law
B. Y. B. Int. L.	British Year Book of International Law
E.S. (with capital roman numeral)	Emergency Session
G.A.O.R.	General Assembly Official Records
García-Mora, *Responsibility*	M. R. García-Mora, *International Responsibility for Hostile Acts of Private Persons against Foreign States* (1962)
Geo. Wash. Univ. L. R.	George Washington University Law Review
Hassouna, *The League of Arab States*	H. A. Hassouna, *The League of Arab States and Regional Disputes: A Study of Middle East Conflicts* (1975)
H.C.D.	House of Commons Debates
I.C.J.	International Court of Justice
Norton Moore (with volume number)	J. Norton Moore (ed.), *The Arab-Israel Conflict* (1974), 3 vols.
Oppenheim-Lauterpacht (with date and edition)	L. Oppenheim, *International Law* (ed. H. Lauterpacht)
Origins	See Introduction, at n.4.
Parkes, *Whose Land?*	James Parkes, *Whose Land? A History of the Peoples of Palestine* (rev. ed. 1970, based on his *A History of Palestine from 135 A.D. to Modern Times* [1949])
Peel Commission Rept.	Report of the Royal Commission, June 22, 1937, G. B. Parliamentary Paper C.M.D. 5479.
Pfaff or Pfaff, *Jerusalem* . . .	R. H. Pfaff, *Jerusalem: Keystone of an Arab-Israel Settlement* (1969)
P.M.C.	Permanent Mandates Commission
Resolutions	See Introduction, at n.4.
Schreuer, "Recommendations"	C. Schreuer, "Recommendations and the Traditional Sources of International Law (1977) 20 *German Yearbook of International Law*, 103-18
S.C.O.R.	Security Law Council Official Records
Self-Determination	See Introduction, at n.4.
Stone, *Legal Controls*	Julius Stone, *Legal Controls of International Conflict* (1954, repr. with Supplement 1959)
U.N. Doc. (with number)	United Nations Document
U.N.G.A.O.R.	United Nations General Assembly Official Records

Introduction

. . . . .

Almost a half-century ago the present writer published his first works on important aspects of the world's first international security organization, the League of Nations.[1] He remains still, more than four decades and a score of books later, fascinated both by the persistence of the central core of international doctrine, and by the kaleidoscopic hues and shapes that its surface texture presents to the first glance of successive generations.

No age has seen more dramatic contrasts between the deep core of international law—in the arcana of state sovereignty for which peoples have for centuries sought in vain a less perilous substitute—and its surface texture, than that since World War II. This generation has a security organization whose charter promises riddance from the scourge of war, but in which continuance of that scourge is perforce assured by the Great Power veto, and various "escapes and evasions"[2] expressed or implicit in the same instrument, not to speak of the innate logic of national control of nuclear weaponry. It has a Security Council that is ostensibly endowed with ample power to keep or restore world peace, but that, except in rare circumstances, cannot use these powers effectively for any but peripheral or parochial conflicts. The General Assembly, at the behest of the Western powers, in 1950 assumed a nonmagisterial peace-keeping role within the framework of the so-called "Uniting for Peace Resolutions"; but operations within this frame can usually be described as "dividing for war" rather than "uniting for peace." The merely hortatory nonmagisterial role of the General Assembly for the support of principles of international law and cooperation under the charter has been steadily transformed into an arena of political warfare in which the principles of international law are travestied, or rather beaten into the shape of weapons, weapons of conflict rather than norms for judgment.

These paradoxes, and many by-products from them, are the combined result of the bipolar power system, underpinned by ideological rift and nuclear armaments, and, within this frame, the decolonization process. This process has almost tripled since the 1950s the number of United

Nations members who each enjoy one vote in the General Assembly, many of them minuscule and of dubious viability. This increase in numbers now produces an almost automatic majority against the Western-type political democracies on any matter in which the "Group of 77" (now mounting to 110) identify a common concern or a common demand against these states. This, of course, turns inside out the position of the 1940s and 1950s, in which, in a restricted membership, American economic and military aid, and hemispheric loyalties of the Latin American states could usually marshal majorities against the Soviet bloc. This formidable shift in the balance of power within that body, however, does not advance the aspiration to make it into a forum of international law and cooperation. The reality of its activities is still embedded in the arcana of sovereignty; *plus ça change, plus c'est la même chose.*

In 1958,[3] when U.N. membership had moved to eighty-two, this writer observed that the thirty-five members of the Afro-Asian and Soviet blocs were already in a position to stop any General Assembly decision favoring a Western state, and that on some matters—for instance economic—on which Latin American states might align with those blocs, they could already marshal fifty-five votes—enough to carry any resolution by a two-thirds majority. He pointed out that the one-state-one-vote principle regardless of population size, contribution, responsibility, or form of government laid no basis for any claim that such a General Assembly was an expression either of democracy on the international plane or of "the conscience of mankind." The continuing story of the General Assembly project for a "New World Economic Order" fits well into this foreshadowing.

Insofar as some redistribution of the world's resources may be regarded as properly on the international agendum, the fact that it was thus opened to discussion is salutary. At the point, however, when the majorities that placed it there began to seek by the same majorities to usurp for the General Assembly magisterial powers over members that the charter very deliberately withheld, we entered a more open and dangerous phase of still persistent *Realpolitik,* only slightly masked by pseudolegality.

Membership of the United Nations has almost doubled since 1958, to the present 150, the increase consisting of states for the most part similarly aligned with the Afro-Asian and Soviet blocs. And the consequences have been aggravated to an extent few recognize even in the chancelleries, by the dual impact of the use of oil boycotts and oil pricing as a political weapon by the Organization of Arab Petroleum Exporting Countries (OAPEC). On the one hand, this has produced a new vulnerability of Western industrialized states to illegal demands of all kinds, weakening the resistance of these states to the pressures from overwhelming majorities in the General Assembly. On the other hand, it has pushed the Third World states, whose community of interests with the Arab oil-producing states is in itself a rather limited one, into an abject dependence on the OAPEC states, which virtually commands the voting behavior of the former on most important issues.

This hitherto skillful use of oil as a political weapon, indeed, may be thought to challenge the present writer's view in *Aggression and World Order* (1958 at 164-65). The view there ventured was:

> Clearly the Western Powers would not, in the long run, continue to assist in strengthening the authority of a General Assembly which might become a protective shield for predatory and imperialist designs against them, and an execution chamber for any State that tried to defend itself against these designs. And it is in part these dangers which have led the present Writer repeatedly to stress the importance of remembering that the General Assembly has no *legal* power of *binding* Members by resolutions as to which State is an aggressor, nor, indeed, as to what should be done by any Member in a crisis. But even the power of the General Assembly based on its claim to represent the conscience of mankind, and its promotion of voluntary action by Members, could also become such a protective shield, if through a regular stacking of votes regardless of the merits it committed a *détournement* of the moral authority of that body.

This change in the political importance of the General Assembly is being pressed at present toward an even more arresting paradox. This is that after the undoubted legal magisterial powers of the Security Council have faded before the practice of bipolarity, the veto, and the nuclear arms race, there is an accelerating drive in certain quarters to promote such powers on the General Assembly. That events were tending in this direction was one of the conclusions of this writer's examination of the definition of aggression adopted by the General Assembly in 1974. Observing there that "the General Assembly is rapidly becoming a committee to execute the will of the Soviet and Arab oil-producing nations, manipulating the numerically overwhelming votes of African and Asian States," we commented:

> How long will the target States permit themselves to be led, one by one, issue by issue, step by step, like sheep to the slaughter?
>
> No doubt, the submissiveness of Western States since 1973 has been mostly due to the brooding threat of renewal of the economic coercion of the oil boycott—a kind and degree of coercion which is certainly a candidate for the title of "economic aggression." In part, however, it was also due to the notion that even such extreme economic coercion is free of legal restraints applicable to strictly military coercion, and is somehow also immune from legitimate defensive action of the victims. The dangers threatened by this chaotic state of affairs may now have arrived. Intransigent and irresponsible majorities in the General Assembly can now, by placing spurious self-serving interpretations on the ambiguities and silences of the Consensus Definition, use it as a political weapon against whichever are the target States for the time being. This would increase enormously "the clout" of that body's *de facto* usurpation of magisterial power. The dangers to the Organisation itself are almost as great as those to target States. The Great Power veto in the Security Council was based on

recognition that the choice was not between an international security organisation with the veto and one without the veto, but between an international security organisation with a veto and no international security organisation at all. The general *lack* of authority of the General Assembly (with a few express exceptions of marginal importance to international security) to take decisions legally binding on members, *was a corollary of this same principle for a body where voting goes by simple majority or even two-thirds majority.*

Insofar as the General Assembly now seeks to arrogate such magisterial authority to itself, it imperils also its true moral and hortatory role in international security matters. As it becomes a mere weapon in one side's political armoury, the effect is to consolidate rather than resolve hostile alignments, to harden rather than temper negotiating positions, and deprive States subject to its pressures of any but military alternatives. Even in terms of the need to avoid military confrontations threatened States may conclude that until these patterns disperse, the only practical step may be a collective withdrawal, not only of budgetary contributions, but of their continued participation. They will certainly recognise, sooner rather than later, that their continued participation is an important source of the legitimacy sought by the manipulating blocs. Such a withdrawal, even if it did not cripple the Organisation by budgetary emasculation, would leave it as a rather empty shell—the fruits of a Pyrrhic victory in the hands of the Third World.

That watershed between the lawful magisterial power of the Security Council, and the usurped magisterial power of a manipulated General Assembly, has not perhaps yet been passed. To pass it would involve a virtual "take-over," a gross dismantling and reconstruction in favor of certain particular states, of the existing international legal order. It can be expected that such a massive operation would be mounted with a degree of circumspection, setting precedents and enouncing precepts of ambiguous import at the time, the meanings of which can be swung by the successive interpretations by automatic majorities against the existing legal order. The present writer exposed what appeared to be this clear design in a major area, in his study (*Conflict Through Consensus* [1977]) of the origins and meaning of the 1974 Definition of Aggression; and further evidence will be offered in the present work. It is to be expected also that the lead-in to such an enterprise would proceed by selecting particular targets that seem specially vulnerable. A practice allowed to be thus established could then serve to base the wider attack on a more openly bloc-aligned basis.

It is remarkable, to say the least, that the further Arab aggression of 1973, which was in law an aggravation of the chronic delinquency of Arab states under the charter, was used as a basis for launching the present assault through the General Assembly on the legal rights of Israel under international law. It would be a very strangely naive, or recklessly biased lawyer, indeed, who would think that a mere repetition of unsuccessful aggression is a reason for stripping the victim state of its rights under international law. It would be nearer to the truth to say that the decisive new factor was the emergence of the full-scale political use of the oil weapon as a part of the 1973 aggression, and that international law, no less than Israel, is its victim. And the present work will, indeed, have to examine a whole series of attempts to rewrite those parts of international law that endow Israel with her undoubted legal rights, and to apply this ad hoc revision retrospectively to the main matters at issue between that state and the rejectionist Arab states. The main materials and process for this operation are accumulations of resolutions in the General Assembly, claims that they are lawmaking, and the diversion of the resources of the United Nations, through committees of that body, to the tasks of eroding the rights of the selected target.

The extraordinary campaign against the State of Israel in the General Assembly since the oil weapon was drawn from its scabbard in 1973 thus involves subversion both of basic international law principles, and of rights and obligations vested in states under them. It has also entailed rather grotesque reversals of the United Nations' own positions of the preceding quarter-century, as part of a wide and illicit rewriting of history. Considered in the context above sketched, this campaign is a kind of pilot operation in a remarkable venture in the *détournement de pouvoir*—an assault with covert as well as overt elements, on the international legal order. It would follow that what is at stake are not only the range of state interests that lie within the lawful concern of the organs of the United Nations, but all interests of states that the General Assembly can by the *ipse dixit* of automatic majorities reach out to control, truncate, or destroy.

The General Assembly's Committee on the Exercise of the Inalienable Rights of the Palestinian People, appointed by Resolution 32/408 of December 2, 1977, has now sponsored and issued a series of "studies" that clearly display this design. The studies prepared by the special unit on Palestinian Rights for and under the guidance of the committee include the following: *The Origins and Evolution of the Palestine Problem* (1978), 2 parts (ST/SG/Ser F/1), is "prepared for" or "under the guidance of" the committee, by "the Special Unit on Palestinian Rights"; *The Right of Return of the Palestinian People* (ST/SG/Ser F/2, 1979) is "prepared for" the committee "in keeping with its guidance"; *The Right to Self-Determination of the Palestinian People* (ST/SG/Ser F/3, 1979) is "prepared for and under the guidance" of the committee. These were followed, also in 1979, by *An International Law Analysis of the Major United Nations Resolutions Concerning the Palestine Question* (ST/SG/Ser F/4) by W. Thomas Mallison and Sally B. Mallison.[4]

The last-mentioned of these "studies" rehearses much that is in its predecessors and overlaps them, and is apparently a kind of coping stone of the series for the time being. The committee has here disclosed the names of the authors, and has also felt it necessary to caution that "the views expressed are those of the authors." The reason for such a caveat in this case, as distinct from the anonymous papers, is not clear. Yet it is very clear that such a caveat cannot disengage the responsibility of the United Nations from any work commissioned and published under its auspices. It is, of course, a proper function of the organization to circulate the partisan positions of member states on contentious matters. It seems, however, highly improper for it to commission, publish, and disseminate, as views of the organization itself, partisan theorizing in support of one side in the contentions among its members.

The appearance at this stage from the General Assembly's Committee on the Inalienable Rights of the Palestinian People, of the above series of studies, catalyzed an interaction between two major interests of the present author, and this book is in a sense a result of this interaction. In one perspective it can be seen as a particular case study in the sociology of contemporary international law. In another it can be seen as a case study of the threatened impact of changes in the constitution and power balance within international organs on the legal rights of a particular state. For both perspectives the above U.N. publications afford examples of what is being done to international law in the theater of the General Assembly. For this reason, rather than because of any basic juridical value in themselves, these publications will often be referred to in the following chapters.

The present writer's concern with the sociology of international law—to the relation of its socioeconomic, political, and psychological substructure to its surface manifestations, is of long standing. It goes back to his Master of Laws thesis about "The Doctrine of Sovereignty and the League of Nations" at the University of Leeds in 1930, and has continued through books on *Legal Controls of International Conflict* (1954, repr. 1958); on *Problems Confronting Sociological Inquiries Concerning International Law* (1956), *Hague Recueil,* vol. 89, pp. 61-180; on *Aggression and World Order* (1958); on *The International Court and World Crisis* (1962), *International Conciliation,* no. 536; *Towards a Feasible International Criminal Court* (1970) especially pp. 315-41; *Conflict through Consensus* (1977), and other writings. He has also contributed much in the last decade to the literature on particular legal aspects of the Arab-Israel conflict.[5]

A mere sampling of some of the issues canvassed in this book will suffice as illustrations for this introduction. What is the standing of General Assembly resolutions as sources of international law concerning matters other than those limited cases in which the charter makes them binding? When, if ever, can they be said to express international law binding on states? When, indeed, is weight to be given even to their assertions of fact? What is the bearing, even on any nonlegal persuasive effect of these resolutions, of the fact that they are adopted by reason of the use by a few members of extreme coercion on others (for example, the duress of the oil weapon)? Is the General Assembly to be given the competence to pass sentence of truncation or even of extinction on states, including members of the United Nations? Is the "sovereign equality" of members under

Article 2 to be made subject to even lesser whims and predations of automatic majorities in the General Assembly? Is the legal establishment of a state on the basis of the self-determination principle, and its admission as a peace-loving, law-abiding state to membership in the United Nations to be subject forever after to such whims and predations of majorities from time to time? Has the adoption of the charter, as most international lawyers believe, reinforced the cardinal principle *ex iniuria non oritur ius* in its application to aggressor states, or has it (as the Arab states now claim) dispensed aggressor states from this principle by entitling them to be restored automatically to the *status quo ante bellum* whenever their aggression is defeated? Is the "self-determination principle" a principle of present international law, or is it still but an important policy or guideline? What, in any case, are the precise content and limits of this principle? What is its intertemporal effect when one application of it is challenged half-a-century later, by another people that has only at that later time recognized itself as a rival claimant? What are the wider implications of any rule adopted as to this matter of intertemporality, that is, the operation of legal principles in the stream of time? Does international law authorize the use of force by some members against others, on the mere allegation that they are vindicating that later claimant's self-determination?

These are only some of the general issues of contemporary international law involved in the positions now taken by a manipulated General Assembly on the Arab-Israel conflict. They are additional, of course, to the specific legal problems involved in the conflict concerning Palestine. These arise from legal events now spread according to one's preferred perspective over the 70 years since the Balfour Declaration, or the 1100 years since the Arab conquest of Palestine, or the 2900 years since the Kingdom of David. Of necessity, this work will have to range mainly over the last 70 years. It will be seen that some events from the early part of that period, like the terms of the mandate for Palestine, remain of great importance even for the problems of today.

In this more particular aspect of the subject, the present work will of course examine the arguments and conclusions of the recent U.N. Secretariat "studies" mentioned above. It will in particular examine their central theses: (1) that the problematic Resolution of November 29, 1947 (Resol. 181[II] on the future government of Palestine [often termed "the Partition Resolution"]) is still legally binding on Israel, requiring her to accept or even facilitate the establishment of an additional Arab state (in addition to Israel and Jordan) within the borders of Mandated Palestine west of the Jordan (Cisjordan); and that (2) this same Partition Resolution also imposes legal obligations on all member states of the United Nations to ensure that such a third state, additional to Israel and Jordan, is established; (3) that repeated recitals in General Assembly resolutions, from Resolution 194(III) to Resolution 3236(XXIX) of Nov. 12, 1974, and others, establish an international law "right of return" of Palestinian refugees; (4) that repeated references in General Assembly resolutions after 1970 constitute a legal determination of the right of self-determination of Palestinian Arabs and that the General Assembly is empowered to remodel the boundaries of Israel accordingly.

The legal merits of these arguments depend not only on internal coherence but also on the legal soundness of the premises from which the authors have chosen to begin. This work will examine them in both these aspects, beginning immediately with two main premises from which they proceed: first, the conflict of claims to self-determination between the Jewish and Arab peoples; second, the standing and force in international law of General Assembly resolutions.

The setting of these interesting (perhaps *too* interesting) legal problems of the current Middle East conflict into the more general problems of contemporary international law on which they finally rest, has made the enterprise here undertaken worthwhile for the author. He ventures to hope that it will likewise seem so to the reader.

1

• • • • •

Jewish and Arab
Self-Determination Rights: The
Time-Frame

PARALLEL LIBERATIONS: "ARAB ASIA" AND JEWISH PALESTINE

The Historical Context. A basic assumption underlying a whole series of United Nations "studies" issuing from the Unit on Palestinian Rights is that the peoples whose competing self-determinations are to be reconciled consist of the Jewish people on the one hand, and the Palestinian Arabs on the other. This assumption is in turn linked with an assumption that the relevant date for applying the self-determination principle in the Middle East is 1947, the date of the Partition Resolution; unless, indeed, it be 1974, when the series of General Assembly recitals about the rights of the Palestinians was transformed in Resolution 3236 of November 22, 1974, into a recital that "the Palestinian people is entitled to self-determination in accordance with the Charter of the United Nations."[1]

Such assumptions fly in the face of the history of the struggle concerning Palestine. The critical importance of the decades before 1947 is testified to not only by the history of the periods before and during the League of Nations mandate over Palestine, the documents of several United Kingdom commissions of enquiry, and reports of the Permanent Mandates Commission of the League of Nations. Even the anonymous authors of *Origins,* the first title in this very series, found it necessary to devote its entire first part (pp. 1-108) to the diplomatic, political, and military history of the struggle of Jews and Arabs over Palestine for three decades before 1947. The Palestine mandate contained safeguards for civil and religious rights of the Arab inhabitants, but studiously avoided referring to their political rights or political standing. This omission seems to confirm what in any

9

case is clear from the post-World War I historical context, that the rival claimants in the distribution of ex-Turkish lands were, at that time, only Jewish nationalism on the one hand and Arab nationalism (with, of course, further dynastic distributions within the Arab allotment) on the other. And the main conclusion of the pamphlet *Self-Determination* in this series is that no such right of Palestinians as a separate people came into recognition "during three decades" of the League mandate, or "the first two decades" of the United Nations.[2]

The importance of this point is that the facts relevant to a correct application of the self-determination doctrine go back to 1917. For whether this doctrine is already a doctrine of international law *stricto sensu,* or (as many international lawyers would still say) a precept of politics or policy, or of justice, to be considered where appropriate, it is clear that its application is predicated on certain findings of fact. One of these is the finding that at the relevant time the claimant group constitutes a people or nation with a common endowment of distinctive language or ethnic origin or history and tradition, and the like, distinctive from others among whom it lives, associated with a particular territory, and lacking an independent territorial home in which it may live according to its lights.

The name Palestine had not for centuries (perhaps millennia) before 1917 referred to a defined political, demographic, cultural, or territorial entity. In the immediately preceding centuries it was a part of the Ottoman Empire designated as "Southern Syria" and governed from Damascus. In 1917, its northern part, from Safed almost to Jerusalem, was part of the Vilayet of Beirut and the whole of it was claimed to be part of Syria. The Arabs living there were not regarded by themselves or others as "Palestinians" or in any major respect as different from their brethren in Syria and Lebanon. This "Syrian" rather than "Palestinian" identification of Arabs living in Palestine underlay the request of the General Syrian Congress on July 2, 1919, "that there should be no separation of the southern part of Syria known as Palestine, nor of the littoral Western Zone, which includes Lebanon, from the Syrian country."[3] A main argument thus made by Arabs in post-World War I negotiations was not that "Palestinians" would resent the loss of Palestinian identity by the establishment of the Jewish national home in Palestine, but rather that they would resent severance of their connection with their fellow Syrians.

That this is correct, so that "Palestine" had no special geographical or political role, and "Palestinians" no specific sociopolitical or cultural identity within the area, during twelve hundred years following the Arab conquest in the seventh century, is clear also from recent historical scholarship. The Princeton historian Professor B. Lewis, in his article "Palestine: On the History and Geography of a Name" in the *International History Review* (vol. 2, no. 1, pp. 1-12, Jan., 1980), made a comprehensive review of the whole matter, from which the following points emerge. First, the term used for the area after its settlement by Jews following the exodus from Egypt was "Eretz Israel," and the two kingdoms that emerged within it after the death of Solomon were called "Israel" and "Judah" (p. 1). Second, the Emperor Hadrian and the Roman invaders attempted to substitute "Palestine" for these names, and "Aelia Capitolina" for Jerusalem, in a calculated design to "stamp out . . . Jewish nationhood and statehood" and "to obliterate . . . historic Jewish identity" (p. 2). Third, after the Arab conquest of the area in the seventh century, Palestine (Filastin) was treated merely as a part of "Syria" (the land of Sham), this being one of a number of major "social, cultural and to some extent even economic and political entities with a continuing identity." Such identities were attributed, along with Syria, to Egypt, Jazira (Mesopotamia), Iraq, Arabia, and Yemen, but not to any area designated as Palestine (pp. 4-5). Fourth, for the Crusaders the area was "the Holy land," or "the Kingdom of Jerusalem," not "Palestine." Fifth, after the Islamic reconquest from the Crusaders, the term "Palestine" ("Filastin") disappeared even as a mere subdistrict of Syria (Sham), (p. 5). Subdistricts under Damascus were identified by reference rather to capital towns such as Gaza, Lydda, Qaqun, Jerusalem, Hebron, and Nablus (p. 5). This is an ironic commentary on recent claims about the centrality for Islam of Palestine and Jerusalem. Sixth, Ottoman rule, after the Ottoman conquest of 1516-17, underscored still further this absence of any distinct sociocultural or political identity of Palestine in Arab and Islamic thought. Not only were the subdistricts ("Sanjaks") still identified merely by townships, but the north of the country was separated off from the rest of it as part of the Vilayet of Damascus, though both sectors remained merely a part of Syria.

By this time, Professor Lewis aptly notes, the very name "Palestine," which for Moslems "had never meant more than an administrative subdistrict . . . had been forgotten even in that limited sense" (p. 6).

Indeed, eventually, Palestine Liberation Organization (P.L.O.) leaders have frankly disavowed distinct Palestinian identity. On March 3, 1977, for example, the head of the P.L.O. Military Operations Department, Zuhair Muhsin, told the Netherlands paper *Trouw* that

there are no differences between Jordanians, Palestinians, Syrians and Lebanese. . . . We are one people. Only for political reasons do we carefully underline our Palestinian identity. For it is of national interest for the Arabs to encourage the existence of the Palestinians against Zionism. Yes, the existence of a separate Palestinian identity is there only for tactical reasons. The establishment of a Palestinian state is a new expedient to continue the fight against Zionism and for Arab unity.[4]

In the light of these facts, the notion that the Arabs living in Palestine regarded themselves in 1917, at the time when Woodrow Wilson's seminal self-determination principle emerged,[5] as a Palestinian Arab people in the sense required by the self-determination principle (or, as I may sometimes here call it, "the liberation of peoples principle" or "the liberation principle") is thus a figment of unhistorical imagination. To respect the historical facts is, therefore, not to impugn the liberation principle; it merely points out that the principle must be applied at the appropriate time to the facts of group life as they truly exist.[6] These historical facts continue to reverberate today in Arab state circles. President Assad of Syria in 1974 stated that "Palestine is a basic part of Southern Syria" (*New York Times,* March 9, 1974). On this, on November 17, 1978, Yassir Arafat commented that Palestine is southern Syria and Syria is northern Palestine (*Voice of Palestine,* November 18, 1978).

The point in time at which it can be confidently argued that a distinctively Palestinian national self-recognition emerged on the scene—if at all—would be around the adoption of the Palestinian National Charter (or Covenant), in 1966 (revised in 1968).[7] And that covenant itself testified with striking clarity that the belatedness of this self-recognition as Palestinians raised grave obstacles to "national" ambitions at so late a stage. For this was nearly half a century after the former Turkish empire had been allocated between the Jewish and Arab liberation claimants, of the latter of which the Palestinians were a part, but not a distinctive part at that time.

The Palestine National Covenant sought to overcome these obstacles by two devices. It claimed that Palestinians were a part of "the Arab nation" to which that allocation was made, and which by 1966 had come to control a dozen new independent states in the Middle East (articles 14-15). But it also insisted in 1966 that Palestinians were a separate people entitled to the whole of Palestine as an indivisible territorial unit for its homeland (articles 1-5). This still left the problem how, assuming the emergence of a distinctive Palestinian people in the 1960s, the covenant could control the application of the "self-determination" or "liberation" principle in 1917. To meet this problem an ingenious fiction was adopted by the Palestinian National Covenant through declaring Palestinian nationhood to have existed in 1917. To this end the Covenant (articles 6, 20, 22-23) provided that only Jews who had "normally resided" in Palestine before the Balfour Declaration and the mandate for Palestine (the Covenant declared both of these illegal) could qualify for membership in the Palestinian state, and, by clear implication, that all others would be expelled.[8]

It is perhaps understandable that the covenant did not seek to go much further back, for instance to Arab entry into Palestine as conquerors in A.D. 663 or to the Kingdom of David one thousand years before the present era. For these leaps in time would, on any principles basing the claims now made for "the Palestinian people," base a no less irrefragable claim to Palestine for the Jewish people, and fix any Arab pretensions of title with the taint of an unlawful breach by past armed invasion of Jewish rights of self-determination. There is on principle no reason why a half-century of time is any more expendable than a millennium or so. Some would even argue that *qui prior est tempore prior est iure*. The facts to which principles are applied may change as completely in a half-century as in a millennium. If a time past is to be reopened, it is still to be explained why one moment in that past rather than other possible moments imposes itself.

For the purpose of examining the assumptions on which the pamphlets on *Self-Determination* and *Resolutions* proceed, however, 1917 may be here accepted for testing the application of the self-determination or liberation principle to the Jewish and Arab nations. At that time the twelve present Arab states of the Middle East had not come into existence, so that "the Arab Nation" on whose behalf wide-ranging claims were made, was certainly an eligible claimant under that principle. By the same token, however, the Jewish people was also a proper claimant under the liberation principle. Historically, indeed, the Jewish claims began earlier than the Arab. In his famous exchange of March 3-5, 1919, with Felix Frankfurter, the Arab leader Emir Feisal recognized the concurrence of the Jewish and Arab nationalist (we would now say "liberation") movements—"having suffered similar oppressions"—and thanked Chaim Weizmann and other Zionist leaders for being "a greater helper of our [the Arab] cause," and expressed the hope that "the Arabs may soon be in a position to make the Jews some return for their kindness." And as a signal reminder that, among Arabs too, in 1919, there was no distinguishable Palestinian nationhood, Emir Feisal added: "Our two movements complete one another. . . . There is room in *Syria* for us both"[9] (emphasis supplied). Even prior to this, the otherwise much controverted Hussein-McMahon exchange of letters referred constantly to "the Arab Nation" as the single undifferentiated claimant on the Arab side in these basic negotiations.[10] It is interesting to juxtapose with this correct record of history the account by the main author of *Resolutions,* who in no way mentions the Arab people generally, or Emir Feisal, in the 1919 negotiation, but names "the Arabs of Palestine" as a "participant."[11]

The correct historical context was clearly set out in the Agreement of Understanding and Cooperation which had been signed on January 3, 1919, by Emir Feisal, representing Arab national aspirations at the Peace Conference of Versailles, and Dr. Chaim Weizmann, representing the Zionist movement at that time. The agreement's preamble envisaged the closest possible collaboration in the development of "the Arab State and Palestine" as the surest means of "the consummation of their [the Arabs'] national aspirations." And it is obvious also from Article 1, providing for the exchange of "Arab and Jewish accredited agents" between "the Arab State" and "Palestine" that what was envisaged was the allocation of "Palestine" for self-determination of the Jewish nation, and of the rest of the region for that of "the Arab Nation." This is no less clear from articles 2 and 3, the latter calling explicitly for all such measures in Palestine "as will afford the fullest guarantees for carrying into effect the British Government's Declaration of November 2, 1917." That Declaration was, of course, the Balfour Declaration calling for "the establishment in Palestine of a national home for the Jewish people."[12] Emir Feisal was, according to the King-Crane Commission, the leader of "the Arab uprising," and the prospective head of the new "Arab State."[13] The significance of this Feisal-Weizmann agreement receives little attention from the U.N. Secretariat in these pamphlets.[14] That the Ottoman Empire was so vast that a dozen Arab independent states came later to be established out of it only reinforces the main point. This is apart from numerous other Arab states that also fulfill the aspirations of the Arab nation, these states together comprising today more than twenty members included in the Arab League.

It is, then, a historical fact that at that time Jewish and Arab national movements (the latter in this undifferentiated sense) appeared simultaneously as liberation claimants. "Jews" constituted a cluster of scattered people in the Middle East and elsewhere; "Arabs" were similarly scattered over the Middle East and elsewhere. Each people within itself shared cultural and religious traditions and experiences deeply rooted in the Middle East region. The Jewish people claimed one part, Palestine, as its historic home with which it had nearly four millennia of unbroken connection. The Arabs claimed virtually the whole of the territories removed by World War I from Turkish hegemony. These were the two claimant peoples, the Jews and the Arabs, between whom the admittedly unsaintly dispensers of justice after World War I, the Principal Allied and Associated Powers, made the allocations that began the modern history of Palestine.

The myth of the 1966 Palestinian Covenant that "the Palestinian people" was unjustly displaced by the Jewish invasion of Palestine in 1917 is widely disseminated, and unquestioningly and dogmatically espoused in these "studies" from the United Nations Secretariat. Furthermore, it is also necessary to recall, not only the Kingdom of David and the succession of Jewish polities in Palestine down to the Roman conquest and dispersion at the turn of the present era, but also that Jews continued to live in Palestine even after that conquest, and were in 1914 a well-knit population there.[15] Hundreds of thousands of other Jews, driven from the Palestine homeland by successive waves of Roman, Arab, and other conquerors, continued to live on for centuries throughout the Middle East, often under great hardship and oppression. And, of course, millions of others were compelled to move to other parts of the world where, too often, as in pogrom-ridden Russia and Poland, they lived in conditions of tyrannous and humiliating subjection, and under daily threat to their very lives.

That the provision for a Jewish national home in Palestine was an application of the principle of self-determination is manifest from the earliest seminal beginnings of this principle. The Enquiry Commission, established by President Wilson in order to draft a map of the world based on the Fourteen Points, affirmed the right of the Jewish people "that Palestine should become a Jewish State" clearly on this ground. Palestine, the commission said, was "the cradle and home of their vital race," the basis of the Jewish spiritual contribution, and the Jews were the only people whose only home was in Palestine. It would be difficult to provide a more succinct statement of the essence of the self-determination principle.[16] The Permanent Mandates Commission, in 1937, provided perhaps the supplementary point when it observed that the sufferings of Arabs and Jews are not comparable "since vast spaces in the Near East . . . are open to the former whereas the world is increasingly being closed to settlement by the latter."[17]

This connection is eloquently stressed by the report in 1937 of what was perhaps the most balanced Commission on Palestine, the Royal Commission, headed by Lord Peel. The zeal with which the U.N. Secretariat's Palestine unit cites passages from this report that favor its own arguments, fails to reach the following:

While the Jews had thus been dispersed over the world, they had never forgotten Palestine. If Christians have become familiar through the Bible with the physiognomy of the country and its place-names and events that happened more than two thousand years ago, the link which binds the Jews to Palestine and its past history is to them far closer and more intimate. Judaism and its ritual are rooted in those memories. Among countless illustrations it is enough to cite the fact that Jews, wherever they may be, still pray for rain at the season it is needed in Palestine. And the same devotion to the Land of Israel, *Eretz Israel,* the same sense of exile from it, permeates Jewish secular thought. Some of the finest Hebrew poetry written in the Diaspora has been inspired, like the Psalms of the Captivity, by the longing to return to Zion.

Nor has the link been merely spiritual or intellectual. Always or almost always since the fall of the Jewish State, some Jews have been living in Palestine. Under Arab rule there were substantial Jewish communities in the chief towns.[18]

On the other hand, when the Peel Report refers to "national aspiration" of Arabs *in Palestine* it is clear in the relevant context of Chapter 20, paragraph 5, that the reference is not to any such "aspiration" of *Palestinian* Arabs as a separate people, but the general "hope of reviving in a free and united Arab world the traditions of the Arab golden age." But this aspiration was, of course, provided for by the vast territorial allocation to the Arab people (including the Palestinians). It accords with this, and with the present view, that in Chapter 23, paragraph 5, of its report the Peel Commission observed wryly: "There was a time when Arab statesmen were willing to concede little Palestine to the Jews provided the rest of Arab Asia were free. That condition . . . is on the eve of fulfilment now." That was in 1937; the reality of the territorial endowments achieved by the Arab nation, constituting now a dozen Arab States in the Middle East alone, has exceeded all former Arab aspirations.

In other words, in terms of modern ideas of self-determination or liberation of peoples, it is critical to identify the two peoples who were thus claimants at the relevant time when the future of the former Ottoman territories in that Middle East was laid out. For it is fatal to any judgment of justice to misidentify the claimants among whom the distribution is to be made. Fallacy arises from ignoring the historical reality that the establishment of a Jewish national home in Palestine was itself an application of the self-determination principle, parallel both in time and principle to the allocation of the great bulk of Middle East territory, "Arab Asia," as the Peel Commission called it, to the Arab people, including the Arabs in Palestine. This fallacy is aggravated by ignoring also the historical fact that the Arab claimants after World War I embraced Arabs of the whole Middle East area, including Arabs in Palestine, who were then in no sense a distinctive national group. The facile assertion that Israel came into existence on the basis of injustice to a *Palestinian* nation proceeds on gross errors of these kinds. To present, in 1980, a "Palestinian nation" as having been displaced by Israel in Palestine, when no such distinctive entity recognized itself or existed at the time of the allocation between the Jewish and Arab peoples after World War I, is an impermissible game with both history and justice.[19]

The distribution between Arabs and Jews after World War I was certainly implemented in succeeding decades as far as Arab entitlements were concerned. Arab claims to sovereignty received extensive fulfillment in the creation of more than twenty sovereign states following World War II, not only in the Middle East but in Africa as well. Altogether this historical process included the following features.

First, despite all the extraneous Great Power maneuverings, Jewish and Arab claims in the vast area of the former Ottoman Empire came to the forum of liberation together, and not (as is usually implied) by way of Jewish encroachment on an already vested and exclusive Arab domain.

Second, the territorial allocation made to the Arabs (as now seen in about a dozen Arab sovereignties in the Middle East [not to speak of many Arab sovereignties elsewhere]) was more than a hundred times greater in area, and hundreds of times richer in resources than the "Palestine" designated in 1917 for the Jewish national home.

Third, by sucessive steps thereafter, this already tiny allocation to Jewish claims was further encroached upon. Thus, already in 1922, a major part of it (namely, 35,468 out of 46,339 square miles, including the more sparsely populated regions) was cut away to establish the kingdom of Transjordan (now known as the the Hashemite kingdom of Jordan).[20]

With so preponderant an Arab allocation capable, as events since 1973 now show, of threatening the economic existence of most of the rest of the world, it seemed reasonable to expect Arab acquiescence in the minute allotment to the people of Israel as their only national home.

The meaning of these historical facts is that the relevant time context for testing the conformity of Israel and Arab (including the present Palestinian Arab) claims in respect of Palestine to the self-determination or liberation principle, is that of the distribution of the former Turkish domains of the Middle East after World War I. And once this is acknowledged, the basic premise on which all these "studies" proceed, namely, that the issue is one of Israel's encroachment on the right of self-determination of the *Palestinian* Arab nation, is exposed as simply incorrect.

The liberation principle was thus, if I may summarize, applied to rival claims of the Jewish people, and the "Arab Nation" (as the Palestine National Covenant still calls all Arabs) in the period following 1917. It was then applied correctly, moreover, according to the facts of peoplehood as they then existed. It was applied by allocating the overwhelming share of territory and resources of the whole Middle East to the Arab Nation (including Palestinians) as that nation then presented itself. This share was ample enough in later decades to form the territorial basis of a dozen independent Arab states. It was also applied by allocating to the Jewish people, as part of the same settlement, a minute fraction of the area, namely the 46,339 square miles embracing both Cisjordan and Transjordan. And that tiny fraction was then reduced by four-fifths in 1922, to create in Palestine what is now called the State of Jordan, leaving the share of the Jewish people under the liberation principle as 10,871 square miles—or about one two-hundredth of the entire territory distributed.

This distribution in no way impaired any right of self-determination of any other nation. As has been seen, neither at the time of distribution, nor until decades later, did any distinct grouping of Palestinian Arabs come to recognition as a separate nation either by themselves, or by other Arabs. There were Arabs who lived in Palestine for centuries, as there were Arabs who had lived in Syria and Iraq and the Hedjaz and Yemen and elsewhere: all of these were then seen as part of the Arab nation to which the vastly preponderant Arab share was allocated. So, similarly, there were Jews who had lived in all these and other parts of the region for centuries. And many of these, Jews and Arabs alike, were to pay a price for the inheritances gained by their respective nations.

This presentation of historical context contrasts violently with the attempt in the Palestine National Covenant in 1964, now repeated by the authors named and anonymous of these "studies" from the U.N. Secretariat, to present the Palestinian issue as a struggle that began in 1917 between the Jews of the world on the one hand, and the Palestinian Arab Nation on the other, in which the Jews seized the major share. It may be appropriate at this point to reconfirm the correct historical content, as here presented, in the light of more recent doctrine of the International Court of Justice. The essential point is not whether self-determination was a legal right in 1919, but rather that, whatever it was, it was duly applied in parallel to the claims of the Jewish people and the Arab people in the Middle East.

Self-Determination and the International Court. The International Court of Justice in the Namibia Advisory Opinion[21] made clear that the self-determination principle, as this was to be understood in 1971, is continuous from its early expression in Woodrow Wilson's Fourteen Points, the mandates system, and Article 22 of the League Covenant, into its embodiment in the United Nations Charter, preamble and Chapters 11 and 12 on the regime of non-self-governing territories and the trusteeship system. This course of history, said the court, left "little doubt that the ultimate objective of the sacred trust was the self-determination and independence of the peoples concerned" (p. 31). The change brought by later developments was not in the principle of self-determination itself, but in extending its benefits to peoples not formerly under the mandate system, extending the sacred trust concept by Article 73 to embrace other "territories whose peoples have not yet attained a full measure of self-government" (p. 31).

The court's stress on the continuity of the self-determination principle since its application in the World War I settlement, confirms the basic submission of the present section, and indeed of this entire opening chapter. The self-determination principle was applied in that settlement for the benefit of the Jewish people and the Arab people (within which Arabs in Palestine were included). As already seen, this resulted in the territorial allocation of the small area known as Palestine for a Jewish national home, and the overwhelming balance of the territories concerned for the Arab people, which later became a dozen Arab states. That allocation under the self-determination principle was accepted at that time, both informally among the states and peoples concerned, and also through the solemn procedures of the international community and the League of Nations. It was confirmed by the admission of the State of Israel, after it was established, to the United Nations. So the principle of self-determination now being used as a weapon for attacking or even dismantling the State of Israel, is the very principle of which that state is among the earliest historic expressions.

To assert that the self-determination principle must now be applied, as if for the first time, for the benefit of a separate Palestinian Arab Nation that emerged in the 1960s, as if the allocations under that same principle more than half a century before had never occurred, is thus extravagant on its face and contravenes the International Court's stress on the unbroken continuity of the self-determination principle from the World War I settlement, into the period of the United Nations. It would perhaps be somewhat more plausible to argue that the earlier allocations under the self-determination principle should be somehow revised or even canceled to take account of the later appearance of a new claimant under the principle, the Palestinian Arabs, a people "post-natus," as it were, to the original disposition. Such an argument, however, would finally have to rest on some vastly expanded notion of *rebus sic stantibus*. The expansion would indeed have to be so vast as to threaten the stable existence of virtually all states and of the whole international order.

A degree of instability is, of course, unavoidable in the dynamically changeful conditions of the present world. Among the sources of it are the extraordinary tempo of technological development in the field of communications and of weaponry, changes in demand for and availability of various basic resources, the conflict of ideologies and *Weltanschauungen* among more than 150 independent states, unprecedented changes in individual ways of life among their peoples, and (without seeking here to be exhaustive) the substantial implementation of the self-determination principle. This last process, in the course of decolonization, has almost tripled the membership of the United Nations in less than a quarter of a century. Most of these factors have operated beyond the control of any authority, national or international. The creation of so many new states under the self-determination principle, on the other hand, is a factor that arises from policies espoused by states individually and through the United Nations, recognizing that the importance of the principle justifies the resulting instabilities and uncertainties in international relations. One assumption of this recognition is that the instabilities and uncertainties of state life would be transitional, and that once the transition was made, the outcome would be a stabler and more peaceful community of states, resting on a closer correspondence of statehoods and peoplehoods.

To accept the above arguments as justifying the use of the self-determination principle in 1980 to attack the existence of a state that was itself a product of this principle sixty-odd years before, would surely be fatal to the assumption that a modicum of international stability is eventually achievable. A state founded or delineated conformably to the self-determination principle at a given time would be exposed forever thereafter to revision of boundaries or even destruction, at the behest of some later-born competing entity. This would be so, indeed (as in the very case of the Palestinian Arabs) even if the new claimant entities did not come to self-consciousness, or to recognition by others, until generations later.

These grave effects would follow, moreover, even if the entities always made their claims in perfect good faith. They would follow even if third states were not prone to promote or exploit or manipulate such entities for purposes of political power, often quite extraneous to, and sometimes quite subversive of, the principle of self-determination. In the actual world, however, this proneness is a notorious and chronic fact of international life. The consequences for the international community would be correspondingly dire and persistent, like those attributed to the intertwined nineteenth-century phenomenon of irredentism, interventionism, and Balkanization. The P.L.O. makes such threats to orderly international life quite explicit. Its leader, Yassir Arafat, again reaffirmed as recently as February 11, 1980: "The destruction of Israel is the goal of our struggle, and the guidelines of that struggle have remained firm since the establishment of Fatah in 1965." And the Soviet Union and other states seeking to manipulate this situation to their adventitious purposes, but to the frustration of peace, expose to open view the threat of subversion to the rights of integrity and sovereignty of all existing states.

This attempted unsettlement of established, lawful title and boundaries would proceed not only ex post facto by reference to later events, but also by reference to past historical circumstances belonging to periods only speculatively related, if at all, to the modern principle of self-determination. It is not necessary to follow in detail the learned explorations of this kind that had to be made by the International Court in the Western Sahara Advisory Opinion (International Court of Justice Reports, 1975, pp. 12 ff., 29 ff.) to appreciate the indeterminate and indecisive outcomes of that opinion with regard to the clarification of the status of the peoples and territories concerned. The court itself in the *Western Sahara* case (p. 33) was constrained to observe upon the obscurities affecting particular applications of the self-determination principle. In the court's words:

> The validity of the principle of self-determination, defined as the need to pay regard to the freely expressed will of peoples, is not affected by the fact that in certain cases the General Assembly has dispensed with the requirement of consulting the inhabitants of a given territory. Those instances were based either on the consideration that a certain population did not constitute a "people" entitled to self-determination or on the conviction that a consultation was unnecessary in view of special circumstances.[22]

And the court was also at pains to emphasize that despite the measure of discretion in the General Assembly's efforts to "realize" the right of self-determination, its opinion would at least "assist" that body in its "future decisions" so that it could continue its discussions "in the light of the Court's advisory opinion" (pp. 36-37).

The questions presented for determination in the Western Sahara were whether that area was "at the time of colonization by Spain a territory belonging to no one (*res nullius*)"; and (if it were not *res nullius*) "what were the legal ties between this territory and the Kingdom of Morocco and the Mauretanian entity" (p. 14). The request referred to an area to which the principle of self-determination had not yet been applied, and in which, indeed, serious competitive interests of states or peoples had only recently arisen. It was made as a preliminary to the conduct by Spain as administering power of a referendum in the Western Sahara.

In the existing uncertainty concerning the future of the territory, the uncertainties of outcome in that case of the self-determination principle were not, perhaps, of particular concern. Should we, however, expose well-established states, themselves founded originally on solemn and open applications of the self-determination principle in the circumstances of the time, to the hazards of repeated reapplications of that principle by votes of states whose attitudes are necessarily affected by the changes and even vagaries of their national interests? To do so would surely be disastrous. It would convert the arena within which states live and have their being into a veritable minefield, in which the location and timing of each explosion remained ever and profoundly uncertain, and in which the only certainty would be a succession of disasters for an endless series of target states.

It is, indeed, precisely to the avoidance of this danger that the final paragraphs of the section on self-determination of the General Assembly's Resolution on the Principles of International Law Concerning Cooperation and Friendly Relations among States, being Resolution 2625(XXV) (hereafter termed the "Resolution on Friendly Relations"), are directed. That section—after referring to the rights of all peoples to determine without external interference their political status and pursue their development, the general duties of states to promote "realization" of the self-determination principle and to refrain from forcible action depriving peoples of the right thereto, and the right of peoples to seek and receive support *in accordance with the purposes and principles of the Charter*—was careful to spell out in its last two paragraphs the limitations in any case implicit in the words here above italicized:

Nothing in the foregoing paragraphs shall be construed as authorizing or encouraging any action which would dismember or impair, totally or in part, the territorial integrity or political unity of sovereign and independent states conducting themselves in compliance with the principle of equal rights and self-determination of peoples as described above and thus possessed of a government representing the whole people belonging to the territory without distinction as to race, creed or colour.

Every state shall refrain from any action aimed at the partial or total disruption of the national unity and territorial integrity of any other state or country (emphasis supplied). (General Assembly Resolution 2625[XXV].)

Professor Schwebel has drawn attention in a related context[23] to the fact that the "battle of words" surrounding "wars of liberation" in U.N. organs has been inconclusive. "Resultant resolutions," he observes, "when they have gained universal support, are so general that they lend themselves to conflicting interpretations on the critical issues." On the other hand, "resolutions which are clearer" lack sufficient support to be thought to express international law.

The matter is much less complicated on the issue here under review. The issue is whether the unity and territorial integrity of established states, based on the application of the self-determination principle to the facts of international life as they existed at the time of establishment are to be respected. Or whether such established states shall continue thereafter to be subject to endless and repeated attacks on their existence, on the pretext that fact situations of a later time—in the case of Palestine, a half-century later—are thought by some to require a different application of the self-determination principle. It is sufficient for the present purpose to observe that the above-quoted paragraphs forbid either partial or total dismemberment or impairment of states conforming to the self-determination principle, and prohibit states from engaging in "any action aimed at the partial or total disruption of the national unity and territorial integrity of any other State or country." Even if this last prohibition were not as un-qualified as it appears to be, these paragraphs clearly bar repeated attempts to use the self-determination principle to threaten "the national unity and territorial integrity of States" themselves founded in their due time on that very principle. That is precisely the case of the state of Israel.

Professor Schwebel concluded,[24] after analyzing relevant General Assembly resolutions and votes thereon, that "the Friendly Relations resolution may not reasonably be interpreted as endorsing support by way of provision of arms—still less by way of armed support itself—to national liberation movements."[25] In this respect the resolution would be consistent with basic principles both of general international law and of the Charter, and of the above analysis of the concluding paragraphs of the self-determination section of that resolution. We shall later show, in chapter 6, that this view is decisively supported by the clear evidence of contemporary State attitudes in the course of the labors of the 1967 Committee on Defining Aggression, and in the outcomes of its work.

THE KINGDOM OF TRANSJORDAN
(JORDAN) AS A PALESTINIAN ARAB STATE

The cutting away in 1922 of four-fifths of the territory within which the Jewish national home was to be established, in order to create the emirate of Transjordan, which later became the present state of Jordan, is in this context of double significance.[26] On the one hand, as already indicated, it drastically reduced the already tiny allocation to the Jewish people's right of self-determination. But it is no less important to note that a reason for this separation, alongside the claims of Hashemite leadership, was to provide a reserve of land for Arabs across the Jordan. Both Cisjordan and Trans-jordan made up historic Palestine.

Thus, the erroneous premise, indulged by these pamphlets from the U.N. Secretariat, as to who were the claimants to self-determination or liberation in 1917 spawns immediately another dramatic error in their *points de départ.* This is their assumption that the Palestinians do not already as a people have a homeland and a base for statehood, so that these must be wrested from the state of Israel. The fact is that after World War I Transjordan arose as a last-minute encroachment on the already small allocation to the Jewish nation in the self-determination distribution, thereafter excluded from the promise of a Jewish national home. Yet these U.N. Secretariat "studies" do not, as far as can be observed, refer to any duty of Jordan as an Arab state in Palestine to accommodate the Palestinians; just as the studies are inadvertent to the moral default of other Arab states in not resettling within their vast domains the hundreds of thousands of Palestinian refugees displaced by the wars initiated by these states. These defaults are the more surprising when it is recalled that the tiny state of Israel did offer and provide such a home for at least as many Jewish refugees from Arab states during the same troubled period, as well as for scores of thousands of Arab refugees. The defaults become astonishing when one also recalls that in the same epoch Western states admitted, resettled, and absorbed as citizens more than nine million destitute persons displaced in the course and aftermath of World War II.[27] Even greater displacements and exchanges of population have been managed in Asia; for example, between India and Pakistan.

The major point for the application of the self-determination principle in 1980, however, is that the origins and present position of the Arab state of Jordan in Palestine rebut the very claim that the Palestinian people lack a homeland. Not only did the state of Jordan arise in Palestine over Jewish protest at the expense of the home allocated for the Jewish nation; it also inexorably became, by the same course of history, a Palestine Arab state. As already seen, the original extraction of Transjordan in 1922 from the area designated by the mandate for a Jewish national home had as a major purpose the assurance of a territorial unit for movement of Palestinian Arabs. Jordanian expansion by unlawful military adventure on to the West Bank in 1948 could only reconfirm this character as a Palestinian Arab state in a triple sense.[28] With or without the West Bank, Jordan is unam-biguously Palestinian territory; and the vast majority—something over 60 percent—of its inhabitants consists of Palestinian Arabs. Moreover, the number of Palestinians within this extended Jordan constituted a majority of all Palestinians.

In terms, therefore, of any intelligible account of the self-determination principle, Jordan was certainly a Palestinian state after 1948. Whether King Hussein and his Palestinian subjects chose to conduct their affairs as a unitary state on democratic majority principles, or whether they chose to establish a separate Palestinian state within the extended territory, the Palestinian Arabs already had a homeland within the state of Jordan. This reality may be concealed from time to time by the difficult relations between King Hussein's regime and his Palestinian subjects. Yet for much of the period 1948 to 1967, and perhaps indeed until the bloody hostilities with the P.L.O. of 1970, the Palestinians in the kingdom of Jordan (forming as mentioned a majority of its population and also a majority of all Palestinians) may well have come to regard Jordan as the Palestine Arab state. Indeed, it seems that in 1970 the Palestinians sided with their own state of Jordan against the P.L.O. The underlying reality continues today. Recent estimates place the percentage of Palestinians in Jordan at 60 percent (London *Observer,* March 2, 1976), 55 percent (*Economist, Annual Supp. on Jordan and Syria*), 66 percent (P.L.O. figures). King Hussein himself, in an interview with the *France-Soir* of February 3, 1977, asserted that Palestinians were the majority of the Jordanian population. In 1979 the population included 1,200,000 Palestinians and 900,000 Bedouin.

This Palestinian Arab affinity with Jordan moreover is deeply embedded in history, and in the consciousness of Jordanian authorities, and even of the P.L.O. Lord Balfour's Memorandum of August 11, 1919, noted that "Palestine" includes all the area east of the Jordan. King Hussein himself in his autobiography, *Uneasy Lies the Head,* asserts the unity of Transjordan and Palestine. He told the paper *Al-Mustakbal* on June 16, 1979, that "the unity of both Banks under one Arab, Moslem rule, will ensure equal rights for the Palestinians." Crown Prince Hassan told the National Assembly on February 2, 1970, that "Palestine is Jordan and Jordan is Palestine." Premier Zaýd al-Rifaʻi of Jordan, himself a Palestinian, told *Al-Diyar* (Lebanon) on December 13, 1974, that "there is one Jordanian Palestinian People." As for the Palestinians themselves, the Conference of West Bank Notables in 1948 called for union of both banks under King Abdullah. Many P.L.O. statements, including statements of the Palestinian National Council, have steadily claimed that Jordan is a part of the future Palestinian state. For example, the 8th Council Meeting of March 1971 declared that "the future State in liberated Palestine will be the Democratic Palestinian Republic . . . in full unity," stressing the unity of the people on both banks of the Jordan, a sentiment repeated at the 9th and the 12th Council meetings, the lattermost in July 1974. And the chief of the Political Department of the P.L.O. was reported (*Newsweek,* March 14, 1977) to have declared that Palestinians and Jordanians are one people. And it is clear that before the realignments of the Rabat Conference the principal Arab states in fact treated Jordan as representing its Palestinian as well as Bedouin population.[29]

Despite the Rabat decisions, a Conference of Syria, Egypt, and Jordan and the P.L.O., on January 4, 1975, asked Jordan to halt the "Jordanization" policy by which it reacted to those decisions. A P.L.O. delegation in Amman announced in *Al-Nahar* (Beirut) on December 18, 1978, the continued responsibility of Jordan for Jordan's Palestinian population. And the central role in Jordan still played by this population was surveyed by *Al-Ahram* (Cairo) on March 5, 1976. Palestinians at that time were reported to control 70 percent of the Jordanian economy; others estimate that Palestinians hold 75 percent of government posts. In Amman itself 85 percent of the inhabitants are Palestinians.

These facts remind us that, despite the common assumption that most Palestinians in Jordan are refugees, even those Palestinian Arabs who moved from Cisjordan to Transjordan were in fact only migrating from one part of Palestine to another, over relatively short distances, averaging perhaps 50 to 100 miles. They continue to live within a similar cultural, demographic, linguistic, religious, and even climatic environment.

The assumption that it is the existence of the state of Israel that deprives the Palestinians of a national home is thus erroneous on these grounds also. It is understandable that the political warfare of rejectionist Arab states and the P.L.O. should refuse even to examine these errors. Only by propagating them can they distort the liberation claims of Palestinians into a demand against Israel, and move toward the destruction of that state, an aim still in 1979 quite explicit in the Palestine National Covenant. But it is strange that a secretarial unit of the United Nations, ostensibly engaged in exposition of international law, should indulge them so unquestioningly.

DISPLACED PALESTINIAN ARABS AND JEWS DISPLACED
FROM ARAB COUNTRIES: PRINCIPLES OF REDRESS

The error underlying Palestinian claims that the self-determination principle entitles them to dismantle the State of Israel and replace it with their own state is, of course, the failure to recognize the intertemporal problems in applying this principle. This principle has to be applied at particular points in the stream of time to the facts as they exist at the particular time. And if we assume that Palestinians became a distinct group entitled to self-determination in the 1960s, and that they have not been given an appropriate portion from the vast territorial allocation to the "Arab Nation" of 1917, of which they were then a part, they may be said to have been wronged by someone or other. Primarily, however, such wrongs would have to be laid at the door of the Arab states, which received this lion's share of the territorial allocation of 1917, enough to create a dozen sovereign states.

Even, however, if it were thought that all the beneficiaries of the 1917 overall distribution, including Israel, should share in the duty of redress to wronged marginal interests such as those of the Palestinians, the obvious resolve of the Mallisons to present the issue as a simple claimant demand of Palestinian Arabs against Israel, is still grossly erroneous. For any wrong to the Palestinians flowed (in proportion to benefits received) far more from the creation of so many Arab states in so vast an area than it did from the creation of the tiny state of Israel. Even on this basis, therefore, principle would require that the burden of redress should fall not on Israel alone, but on the Arab states and Israel in common and in some due proportion to benefits they respectively received in the overall allocation of 1917.

This principle, moreover, also seems applicable to Jews fleeing from Arab lands, as well as to Arabs fleeing from Palestine, all in the course of the same Arab-Israel conflict. The members of each of these groups suffered similar wrongs incidental to the overall distribution. The duty of providing homes for the 700,000 Jewish refugees was assumed by Israel in its fundamental Law of Return, as a first responsibility of the new state. The great burden of rehabilitation was assumed by the state of Israel and should, both in law and justice, be brought into account in assessing contributions to be made by the Arab states and Israel to what Security Council Resolution 242 called a "just" solution to the refugee problem. Surprisingly again, the authors of the studies entitled *Resolutions* and *Right of Return*, show no advertence to the principles involved.[30]

2

. . . . .

General Assembly Resolutions and International Law

Pronouncements on Palestinian Self-Determination. It has been shown, thus far, that the chronology and circumstances of the primary application of the self-determination or liberation principle in the Middle East took account of the rights of both the Jewish and the Arab nations as they then existed. This removed any basis on which a claimant to separate Palestinian peoplehood, emergent forty-odd years later, could claim to dismantle statehoods properly established in their due time on the liberation principle. The erroneous assumptions of the Mallisons on these critical matters undermine much of their analysis of the major U. N. resolutions.

The Mallisons are, for example, at pains (and necessarily so since it is crucial to their themes) to explain away the absence of General Assembly resolutions before 1970,[1] affirming the right of self-determination of Palestinian Arabs as an issue between Israel and the Palestinians. Up to then (the Partition Resolution apart—to be considered hereafter) General Assembly resolutions concerned themselves with the claims of Arab refugees to return to their homes and "their repatriation, resettlement and economic and social rehabilitation and payment of adequate compensation for the property of those choosing not to return."[2]

It is only with Resolution 2672C, as late as December 8, 1970, as the *Resolutions* "study" has to admit[3] that "the General Assembly moved towards acknowledging the correlation between the right of self-determination and other inalienable rights." From this and from a phrase in Resolution 2649 of November 30, 1970, its authors make bold to argue that prior resolutions of self-determination of peoples, which the General Assembly had not at the time applied to the Palestinian people, "are now specifically

27

applicable to the Palestinian people."[4] They are thus accepting as a historical
fact that, even so far as the General Assembly is concerned, the peoplehood
of the Palestinians begins in 1970. And the elaborate structures that they
try to build on this then proceed on the gross error, exposed in preceding
sections, that the basic application of the self-determination principle to
the claims of the Jewish and Arab nations had not already been made half a
century before. And it is to be noted that even Resolution 2672C in 1970,
which is thus claimed as an epoch-making recognition of Palestinian self-
determination was hesitant even at that late stage. No less than 72 states
out of a total of 139 then Members of the United Nations either opposed,
or abstained from, this vote, and only 47 States voted for it. This scarcely
signals a wholehearted flash of recognition, even a belated one, by the
international community of an age-old self-evident truth!

It is also curious that in a ten-page section on "The National Rights of
the People of Palestine," these authors avoid reference to what many
regard as the most important of resolutions on the Middle East, namely,
Security Council Resolution 242 of November 22, 1967, and Resolution
338 of October 22, 1973, which emphatically reaffirms Resolution 242 as
the basis on which a Middle East settlement is to be negotiated. As international lawyers, the authors must be aware of the importance of Resolution 242, accepted by Egypt, Jordan, Syria, and Israel, as the only authoritative formulation of a unanimous Security Council on the issues between
Israel and the Arabs requiring resolution by negotiation. Indeed, the
authors enthusiastically cite it in the preceding section of their pamphlet
as supporting the "right of return" of Palestinian refugees, since it calls
for "a just settlement of the refugee problem." But they do not deign to
notice that on the self-determination issue Security Council Resolution
242 significantly excludes any reference to any national claims of
Palestinian Arabs against Israel. This was not an issue in the Middle East
conflict in 1967; nor was it even in 1973 when Resolution 338 reaffirmed
Resolution 242. (Nor, I may add, on "the right to return" aspect, do
these authors care to notice that the "just settlement of the refugee
problem" called for embraces on its face all refugees, Jewish and Arab.)

In the General Assembly itself it required the unprecedented coercion
of the Arab states' oil boycott in support of the Syrian-Egyptian attack
on Israel in 1973, and its aftermath of pressures in subsequent years, in
alignment with the Soviet bloc, to move a majority of the membership to
vote for a resolution asserting the existence of separate Palestinian Arab
national identity. And under such threats and duress the pertinent
Resolution 3089D of December 7, 1973, marshaled only eighty-seven
affirmative votes (with thirty-nine states voting against or abstaining).
When, a year later, Resolution 3236 of November 22, 1974, attempted to
strengthen the self-determination claim by "reaffirmation," there were
increases in both the number of members who opposed, and the number

who abstained.[5] The authors of *Resolutions* are willing, at any rate, automatically to translate such resolutions into rules of international law. This, however, raises another set of international law questions about the legal effects of General Assembly resolutions, to which I now turn.

STANDING OF RESOLUTIONS: SIMPLISTIC ASSUMPTIONS

The basic general rule as to the legal effect of General Assembly resolutions is that stated by Sir Hersch Lauterpacht, concurring in the South West Africa Voting Procedure Advisory Opinion of 1955. He there observed that, save where otherwise provided, as (for example) with regard to budget under charter, Article 17, or admission of members under Article 4(2), "decisions of the General Assembly . . . are not legally binding upon the Members of the United Nations." Apart from such charter exceptions, "resolutions" of this body, even if framed as decisions, "refer to recommendations . . . whose legal effect although not altogether absent, . . . appears to be no more than a moral obligation."[6] Beyond this, legal bindingness of such resolutions has to be established by criteria of some recognized process for creating international law, as by conformity to the requirements for creation, for example, of customary law or treaty law. Before, therefore, their massive reliance on General Assembly resolutions as creating legal obligations for members, the Mallisons owed their readers a full and careful consideration of these requirements.

A generation after the above opinion of Judge Lauterpacht, in an equally considered pronouncement, still another distinguished former judge of the International Court of Justice, Sir Gerald Fitzmaurice, was no less unequivocal in rejecting the "illusion" that a General Assembly resolution can have "legislative effect." First, he pointed out, a Philippine proposal[7] for such a legislative effect was rejected in Commission II at the San Francisco drafting of the charter by an overwhelming vote of 26-1 (United Nations Conference on International Organisation Documents [1945] 316). Second, the general structure of the charter limits the General Assembly (as distinct from the Security Council) to merely recommendatory functions. Third, it was precisely this limitation that explained why U.N. members are so often prepared to allow Assembly resolutions to be adopted, for example, by abstaining rather than opposing them. Fourth, Sir Gerald pointed out, General Assembly resolutions do not and cannot become a formal source of international law additional to those already well recognized. He adopted the conclusions as to this in H.W.A. Thirlway, *International Customary Law and Codification* (1972), Chapter 5, and the authorities there cited. Fifth, such relevance as General Assembly resolutions might have to international law was, at most, that the content of a particular resolution might come to be considered for adoption by states in "a separate treaty or convention." (This, of course, would become binding by virtue of such treaty adoption, whatever its literary or material source, and not because of any legal force of the resolution.) Finally, the "complete imbalance" arising from the entry of scores of new states into the United Nations promotes resolutions in the General Assembly reflecting political, economic, or sociological aspirations rather than a responsible assessment of the relevant legal issues and considerations. It would greatly enhance the dangers inherent in this imbalance in the United Nations, if the above illusion were thoughtlessly indulged.

In the following year, at the 1492d meeting of the General Assembly's Sixth Committee, on November 5, 1974, there was a remarkable manifestation of similar views by United Nations members. The Committee had before it a draft resolution on the role of the International Court of Justice, the preamble of which referred vaguely in its eighth paragraph to the possibility that the court might take into consideration declarations and resolutions of the General Assembly. A wide spectrum of states, including Third World, Soviet bloc, and Western states, rejected even this indecisive reference. It was, some said, an attempt at "indirect amendment" of Article 38 of the Statute of the International Court—a "subversion of the international structure of the United Nations" (Mr. Sette Camara [Brazil] United Nations General Assembly [U.N.G.A.] A/C6/SR1492, p. 166, with whom U.S. representative Rosenstock agreed on this point). It contradicted the U.N. Charter and the court statute, so that on a separate vote the Soviet Union would not have supported it (Mr. Fedarov, Union of Soviet Socialist Republics, ibid., p. 167). It was capable of meaning that "General Assembly resolutions could themselves develop international law" (Mr. Steel, for United Kingdom, ibid., p. 167). It was "inappropriate in the light of Article 38" of the Court's Statute (Mr. Guney, Turkey, ibid., p. 168). It was subject to "serious doubts" (Mrs. Ulyanova, Ukraine, ibid., p. 168). It was an attempt to "issue directives regarding the sources of law," departing from his delegation's view that resolutions and declarations of the General Assembly are "essentially recommendations and not legally binding" (Mr. Yokota, Japan, ibid., p. 168). Mr. Rasoloko, Byelorussia, declared roundly (ibid., p. 169) that "declarations and resolutions of the General Assembly could not be sources of international law"; and Mr. Prieto, Chile (ibid., p. 169) added that they could not be so considered "particularly in view of their increasing political content which was often at variance with international law." The eighth paragraph, it was also objected, attributed to the General Assembly "powers which were not within its competence" (Mr. Foldeák, Hungary, ibid., p. 169). Also, the preambular paragraph in question had already been amended at the instance of Mexico in a sense explained as in no way altering or introducing any new source of international law to those enumerated in Article 38 of the Statute of the International Court of Justice (A/C6/L 989).

The authors' lack of assurance as to the legal basis afforded for their thesis by recent General Assembly resolutions, moreover, is manifest in the whole structure of *Resolutions*. They open with a section devoted to "The Juridical Competence of the Political Organs of the United Nations," obviously designed to maximize the legal effect of those General Assembly resolutions favorable to their theses.

Whole volumes have been devoted, and more no doubt will be, to the contentious issue whether, and if so within what limits, the conduct of states in the course of debating and voting on resolutions in the General Assembly, can establish new rules of international law. The authors of *Resolutions*, however, purport to dispose of the matter by two carefully selected quotations. One is from Professor Rosalyn Higgins's opening general statement[8] that votes and views of states in international organizations have "come to have legal significance," and that "collective acts of States repeated by *and acquiesced in by sufficient numbers [of states]* with sufficient frequency, *eventually* attain the status of law" (emphasis supplied). The other is Judge Tanaka's dissenting opinion in the *South West Africa* cases.[9] That learned judge there pointed out that the requirements of practice, repetition, and *opinio iuris sive necessitatis* in the relevant conduct of states, traditionally required for the creation of a new rule of customary law are still required, but may mature at a quicker pace under modern techniques of communication and international organization.

From these carefully qualified generalities the authors of *Resolutions* proceed immediately to their own statement of the desired law, namely that "the State practice requirement for customary law-making [is to be found] in the collective acts of States (as in voting in favor of a particular General Assembly resolution) as well as in their individual acts."[10] For this summary to represent correctly the learned authorities whom they quote, the authors should then have proceeded to add, with the same care as Professor Higgins and Judge Tanaka, the requirements as to acquiescence of states, and the exact meaning of acquiescence by reference to the essential requirement of *opinio iuris sive necessitatis;* as to the sufficiency of the number of states involved, including the nature of their interest, self-serving or adverse, in the subject matter, as well as the sufficiency of the number of instances when these requirements are met. The authors, however, do not trouble to explore these vital questions, and I shall have to return to them below under "Standing of Resolutions: Actual Legal Complexities" and "Taints in General Assembly Process as Lawmaking."

Instead of exploring those questions, they fill the lacuna rather with a superficial summary of the subject matters on which the Security Council and General Assembly are authorized to pass resolutions under articles 33-38, and articles 12-14. It is surprising that in doing so, they make no reference to the point, rather important for their thesis, that it is only as to decisions of the Security Council that Article 25 of the charter creates legally binding obligations for members. No such legal force is attributed by the charter to resolutions of the General Assembly except on certain specific and narrowly delimited matters, such as apportionment of expenses among members (Art. 17[2]).

The most serious matter remains the use (or abuse) of quotations from Professor Higgins's and Judge Tanaka's careful specifications, followed by a summary, which is then attributed to these authorities, but which ignores those specifications. On this basis the authors invite the reader to accept that all assertions of fact or law repeatedly found in General Assembly resolutions become ipso facto international law by consensus.[11] Indeed, by a singular petitio principii, the only real guidance offered by *Resolutions* as to the requirements for General Assembly resolutions to qualify as customary law, is to say that "this practice [i.e. of expressing consensus on legal issues through the General Assembly] is particularly evident in General Assembly resolutions concerning Palestine, Israel and the Middle East."[12] Thus, after setting out to establish, as a basis for their claim that certain resolutions on the Palestinians are law, the limits within which General Assembly resolutions may be offered to establish the existence of new international law by direct action of the participating states, the authors then simply beg that preliminary question by tendering those very resolutions as examples of how such new customary law is created in the General Assembly.

This vice in the legal foundations that the authors attempt to lay for their interpretation of General Assembly resolutions affects all their main submissions in the rest of the pamphlet. These submissions are that a formidable series of legal obligations arising outside traditional international law and the charter have been imposed on Israel by General Assembly resolutions.

STANDING OF RESOLUTIONS: ACTUAL LEGAL COMPLEXITIES

The desire of the authors of *Resolutions* for a simplistic rule translating General Assembly resolutions into international law, and their failure to establish such a proposition, are understandable. What is difficult to understand is that as international lawyers they show so little awareness of the range and depth of controversies among their colleagues that forbid such simplification.

The two quotations resorted to by the authors proceeded by analogy with customary law, an analogy that the authors then distort into a vague notion of *consensus*. But half a dozen other hypotheses—each with its own consequential criteria and limits—are current in the literature and divide the authorities. These hypotheses include the treatment of voting behavior—(1) as an extension of treaty-making; (2) as authoritative interpretation of existing treaties; (3) as expression of "general principles of law"; (4) as declaratory statements about the existence of rules of international law; (5) as a new source of international law supplementing the inadequacies of the sources laid down in Article 38(1) of the Statute of the International Court of Justice; (6) as a means of creating informal expectations among states. On this sixth hypothesis, expectations have been thought only to mature into binding rules according to whether the votes of states (a) represent the interests of all affected sides in controversial matters; (b) avoid extreme and intransigent positions; (c) are free of vague and indeterminate language; (d) are free of politically motivated double standards; (e) are not used to champion ex parte positions in political quarrels; (f) proceed from an international organ that maintains on the particular matter impartial methods of deliberation and resolution between parties in conflict.

Hypotheses 1-5, as well as that which proceeds on the analogy of customary law, all remain rather inchoate, with applicable criteria surrounded by doubt and dispute. As to hypothesis 6, it will be apparent, as this examination proceeds, that much recent General Assembly action on the Middle East, especially since the deploying of the oil weapon in 1973, is a veritable paradigm of that kind of action in United Nations organs that will *not* mature into law.[13] And I shall in the concluding sections of Chapter 6 show, by a study of the work of the General Assembly's Fourth Special Committee on Defining Aggression, that the conclusion of that committee and the very many states represented on it (and indeed the General Assembly when it adopted the Definition of Aggression proposed by that committee) contradicts the simplistic thesis of the *Resolutions* study about the law-making effects of General Assembly resolutions.

TAINTS IN GENERAL ASSEMBLY PROCESS AS LAWMAKING

Double Standards and Credibility of Resolutions. Professor Schreuer wisely observed in his survey of the state of international law authorities in 1977 on this matter:

A recommendation's significance will not least depend on the moral authority of the adopting organ. Only the maintenance of high and impartial standards of decision-making in the international organ will endow its recommendations with persuasive force for all sectors of the international community. The application of politically motivated double standards or the use of general resolutions to champion positions in political quarrels are liable to undermine the credibility of the international organ even in areas of relative agreement.[14]

There are several reasons for suspecting that this rather self-evident prerequirement for attributing binding force to resolutions of the General Assembly not invested with such force by the charter has often not been fulfilled in recent years.

One obvious reason is that some pronouncements of that body, even when they purport to "declare" or "interpret" law, smack of short-term power politics rather than legislative process. Law, of course, may sometimes issue rather directly from power politics, as in the nineteenth-century Concert of Europe, when the ambitions of major powers checked and balanced each other over the long run. In a General Assembly of over 150 Members, on a one-State-one-vote basis, major powers like the Soviet Union, or powers controlling a major resource like oil, allying themselves to large blocs of Third World states, are in a position to use that body as a mere instrument of their own political warfare. In the General Assembly with limited powers sanctioned by the charter this would be a tolerable (perhaps even a desirable) arena of international politics. It becomes unacceptable and dangerous when the majority groupings for the time being attempt to attribute to the resolutions of this body, passed by these same groupings, legally binding power over members. Such usurped power is at present being targeted against much of the Western World, and against the state of Israel in its historic relations with this world. Neither the United Nations nor the traditional international legal order could sustain fuller development of these usurping tendencies.

Resolutions Carried under Duress.   A second reason for suspecting the moral authority of the General Assembly is that the coercive powers wielded by a few states that may be diminutive in population but formidable in importance of the resources they control may frequently inhibit members who might wish to vote no, or even to abstain, on a range of matters notably but not exclusively affecting the Middle East. In the light of the experience of recent years, it is not difficult to imagine most outrageous manipulations of voting in the General Assembly. It is no great distance from the General Assembly's equivalation of "Zionism" with "racism," to categorizing the United States or the United Kingdom or Australia as "racist" states.

The United Kingdom, for example, could be declared in violation of the principle of self-determination; Welsh and Scottish and Irish "liberation organizations" could be recognized, and made into international legal "entities" represented at the United Nations; so with the Basques and Catalonians against Spain; the Bretons and Corsicans against France; the Croats against Yugoslavia; the Walloons against Belgium; and numerous others. It is unnecessary to list the more well-known contexts of liberation claims in Asia and Black Africa, or of Chinese in Malaysia, Malays in Singapore, or the proliferating claims of tribal groupings within many new Black African states.

Committees on the inalienable rights of this or that "people" could be established in the Secretariat, publishing to the world under the U.N. emblem "studies" prepared by propagandists. Australia's immigration policies could be pronounced in violation of the charter, so that levels of immigration there from overpopulated countries elsewhere could be prescribed by the General Assembly, after reciting references in the Charter preamble to promotion of "social progress and better standards of life in larger freedom," and in Article 1 to the goal of solving "problems of an economic, social, cultural or humanitarian character and encouraging respect for human rights."

Faced with sufficient duress, sufficient members can be "obliged" to support, or at least abstain from opposing, so as to secure a majority for such resolutions, and, indeed, for a resolution that the earth is flat. States would be obliged to vote in this way; but to be "obliged" in this manner certainly does not satisfy the time-honored requirement of *opinio iuris sive necessitatis* in the international lawmaking process. In the jurisprudential commonplace, to be "obliged" to yield to an armed bandit is not to have a legal obligation to do so. Nor can any process of this kind, whether on Middle East or other issues, create international legal obligations.

The General Assembly resolution 34/65B of November 29, 1979, purporting to declare that the Camp David Accords and other agreements such as the Treaty of Peace between Israel and Egypt, have no validity, poses, at a new height of visibility, the threat to international law from automatic attribution of legal (or even moral) force to resolutions of the General Assembly. This extraordinary pronunciamento on "legal validity" blatantly expresses the policy of the Arab "rejectionist" states, including the Organization of Arab Petroleum Exporting Countries (OAPEC), and the Soviet determination to maintain its power role in the Middle East. That is as it may be. But the present point is that these policies cannot be made into "law" by such a vote in the General Assembly. In a United Nations of more than 150 members, 100 members can pass any resolution they wish, however irresponsible, and it cannot be overlooked that the so-called Group of 77 Third World states in the United Nations is now alone well over 100.

That this is now a regular pattern in General Assembly voting is clear from a comparison with the notorious Resolution 3379(XXX) of November 10, 1975, which solemnly pretended to "determine" that "Zionism" is a form of "racism." On that resolution more than half the members voted against, abstained, or absented themselves the "majority" consisting of 72, with no less than 75 against, abstaining or absent. From the roll-call of this vote the inference of coercion by oil-producing states, in alliance with Communist states, is very difficult to avoid.

It is obviously not possible to prevent such resolutions' being passed. But that is not the pertinent issue. This issue is whether to these extravagant expressions there should be added, as the manipulators demand, an attribution of binding force in international law that would be grossly inconsistent with the provisions of the charter.

Transitional Confusions in Doctrine. It would indeed be extraordinary if at a time when treaties induced by the application of unlawful coercion to a state party thereto have been declared to be void, the international community should for the first time attribute legal binding force to the resolutions of the General Assembly for which states vote under extreme duress such as threats of deprivation of essential oil supplies. No doubt the use of bargaining power, of which the possession of oil resources no less than the possession of great military power is an example, cannot be prevented altogether from influencing the outcomes of negotiations between states. Yet just as Article 52 of the Vienna Convention on the Law of Treaties sets limits to the lawful role of military power in inducing a party to accede to a demand, there must be corresponding limits to other means of coercion, for instance, by economic strangulation.[15]

The "Declaration on the Prohibition of Military, Political and Economic Coercion in the Conclusion of Treaties," adopted by and annexed to the Final Act of the United Nations Conference on the Law of Treaties, of May 23, 1969, clearly asserted such limits. It "solemnly condemns the threat or use of pressure in any form, whether military, political or economic, by any State in order to coerce another State to perform any act relating to the conclusion of a treaty in violation of the principles of the sovereign equality of States and freedom of consent." What was thus declared to limit even the axiomatic principle that every treaty in force binds the parties to performance in good faith, must *a multo fortiori* also limit any force as law of General Assembly resolutions, problematical in any case as such force is on other grounds.

At least three such limits are suggested by the oil measures launched in 1973 in support of the armed attack initiated by Egypt and Syria against Israel.

One limit pertains to the degree of severity of the duress of any kind, including economic duress, that states in the relations of peace may use against each other as a means of inducing acceptance of otherwise lawful demands. This, of course, is the problem of economic aggression, *stricto sensu*, which has been frequently discussed since 1956 in the course of attempts to define aggression. The best known Soviet proposal, to the 1956 General Assembly Special Committee on that matter, included under "aggression" measures of economic pressure "violating the sovereignty and economic independence" or "threatening the bases of the economic life" of another state.[16] Serious discussion of this continued into the work of the General Assembly's 1967 Special Committee on the same matter from 1967 to 1974. For various reasons, centrally the importance of focusing in the first stage of definition on armed force as "the most dangerous form of the illegal use of force,"[17] the definition of aggression then arrived at and adopted by consensus of the General Assembly on December 14, 1974, did not expressly refer to economic aggression. It is clear however from the *travaux* that many participating States asserted nevertheless that extreme economic pressure, such as that of withholding oil supply, constituted a grave international delinquency, if not a form of aggression. At the very least, as Special Committee Chairman Professor Bengt Broms declared, the use of economic coercion by a state could be a legal justification for a response of the victim state by the use of armed force against such economic coercion.[18] And it is of the utmost significance, as indicating importance of this matter for all states, rather than merely Western states, that the main pressures in 1974 for thus establishing the unlawfulness of economic duress came from other than Western states and the main defense of such duress came from OAPEC states.[19]

The second limit proceeds *a fortiori* from the first above discussed, which applies in all cases even when the demands pressed by economic coercion are demands against the victim state. *A fortiori* extreme economic coercion must be unlawful when it is used against third states in order to compel their foreign policy or other alignment as between the coercing state and its opponent.[20] The most notorious instance is, of course, the oil boycott of 1973, which went far beyond any plausible use merely to advance the foreign policies of the oil-producing states concerned, favoring return of some Arab lands and the cause of the Palestinians. The boycott was an attempt to force terms of settlement on Israel, not by means of oil pressure against Israel, but by coercing third states, for instance Japan, to change their own foreign policies, and even to compel them to take coercive measures against Israel. It openly inflicted severe coercion as punishment against states classified as "supporting Israel." It aimed explicitly to force third states to sever diplomatic and trade relations with Israel, as well as to extend military and economic aid to Arab states. In all these respects it was an invasion of the sovereign prerogatives of the third states by the use of coercion no less extreme than most conventional military aggressions.

The third legal limit, which already seems clear, on the use of economic duress by States is that it must not be used to support activities that are themselves independently unlawful. The seizure of the United States

Embassy and personnel in Teheran in 1979 was unlawful. It must surely follow that proposed action by other oil-producing states such as Libya by way of oil boycott, in support of the extraordinary conduct of the Iranian authorities, must surely be tainted on this ground also.

If the exercise of modes and degrees of duress against individual states violating such limits is thus unlawful, it would be strange to think that it could remain lawful when exercised against the collectivity of member states of the United Nations in the General Assembly. And it would become correspondingly grotesque to argue, as do all the pamphlets from "The Committee on . . . Rights of the Palestinian People," that once assertions in resolutions of that body are sufficiently repeated, they are transformed into international law, regardless of any duress by way of oil pressures, which induced many members to act so as to permit them to pass. The grotesqueness arises not merely from ignoring the unlawful pressure by which the appearance of consensus is produced, which, in principle, should taint the resolution *qua* resolution. The grotesqueness is raised to breath-taking proportions by the claim that such resolutions not only remain unexceptionable *as resolutions* despite this taint, but are transmuted into precepts of international law binding on all states. What is wrong here, of course, is not merely the *ad hoc* biased nature of much of this research. It also rests on the researchers' failure, as I have pinpointed above, to understand or even attend to the precise criteria that must be satisfied for voting behavior in international bodies to qualify as lawmaking.

We have up to now considered the effects of extreme duress on the legal validity of outcomes on general principle. Though it is not possible here to discuss them, it should also be mentioned that there are a number of specific provisions of the charter that are violated by measures of extreme economic duress such as oil pressure. First, Article 53 of the U.N. Charter expressly commands that "no enforcement action shall be taken under regional arrangements, or by regional agencies without the authorization of the Security Council." This is exactly what the 1973 Arab state oil measures against the U.S., Netherlands, Japan, and other states amounted to, even if their demands had conformed (which they did not) to the Security Council resolutions involved. Second, the extreme coercion of the concerted oil measures, arising from the near monopoly power involved, probably constituted a threat or use of force, forbidden by Article 2(4) of the charter. There is a great difference between this degree of economic coercion, and mere embargoes by one state against another when a monopolistic position of a group of conspiring states in the particular commodity is not involved. Third, as already seen, many U.N. members have taken the view in connection with the definition of "aggression" (for instance, under Article 39 of the charter) that this international crime includes "economic aggression," and that the victims of such aggression may lawfully take appropriate measures of self-defense. Fourth, this kind of conspiratorial design by a group of members to cripple the economies of other members for collateral political ends obviously flouts the "Purposes" and "Principles" of articles 1 and 2 of the charter, as well as the Declaration on Principles of International Law Concerning Friendly Relations and Cooperation among States adopted by the United Nations General Assembly in 1970. Fifth, as a number of states urged in the 1967 Special Committee debates, the "sovereignty" of states protected by Article 2 of the charter, as well as by the Consensus Definition of Aggression, embraces attributes other than mere "territorial integrity" and "political independence."[21] In addition, the extreme coerciveness and dubious legality of the Arab oil boycott would also seem to constitute "a threat or use of force in violation of the principles of the Charter," the presence of which under Article 52 of the Vienna Convention on Treaties of 1969 renders void any consensual obligation that states are induced to accept by this means.

Among the main objections to claims that General Assembly resolutions as such create binding law is the rather indiscriminate fashion in the General Assembly, in the aftermath of decolonization, of endorsing or even promoting assertions made in the name of "international law," merely because they seem "progressive" in the sense of constricting the legal rights of states that do not belong to the so-called nonaligned group. Such positions are often taken by publicists of some sincerity, but they often represent a naive view, not only of international law, but also of both morality and international politics, occasionally to the point of self-contradiction. They can be found to take stern restrictive views of the range of lawful resort to force by states, while insisting, with no sense of the incongruity, that states are also free to initiate or support "wars of liberation" of their own choice, provided that they can control by any means sufficient protective votes in the General Assembly. Such doctrines are a veritable forcing-bed for the double standards that Dr. Schreuer correctly stigmatizes as fatal to lawmaking by General Assembly resolutions. (See above under "Double Standards and Credibility of Resolutions.")

This "softening" of some Western publicist doctrine, doctrine which had been a mainstay of statecraft since before the Peace of Westphalia, is of course due in part to changing power-constellations, and cultural styles, to ideological commitments, and sometimes to postcolonial guilt feelings. But it is also in part due to the skill, political imagination, and energetic persistence with which Soviet, Arab, and other Third World diplomats and publicists have coordinated, disguised, and pressed the accumulation of their demands against the existing legal order. It is not the present thesis that in this new situation give and take in the conflict of claims and the power that backs them may not yield new principles in a viable legal order, as perhaps they have already done to some extent for the law of the sea. Yet to sanctify as international law any assertion for which a majority can be marshaled in the General Assembly (claiming, for instance, that since the United States had not accorded full self-determination to American Indians, force may be used against it by third states in support of the American Indians) would quickly undermine both the United Nations and the international legal order as hitherto understood. The too facile attribution by some Western publicists of legal force to such resolutions of that body may also sometimes represent in Freudian terms a yearning for authoritative shelter from the storms of legal and political change. Yet such fantasies, however helpful to the publicist's psyche, are at odds with basic assumptions of the charter, and of international law. And their effect may be so to block or vaporize that law as to foreclose any chance of adjusting it to changing conditions, as well as to invite political and military disasters.

Professor Gaetano Arangio-Ruiz's work, *The Normative Role of the General Assembly of the United Nations and the Declaration of Principles of Friendly Relations,*[22] is perhaps the most comprehensive and up-to-date treatise on this matter (though the authors of none of these U.N. Secretariat "studies" have apparently seen it). That learned and experienced diplomat has diligently assembled, scrupulously explicated, patiently organized, and critically analyzed, not only the practice but the growing literature that seeks to establish, explain, or support pretensions to lawmaking authority of the General Assembly, beyond the rare situations where the charter empowers that body to make law. It is a work that commands attention from all who value juristic and intellectual integrity above mere fashion and ideology.

Professor Arangio-Ruiz (like Professor Schreuer after him) ranges over numerous theorems offered for attributing lawmaking authority to the General Assembly. These include the supposed legitimation by the charter or other contractual rule; a supposedly authorizing rule of customary law; the supposed "will" of the "Organized International Community"; the supposed binding force of particular resolutions seen as the practice of states maturing into custom, or seen as "treaty" obligations based on "consensus," or as "declaring" "principles of international law," or as "determining" or "interpreting" international law. As to every such ground, he is led to conclude that the General Assembly lacks legal authority either to enact or to "declare" or "determine" or "interpret" international law so as legally to bind states by such acts, whether these states be members of the United Nations or not, and whether these states voted for or against or abstained from the relevant vote or did not take part in it.

He observes upon the "futility of grandiloquent theories" (among which he would certainly rank those here under discussion), and upon the dangers *de lege lata* as well as *de lege ferenda,* which may accompany this futility. His demonstration is cogent both for such projects of abstract "declaration" of law by the General Assembly, and for usurpation of the power to "determine" matters on which states are at variance, and which the charter does not empower that body to "determine."

Professor Arangio-Ruiz summons international lawyers to resist and reject under whatever guise what he calls the "soft-law method" associated with loose attribution of independent lawmaking power to the General Assembly. The summons should be heeded, because such paths may be no guide either to law or to the objective facts. They rather lead to a legal chaos that is a sinister medium for subjugating particular members and indeed the organization itself to adventitiously voting blocs whose predominance may rest on elements as meretricious as economic duress and strangulation. In response to arguments like those made in the pamphlets from the U.N. Secretariat that a sufficiently frequent repetition of an alleged rule in the General Assembly can in itself convert that statement into a rule of customary law, Professor Arangio-Ruiz offers a fitting peroration:[23]

It would be too easy if the "shouting out" of rules through General Assembly Resolutions were to be law-making simply as a matter of "times" shouted and size of the choir. By all means, we would urge that one let the General Assembly shout as often and as loud as it is able and willing to shout. However, for the shouted rule to be customary law there still remains to consider the conduct and the attitudes of States with regard to the actual behaviour, positive or negative, contemplated as due by the rule.

LEGAL PERVERSIONS IN GENERAL ASSEMBLY RESOLUTION 3236

Among the more dramatic examples of the dangers to the international legal order from loose attempts to turn General Assembly resolutions into international law, is that body's Resolution 3236(XXIX) of November 22, 1974. Since this resolution is also a centerpiece of all the pamphlets under scrutiny, especially that of the Mallisons, it may here be characterized in terms of the preceding general analysis.

As is well known, the basic issues and principles for settlement of the Middle East dispute were set forth in Security Council Resolution 242 of November 22, 1967, reprinted in an appendix hereto. And Resolution 338 of 1973 reaffirmed these and even more explicitly provided that the states involved in the 1967 and 1973 wars should proceed forthwith to negotiations for a just and durable peace.[24] During the 1967-73 period, cease-fires ordered by the Security Council and consented to by the parties were beyond any doubt in full legal force.

Under these circumstances, the hostilities initiated by Egypt and Syria in 1969-70 and 1973, and the Arab states' harboring and support of terrorist operations against Israel under the auspices of the Palestine

Liberation Organization (P.L.O.) and its military wings, should therefore have incurred the censure of the United Nations. However, the geopolitical drives of Soviet policy, the multiplication of U.N. members aligned in voting blocs with Communist and Arab members, the legal use of the Soviet veto, and the political use of the oil weapon rendered the Security Council impotent through most of the 1973 October War to give effect to international law or charter principles.

Then, on November 22, 1974, the General Assembly passed Resolution 3236 which made explicit this travesty of the applicable principles of international law and the charter law. No one can predict what the voting fate of these resolutions would have been had not the Damocles sword of an oil boycott hung over the proceedings. Even under such coercion, a third of the members either voted against or abstained from voting on it. Resolutions adopted in such circumstances are not likely to reflect or promote international law, much less justice or morality.

In this resolution on the Palestinians of November 22, 1974, the General Assembly purported (by a vote of eighty-nine to eight, with thirty-seven abstentions and four states absent) to "reaffirm the inalienable rights of the Palestinian people in Palestine" and to recognize the P.L.O. as the appropriate claimant in respect thereof.[25] In so doing, the General Assembly, first, impliedly endorsed prior P.L.O. terrorist activities deliberately aimed not only at the State of Israel but also at civilian men, women, and children, as well as the citizens, airports, and aircraft of numerous states not involved in the Middle East dispute.[26] By the same token, and by a later express provision to be mentioned below, it also offered dispensation for the continuance of such activities.

Second, this resolution violated various legal principles and rights guaranteed under international law and other long-standing U.N. resolutions. By its implied endorsement of the P.L.O.'s aspirations, which (under Art. 6 of the Palestinian Covenant) included and still include the destruction of the state of Israel, the measure violated Israel's right of sovereign equality guaranteed under Article 2(1) of the U.N. Charter, not to speak of its right to be free from the threat or use of force and armed attack under Article 2(4) and Article 51. Article 2, paragraph 1, of the charter provides that "The Organization is based on the principle of the sovereign equality of all its members." Article 2, paragraph 4, provides that "All members shall refrain in their international relations from the threat or use of force against the territorial integrity or political independence of any state, or in any other manner inconsistent with the Purposes of the United Nations." Article 51 further provides that "Nothing in the present Charter shall impair the inherent right of individual or collective self-defense if an armed attack occurs against a Member of the United Nations, until the Security Council has taken measures necessary to maintain international peace and security."

Third, the resolution contradicted the assurance embodied in Security Council Resolution 242 of Israel's right to "live in peace within secure and recognized boundaries free from threats or acts of force."[27]

Fourth, by reaffirming what it called "the inalienable rights of the Palestinian People in Palestine," with no geographical limitation placed on those last two words, Resolution 3236(XXIX) of Nov. 22, 1974, contradicted Resolution 181(II).[28] Even though that resolution was prevented by Arab rejection and aggression from ever coming into legal operation, it certainly committed the General Assembly to the entitlement of the state of Israel to some part of Palestine. Historic and geographic "Palestine" includes not only Judea and Samaria (the West Bank) and Gaza, but also the whole of Israel and Jordan.[29] Yet the Jordanian representative in the debate on the Palestinian resolution made clear his country's view that Israel was indeed included in the "Palestine" claimed for the Palestinians but that Jordan was not! The fact is that the state of Jordan accounts (east of the river) for 35,468 of the 46,339 square miles of "Palestine," or almost four-fifths of the latter.[30] As already seen, most of Jordan's citizens are Palestinians and constitute, together with those on the West Bank, the great majority of all Palestinians.[31] Thus, Jordan was already, as above observed, a state of the Palestinian Arabs.

Fifth, the Palestinian Resolution impliedly reflected on the General Assembly's deliberate and well-considered endorsement of the establishment of the state of Israel. (But of course the establishment and the legal existence of the State of Israel, like that of most U.N. members, did not and does not depend on such endorsement.)

Sixth, the General Assembly in its Resolution 181(II) of November 29, 1947, had requested the Security Council to treat the use of force by Arab states to "alter by force the settlement" there proposed, as "a threat to the peace, breach of the peace or act of aggression." By contrast, the General Assembly in 1974 placed itself virtually in the role of accomplice in encouraging renewal of that very kind of aggression that it formerly singled out for peremptory condemnation.

Seventh, this lamentable role is underscored by the resolution's express approval of the use by the P.L.O. of "all means" to achieve its ends,[32] and its appeal to all states and international organizations to assist with such means![33]

The U.S. representative spoke for many members whose votes in no way reflected their view of the standing of these extraordinary assertions in international law, whether *de lege lata* or *de lege ferenda*. Referring to the dangers posed by one-sided resolutions to the authority of the United Nations, he cited the handling of the global economic crisis and the Middle East conflict as examples of what he viewed as arbitrary disrespect for the U.N. Charter. He warned that if the United Nations continued to proceed on the basis of arithmetical majorities, a "sterile form of international activity" would result and the United Nations would no longer be regarded as a responsible forum of world opinion.[34] Yet this resolution is a veritable paradigm of the resolutions of the recent period on which in the final analysis the authors of these Secretariat productions, including that authored by the international lawyers selected by the Committee on . . . Rights of the Palestinian People, have to base their final positions.

3

. . . . .

Territorial Rights in Palestine Under International Law

ISRAEL'S RIGHTS FROM LAWFUL SELF-DEFENSE

We shall return in due course to the legal standing of the specific contents of various resolutions of the General Assembly that the U.N.-sponsored authors of the study here briefly termed *"Resolutions"* try to qualify as international law. And we shall also consider the distinct question of the legal standing to be attributed to the Palestine Partition Resolution 181(II) if it had ever come into force, as well as the effect of its abortion through its rejection by the Arab states and their armed aggression against it, and against the state of Israel.

Any legal import, however, of United Nations resolutions would not in any case operate in a legal vacuum. It would operate within the frame of the rights and duties of the states concerned under international law, including the provisions of the charter and any pertinent determinations of the Security Council under the charter. It is essential, therefore, in this and the succeeding sections to set out this framework.

The axiomatic base of international law, even under the charter, is that states live under an international legal order in which force is not the monopoly of the organized community, but in the hands of individual nations. Nor can the organized international community change the legal order as it affects particular nations, without the consent of these same nations. Internationally what we have is the absence of predominant community force, and the constant accumulation of force (including military power) in the private control of states. Consequently, the most that can be done in support of legal order and community is to marshal some private forces against others for public ends. And these forces are also, in fact, marshaled from time to time against the international legal order.

It is for these reasons that international law has always, right into the present century, given legal effect ex post facto to the outcomes of its collision with overwhelming power of individual states. By allowing the military victor through the imposed treaty of peace to incorporate his terms for peace into the body of international law, international law preserved at least the rest of its rules and its own continued existence.

In traditional international law these legal positions held for the relations between states, whether the victor himself initiated the use of force, as with the Soviet invasion of the Baltic States during World War II, or whether the force was initiated by the defeated state to which the victor responded by way of legitimate self-defense, as with Israel's response in 1967 to the closing of the Straits of Tiran, the marshaling of Arab state forces at its borders, and the expulsion of the United Nations buffer forces.

The recent modification of this classical legal position, especially under the Covenant of the League of Nations and the Charter of the United Nations, arises from the application of the principle *ex iniuria non oritur ius.* Whether as applied to treaties procured by duress, as in Article 52 of the Vienna Convention on Treaties, or to the acquisition of territory, this modification seeks to strip of legal effect, not use of force as such, but *unlawful* use of force.

From its beginnings the state of Israel has had an unusual record of law observance despite endless aggressions against her by her neighbors. Her statehood rests on her people's Declaration of Independence and her successful repulsion of multiple aggressions from surrounding Arab states. Her immediate admission to the United Nations added world acclamation and endorsement to that existing legal reality. It was armed aggression by Arab states (denounced as such in the Security Council) that aborted the Partition Plan accepted by Israel in 1947. It is no less clear, as will be elaborated in Chapter 7, under "Bases of Sovereignty under International Law," that the hostilities of 1967 were a case of lawful self-defense by Israel, even if we did not know that the General Assembly by an overwhelming vote defeated, on July 4, 1967, the Albanian draft resolution seeking to declare Israel the aggressor.[1]

From that point onward, right up to President Sadat's journey to Jerusalem in 1977 and recognition of the state of Israel, Egypt as well as other Arab states persisted in belligerency against Israel. For three decades they flouted their basic obligations as members of the United Nations to refrain from the threat or use of force and armed attack against Israel's independence and territory.

They did so, after 1948, not merely by threats of wars and wars of 1967 and 1973, of which the facts are notorious, violating their obligations under Article 2 of the U.N. Charter. They also less openly hosted and promoted attacks by armed bands against Israel from Syria, Egyptian-controlled Gaza, Jordan, and Lebanon, which massacred and maimed hundreds of civilian men, women, and children. From Lebanon, the P.L.O. and its associated terror organizations have operated for years with the aid of other Arab states and the toleration of the authorities of Lebanon, a situation reendorsed by the members of the Arab League at their Tunis Conference as recently as November 22, 1979. Israel's repeated requests, directly or in the United Nations, that these unlawful attacks be stopped have been fruitless. Her own military actions in southern Lebanon were accordingly designed to abate them, and conform to international law, as set out, for example, in such authoritative textbooks as Oppenheim-Lauterpacht's *International Law.* This work states that on failure of the host state to prevent or on notice abate these attacks, "a case of necessity arises and the threatened State is justified in invading the neighbouring country and disarming the intending raiders."[2]

The Israel government is thus legally correct in not speaking of "reprisals" or "retaliation" here, and it is unnecessary, and even misleading, to do so. The rule of international law makes clear that this is "a case of necessity," of self-defense authorizing her to enter and destroy or remove the weaponry and bases used against her. In the language of the Soviet Union, in an analogous situation, such action is by way of necessary "countermeasures" and "legitimate defence."[3] The leading statement on this matter is, indeed, Secretary of State Webster's statement of the conditions of self-defensive action by the aggrieved state.[4] Majorities in the United Nations and its committees, which, from time to time, have by silence appeared to condone such attacks by armed bands, and even purported to condemn measures taken by Israel to abate them, have no standing to alter such fundamental precepts of international law. The somewhat speculative rider on the traditional law suggested by Professor García-Mora is examined under "Aggression by Attacks by Armed Bands" below.

After the cease-fires accepted by the Arab states concerned in the 1967 and 1973 wars, the illegality of continued hostilities by them became even more heinous. They flouted not only the charter, but the very cease-fires that they had requested and that they had solemnly accepted. Here again the fact that Soviet and other pro-Arab interests in the United Nations marshaled majorities to shield these illegalities from U.N. censure in no way legalized them, or impugned the legality of Israel's responses.[5]

Nor is this conclusion as to the Arab states' violations of international law a mere inference from their behavior. It has also been quite explicit in their own repeated declarations of position.[6] As recently as February

20, 1980, in a letter to the secretary-general, transmitting for U.N. circulation to the General Assembly and the Security Council in connection with items 26 (Situation in the Middle East) and 106 of A/35/50 (Report of the Special Committee on Enhancing . . . Non-Use of Force in International Relations) a "National Charter of Iraq" (A/35/110-S/13816). This declared *à propos* of inclusion in the charter of a principle of nonuse of force: "The principle of non-use of force . . . shall apply to the relations of the Arab Nation and Arab States with the nations and countries neighbouring the Arab Homeland. Naturally, as you know, the Zionist entity is not included, because the Zionist entity is not considered a State, but a deformed entity occupying an Arab territory. It is not covered by these principles." After all, every state concerned (including Israel) is a member of the United Nations, bound by the charter, and in particular by Article 2. Refusal by a member to acknowledge the statehood and membership of a state duly admitted seems incompatible with the charter, and in particular with Article 2(1) declaring the "sovereign equality" of all members. This seems *a fortiori* so when the refusal carries with it the claim to be at liberty to destroy that state by force, despite Article 2(4) of the charter. However wide or narrow be that last difficult text, the open claims of the Arab states since 1948 to destroy Israel and drive her people into the sea seem to violate its prohibitions against "threat or use of force," and the positive duties implied in Article 2(1) above, as well as of Article 2(2) and 2(3) concerning the assurance to them of the benefits of membership, and the peaceful settlement of disputes.[7]

AGGRESSION BY ATTACKS BY ARMED BANDS

Even before the work of the 1967 Special Committee on . . . Defining Aggression, to be examined in Chapter 6 below, beginning with "The 1974 Definition of Aggression . . .," doctrinal writings were concerned to reinforce the delinquency of hostilities by armed bands from one state's territory against another, both on the part of the bands themselves, and of the state harboring them. Professor M. R. García-Mora, in his *International Responsibility for Hostile Acts of Private Persons* (1962), makes the following emphatic propositions relevant to the present discussion:[8]

(1) ". . . even in terms of the traditional law, if a State has obviously used all the means at its disposal to prevent a hostile act of a person against a foreign nation, but is physically unable to suppress it, it has certainly not discharged its international duty,"[9] and may be guilty of aggression.

(2) The delinquency of the host state, the character of this delinquency as aggression, and the responsibility of the host state are established by a "consistent tendency" of international practice.[10] This practice is found

in a long series of proposals and international instruments, including the Draft Declaration on Rights and Duties of States (Article 4), and the Draft Code of Offences against the Peace and Security of Mankind (Article 2, (4), (5), and (6). Article 2(4), as revised in 1954, stigmatized as such an offense:

The organisation, or the encouragement of the organisation, by the authorities of a State, of armed bands within its territory or any other territory for incursions into the territory of another State, or the toleration of the use by such armed bands of its territory as a base of operations or as a point of departure for incursions into the territory of another State, as well as direct participation in or support of such incursions.

(3) The emergence of criminal responsibility of the host state is evidenced by Article 2(4) of the Draft Code of Offences against the Peace and Security of Mankind quoted above and the related Article 2(12).[11] ". . . [A] more effective legal order can only be attained if States and individuals are constantly made aware that the values of the international community will scrupulously be enforced by the establishment of a criminal law reaching individuals."

(4) This development is harmonious with pronouncements of the founding writers of international law, for instance de Vattel, who thought the injured sovereign "may justly lay the blame upon the whole [host] nation." De Vattel went even further: "Nay more, all Nations may unite to repress such a Nation as the common enemy of the human race."[12]

(5) The imputation of criminal responsibility under international law, as well as the municipal law of injured states, to members of such armed bands (as well as to the culprit state) is now rendered the more imperative by the increased use by states of armed bands as a way of "preparation of a larger scale military invasion into foreign territory, the undermining of the morale . . . of the selected target and the establishment of bases . . . for . . . eventual annexation."[13] This peril lies behind the cumulative pattern of inclusion in lists of "acts of aggression" of support by a state of incursions by armed bands from its territory against neighboring states.[14]

Even authorities who are not as stern as Professor García-Mora in imputing responsibility for armed bands to the host state, for instance the late J. L. Kunz, still emphatically insist, like L. Oppenheim and H. Lauterpacht, and the present writer, that the victim state is entitled on this default to enter the host state's territory to abate the illegal hostilities.[15] Professor García-Mora, however, speculates rather paradoxically that while those hostilities are grave enough to constitute "aggression," and certainly give the victim state a right of forceful abatement under customary international law, as evidenced by the U.S.-U.K. correspondence in the *Caroline Affair*,[16] this legal right of the victim to take measures of abatement may now be prohibited by the U.N. Charter provisions concerning the use of force.[17]

De lege lata his argument rests on one possible interpretation that I have elsewhere called "the idealist-restrictivist view," as opposed to "the realist traditional view," of the final meaning of complex charter provisions. The issue is not whether the license to use force is limited by the charter, but what precisely, bearing in mind all its provisions, including its voting rules, and the clauses of escape and evasion,. these limits are. Others, including the present writer, have taken an opposed view.[18] The learned writer bases his argument on Article 2(3) requiring members to settle their disputes "in such a manner that international peace and security, and justice, are not endangered," as well as on the better-known prohibition in Article 2(4) of "the threat or use of force against the territorial integrity or political independence of any State or in any other manner inconsistent with the Purposes of the United Nations."[19]

This view, as he perforce admits, confronts puzzles of how these and other charter provisions are to be read together. It does not, either, explain why the Article 51 liberty of self-defense "if an armed attack occurs against a Member" should not apply to a type of armed attack that he himself so emphatically stigmatizes as aggression and regards as an escalating threat to all nations. Nor does it attend sufficiently to the limits on the prohibition of Article 2(4) that arise if the word "against" in the phrase "against the territorial integrity or political independence of any State" is given its quite ordinary meaning of "directed against." Action by an attacked state to abate the hostile action of armed bands across a frontier is correctly described as action directed against those armed bands, and not against the territorial integrity of the host state, much less against its political independence.

Professor García-Mora's main position, therefore, well illustrated by his thoughtful critique on the Caroline Affair,[20] reinforces the generally accepted view that a state's failure to prevent incursions by armed bands against a neighboring state, involve that state's responsibility, and may involve its criminal responsibility for aggression, and that customary international law permits the victim in such cases, if necessary by entry into the host state's territory, to abate the hostilities. He is inclined to think, however, that this latter remedial license of forcible abatement or self-defense is now excluded by the U.N. Charter provisions as to use of force. This offered caveat is, however, both sanguine and dubious. It rests no doubt on a utopian vision of "orderly world community processes" to replace abatement and self-defense. This is a desire that many (including this writer) share. But it is going too far to hope that this transformation has begun (or indeed could begin) at the extreme point of international conflict that he himself insists on characterizing as aggression by or by means of armed bands.[21] Such a hope flies in the face of the facts of contemporary international life and law. When international law falls short of the model of "world community processes," we are neither wise nor correct to pretend otherwise. The harsh realities of the *lex lata* are still the base from which we must struggle towards the *lex ferenda.* It will be shown beyond doubt, at the end of Chapter 6, below, under "The 1974 Definition: . . .," that the present attitudes of states reject so hazardous a caveat on the undoubted license granted by customary international law.

EX INIURIA NON ORITUR IUS AND TERRITORY

The basic precept of international law concerning the rights of a state victim of aggression, which has lawfully occupied the attacking state's territory in the course of self-defense, is also clear. And it is still international law after the charter, which gave to the U.N. General Assembly no power to amend this law.

This precept is that a lawful occupant such as Israel is entitled to remain in control of the territory involved pending negotiation of a treaty of peace. Both Resolution 242 (1967) and Resolution 338 (1973), adopted by the Security Council after the respective wars of those years, expressed this requirement for settlement by "negotiations between the parties," the latter in those very words. Conversely both the Security Council and the General Assembly in 1967 resisted heavy Soviet and Arab pressures demanding automatic Israel withdrawal to the pre-1967 frontiers. Through the decade 1967-77, Egypt and her Arab allies compounded the illegality of their continued hostilities by proclaiming the slogan "No recognition! No peace! No negotiation!" thus blocking the regular processes of international law for postwar pacification and settlement.[22]

In the meantime, blackmail pressure by the Organization of Arab Petroleum Exporting Countries (OAPEC) upon Third World states, as well as Western states and Japan, and the propaganda machines of the Arab-Soviet blocs, set out to conceal these gross illegalities. Though the general law (as well as Resolutions 242 and 338) required the Arab states to negotiate with Israel (*inter alia*) the extent of Israel's withdrawal from the territories, these states demanded withdrawal from all the territories *before negotiation.* There is no historical instance in which aggressor states have been granted that kind of prerogative after the defeat of their aggression.

Israel's territorial rights after 1967 are best seen by contrasting them with Jordan's lack of such rights in Jerusalem and the West Bank after the Arab invasion of Palestine in 1948. The presence of Jordan in Jerusalem and elsewhere in Cisjordan from 1948 to 1967 was only by

virtue of her illegal entry in 1948. Under the international law principle
ex iniuria non oritur ius she acquired no legal title there. Egypt itself
denied Jordanian sovereignty; and Egypt never tried to claim Gaza as
Egyptian territory.[23]

By contrast, Israel's presence in all these areas pending negotiations
of new borders is entirely lawful, since Israel entered them lawfully in
self-defense. International law forbids acquisition by unlawful force, but
not where, as in the case of Israel's self-defense in 1967, the entry on the
territory was lawful. It does not so forbid it, in particular, when the force
is used to stop an aggressor, for the effect of such prohibition would be
to guarantee to all potential aggressors that, even if their aggression
failed, all territory lost in the attempt would be automatically returned
to them. Such a rule would be absurd to the point of lunacy. There is no
such rule.

Nor, even if some degree of legal effect were given to the relevant
provisions of the 1970 General Assembly Declaration on Principles of
International Law Concerning Friendly Relations and Cooperation
Among States, can any legal basis be laid for so absurd a rule. Those
provisions preserve the above distinction between lawful force and
unlawful force, and they seek to forbid "military occupation" as well as
"acquisition" of territory. The whole paragraph in which these are
forbidden is qualified by the description "resulting from the use of force
in contravention of the provisions of the Charter." Moreover, the paragraph concludes, apparently *ex majore cautela,* that "nothing in the
foregoing shall be construed as affecting (a) Provisions of the Charter
. . .; or (b) the powers of the Security Council under the Charter." The
exercise of self-defense against armed attack is thus doubly removed
from any impact of these provisions and remains governed by the well-
recognized principles of international law discussed in this section.

It will be shown, at a later point, that the 1974 Definition of Aggression
is, if anything, even more emphatic in its maintenance of the principle
ex iniuria non oritur ius, and of the crucial resulting distinction between
lawful and unlawful force.

International law, therefore, gives a triple underpinning to Israel's
claim that she is under no obligation to hand "back" automatically the
West Bank and Gaza to Jordan or anyone else. In the first place, these
lands never legally belonged to Jordan. Second, even if they had, Israel's
own present control is lawful, and she is entitled to negotiate the extent
and the terms of her withdrawal. Third, international law would not in
such circumstances require the automatic handing back of territory
even to an aggressor who was the former sovereign. It requires the
extent and conditions of the handing back to be negotiated between the
parties. Precisely for such reasons many international lawyers of standing
concluded that international law presented no obstacles even to formal
annexation by Israel if she were so minded. It testifies the more power-

fully to the state of Israel's steady concern for peace rather than territorial gains, that its governments have for so many years maintained
their readiness to negotiate a comprehensive treaty of peace with each
of her neighbors. She has fully manifested this dedication in the peace
treaty recently negotiated with Egypt, and the agreed territorial regime
between them in Sinai.

Arab states and their protagonists have been concerned, of course, to
conceal not only their own illegal courses, but also this strong and clear
legal basis of Israel's territorial standing in Jerusalem, Gaza, and the
West Bank. They have made strenuous efforts to cover over or even
rewrite the precepts of international law, especially through resolutions
of the General Assembly promoted and pressed under threats of oil
deprivations. The foresight, ingenuity, and persistence displayed in that
regard does not protect the outcomes from being, as here submitted, a
veritable travesty of international law. The next section will examine
another example of this travesty of established law that the Arab states
have sought to design and build on the preambulatory recital in Resolution 242 of "the inadmissibility of the acquisition of territory by war."

ARAB STATES' RESISTANCE TO *EX INIURIA NON ORITUR IUS*

As many (including this writer) have shown, attempts to amend the
draft of Security Council Resolution 242 of 1967 so as to call for Israel to
withdraw to the 1967 frontiers, failed.[24] That resolution did not call for
withdrawal from *all* the territories captured in the 1967 War, but only
withdrawal to lines to be negotiated, which were then to become "secure
and recognized boundaries." Indeed, any other provision would have
been at odds with the plain fact that, immediately after the Six Day War,
the Soviet resolution seeking to brand Israel as the aggressor failed of
adoption by 11 votes to 4. And the General Assembly at that time, long
before the entry of the oil weapon into that voting arena, also repeatedly
refused to endorse such a proposition.[25]

Because of these votes, and of the terms of the operative parts of
Resolution 242, Arab arguments moved off to focus on the preambulatory recital in that resolution of "the inadmissibility of the acquisition of
territory by war." They have sought to bury under that Delphic phrase
the clear international legal basis of Israel's territorial standing in Gaza,
the West Bank, and other administered territories. They have had to
argue that this phrase must be taken literally in its widest ambit. When it
is thus stretched, they draw from it a meaning that other states have not
been willing to accept. That meaning indeed yields such absurd results
that while they press it against Israel, they implicitly deny that it applies
against themselves. It is a rule offered as it were, to kill a particular
goose, not even other geese, and certainly not a gander.

The international lawyer, faced with this recital in Resolution 242, juxtaposed with its well-known operative provisions, will recognize no less than three logically possible interpretations of it. He has then to ask which of these three makes sense in its immediate context, in relation to the existing principles of international law, and in relation to what many call the "world order" policies that underlie these principles.

The above Arab states' version is certainly one logical possibility, and that version would yield their desired result, that the occupying state — here Israel—must automatically and fully withdraw, however perfectly lawful its presence. A second possibility is that the recital merely recalls, with the eloquent flourish common in preambles, the established *ex iniuria* principle of international law as this applies to unlawful war. (In this reading "acquisition . . . by war" would refer to the initiation of war for the purpose of acquiring territory. Such initiation, being unlawful, would bring the *ex iniuria* principle into play.) Third, also plausibly, the recital could be a restatement of the rather commonplace technical principle of international law that mere occupation of territory does not itself vest in the occupant sovereign title over it. Transfer of title requires some further act, such as formal annexation or cession by a treaty or other accepted instrument. And, of course, this third meaning would also fit well with the operative provisions calling for negotiations on such matters as "secure and recognised boundaries," the fixing of "demilitarized zones," and the like.

The Arab-favored first meaning above would, as already observed, be at odds with the operative provisions of Resolution 242. It would, moreover, contradict existing international law. Even then, could it be said to be an amendment of this law, offered by the Security Council *de lege ferenda* for the international future?

So offered *de lege ferenda* the recital would mean that an occupant must withdraw even before peace terms are agreed, even if he entered lawfully in self-defense against an aggressor. A rule presented *de lege ferenda* must by definition be a rule the consequences of which would be regarded as desirable for members of the community generally. But it is apparent that this proposed rule would be disastrously undesirable. It would assure every prospective aggressor that if he fails he will be entitled to restoration of every inch of any territory he may have lost. It would do this even if the defeated aggressor still openly reserves the liberty to renew his aggressive design, and even if (as with Egypt in Gaza and Jordan on the West Bank), the territories in question were formerly seized unlawfully by the claimants, who have consistently used them since then as a base for aggressive activity against the present occupant.

In short, the Arab state-favored meaning would underwrite unconditionally the risks of loss from any contemplated aggression. By such a rule an international law that sets out by the *ex iniuria* principle to discourage aggressors would end with a rule encouraging aggressors by insuring them in advance against the main risks involved in case of defeat. To offer such a rule *de lege ferenda* would sanctify a new and cynical legal maxim that might run: "If you cannot stop the aggressor, help him!" A meaning of the preamble yielding such a result cannot, therefore, be preferred when the two others above-mentioned are available. It may perhaps be added that Soviet and Arab voting patterns in the West Irian and Goan affairs showed no particular support for a norm in that context barring *simpliciter* acquisition of territory by force.[26]

Finally, as to this point, it must be added as to Egypt in Gaza and as to Jordan on the West Bank, that even if their entry there had not been unlawful, nor in defiance of the Security Council resolutions of April and May 1948, the proposed rule would bar any right of theirs to be in those territories either. For their entry (even if not unlawful as it was) would fall within the meaning they seek to give to "the inadmissibility of the acquisition of territory by war." So that even if the rule were now newly legislated with retrospective effect it could not improve *their* present legal position vis-à-vis Israel except by an entirely unprincipled discriminatory application of the new rule to one side and not the other.[27]

This kind of Arab state activity, designed to "amend" international law for ad hoc use against Israel, has become persistent since 1967 in all fora and contexts of international activity. The Fourth Special Committee on the Question of Defining Aggression, appointed by the Twenty-Second General Assembly in 1967, reported a draft definition, which was finally adopted by consensus of the twenty-ninth session on December 14, 1974. It had had an interesting history of Arab state efforts to include in it a provision that territorial acquisitions obtained even by *lawful* force would be invalid; those efforts failed abjectly.[28] The only operative provision concerning acquisition of territory by force (Article 5, para. 3) strictly limits any invalidity by reference to no less than three requirements. First, it is not acquisition by mere threat or use of force, but only acquisition by "aggression" that is so tainted. Entry in the course of self-defense, as in the case of Israel in 1967, is not within this. Second, the acts of force there enumerated in articles 2 and 3 are stated to be aggression *only if first committed by the acquirer,* thus doubly excluding acts in self-defense from the taint. Third, even such acts, to be tainted, must be "in contravention of the Charter," thus triply excluding acts of self-defense. (This limitation of any taint to acquisition of territory to acts "in contravention of the Charter" is also explicitly made in the reference to the matter in paragraph 7 of the preamble.)

Through more than one hundred meetings of the thirty-five-state Fourth Special Committee, not to speak of the Sixth Committee of the Twenty-Ninth General Assembly between 1967 and 1974, a version of the rule concerning acquisition of territory by force based on the principle *ex iniuria non oritur ius* maintained itself against all Arab state efforts to change it into a form targetable against Israel. The attempted twisting of this principle of international law for ad hoc use against a particular target state thus wholly failed. This must be attributed not merely to the legal skills and learning of most state representatives, but also to awareness by many of them of the dangers to the security of all states that would ensue from a change in international law of which the policy implications are (as seen above under *"Ex Iniuria non Oritur Ius* and Territory.") quite absurd.[29]

OBSERVATIONS ON CERTAIN METHODS OF ARGUMENT

The preceding pages have reviewed the international law context, and the prevailing rules, as to the territorial entitlements of states in situations emerging from the use of force, lawful and unlawful. They have also examined, in that context, the assumptions as to the legal effects of the General Assembly resolutions on matters as to which the charter itself endows them with no binding legal effect. This conscientious inquiry in the context of international law is also what the authors of the legal theses of *Resolutions* claim to pursue. It is thus dismaying to find that major questions and principles that have been shown to be part of the essential international law context of the matters they discuss, receive virtually no consideration or even mention from these authors. And where, as with the question of the legal value to be attributed to General Assembly resolutions, they do consider this context, the consideration is slight, if not perfunctory, ignoring most of the authorities, and is in the end patently question-begging.[30]

Those authors are presumably not aware of the inadequacies cited above. Other inadequacies are, however, highlighted by the authors themselves in their introduction. This makes their own inadequacies even more puzzling. One passage highlighting inadequacies is the authors' declaration that "consistent with the consulting arrangements with the United Nations, no direct use has been made of the formal negotiating history of the resolutions or of the informal unrecorded[31] consultations which led to the adoption of particular wordings."[32] Consultation of the *travaux préparatoires* is, of course, an essential part of international techniques of interpretation. The reader is entitled to wonder why either any U.N. officials concerned or the Sponsoring Committee or these authors should wish to renounce it. And this is especially so since such preparatory materials are sometimes quite critical for Middle East issues on which the authors engage. As Lord Caradon himself testified, for example, the *travaux* are essential background for understanding the effect of the references to "withdrawal of Israel armed forces" in Security Council Resolution 242,[33] just as they are to ascertaining the meaning of references to acquisition of territory by force in contravention of the charter in the 1974 Definition of Aggression adopted by Resolution 3314 of the General Assembly's twenty-ninth session.

The renunciation of the *travaux* was not necessarily inspired by a sense that foreshortened inquiries would yield better outcomes for their own particular theses. No such neutral explanation is plausible for another stipulation of their introduction, namely: "The terms 'Jew' and 'Jewish' are used to refer to adherents of a particular monotheistic religion of universal moral values. The terms 'Zionism' and 'Zionist' refer to a particular national movement, with its political programme of first 'a national home' and then a national state located in Palestine."[34] The authors innocently declare that this is a "basic distinction" that it is necessary to make "because this is a juridical study." But it is no more "basic" from a juridical point of view than an analogous distinction between "Irishmen as adherents to a particular form of Christian Catholicism," and "Tykes" (or some corresponding expletive) "who are adherents to a political programme of securing (formerly) the independence of Ireland, or now of Northern Ireland." For the authors are certainly aware that the symbols "Zionism" and "Zionist" have been falsely and arbitrarily translated into "racist" by one of the lamentable recent resolutions (3379[XXX] of Nov. 10, 1975) of the General Assembly, which they are thus attempting to rescue from the morass of international power politics to the more sheltered level of international law. No reputable international lawyer has accepted that meretricious pronouncement as other than an adventure in expedient pejoration. The authors should, as international lawyers, have avoided demeaning their arguments in this way, especially since it is difficult to find any important legal argument that they make that would not be equally strong (or equally weak) without this so-called "basic distinction."[35]

There is, on the other hand, another distinction that would indeed have been "basic," not only for the juridical study that these authors set out to write, but also for their exposition of what they claim to be "the background of the Partition Resolution."[36] This is the distinction in time that was demonstrated in Chapter 1 under "Parallel Liberations: 'Arab Asia' and Jewish Palestine" between what the authors in 1979 identify as "the Palestinian Nation," on the one hand, and the "Arab Nation" of 1917, on the other. This distinction is no invention of the present writer. The Palestine national movement in its constituent document insisted precisely on this distinction. It was to the "Arab Nation" (understood in 1917 as including Arabs living in Palestine, who were not yet identified as a separate people) to whom virtually the whole of the Middle East domains of Turkey were allocated, in the distribution after World War I between the Arab liberation movement, on the one hand, and the Jewish liberation movement (to which a tiny sliver of this vast area was allocated), on the other.

It was shown, in Chapter 1, under "Parallel Liberations: 'Arab Asia' and Jewish Palestine," that there is neither juridical nor moral basis for undoing that initial application of President Wilson's self-determination principle after World War I in its own time context, merely because, half a century later, the Arabs of Palestine came belatedly to distinguish themselves as a separate people from the "Arab Nation" whose self-determination was already so amply endowed. The authors of *Resolutions* might or might not agree with that analysis and the conclusion that the burden of redress due to Palestinians, like the redress due to Jews displaced by this distribution, should be shared equitably between the Arab states of the Middle East and Israel, perhaps in proportion to their respective endowments. But it is difficult to see how they could fail to address themselves at all to a distinction so relevant and central, but also so damaging by its omission, to both the structure of their argument and its main conclusions.

Still another observation must be made at this point, particularly as I approach in the succeeding section these authors' efforts (sometimes even to the point of misquoting important documents) to show that the General Assembly's Partition Resolution is "the preeminent juridical basis for the State of Israel," and that Israel is bound by this resolution even though the Arab states rejected it and, by blatant acts of armed aggression, wholly aborted its operation. These authors have, as here shown, an exalted but somewhat undiscriminating view of the legal effects of General Assembly resolutions. They are, as just observed, particularly enthusiastic about Resolution 181(II). But there is one central provision of that Resolution, reference to which they assiduously avoid. This is the General Assembly's request that: "The Security Council determine as a threat to the peace, breach of the peace or act of aggression, in accordance with Article 39 of the Charter, any attempt to alter by force the settlement envisaged by this resolution." By this omission, they can also avoid considering the consequences of the Arab side's rejection of the Partition Resolution, and their armed aggression against it and against Israel, which prevented its ever coming into legal operation. Such consideration, as will immediately be submitted, is fatal for the main legal conclusions to which they seek to lead their readers.

These aspects of purportedly objective studies are perhaps in part explained by the need of the Committee on . . . Rights of the Palestinian People to find international lawyers whose opinion on points at issue would produce the outcomes that the committee desired. There is a dramatic instance of this in *Origins,* part 1, in relation to the "validity" of the Palestine mandate. Mr. Henry Cattan is the main authority whom the Committee can apparently marshal to support the desired conclusion.[37] Mr. Cattan is a lawyer of ability and distinction, but he is also a former member of the Palestine Higher Arab Committee led by the notorious Haj Amin al-Husseini, Mufti of Jerusalem. He also later presented the Arab case at the United Nations in 1947. The only other international law "authority" offered is Professor W. T. Mallison, an associate of Mr. Cattan, who wrote an introduction to Henry Cattan's book *Palestine and International Law* (1973).[38] And it conformed to this pattern, of course, that the committee also chose Professor Mallison as the consultant to enunciate versions of international law worthy of its sponsorship, in the final study on *Resolutions.*

4

· · · · ·

Abortive Partition
Proposals

Three distinct and basic questions are wholly overlooked by the analysis, in the United Nations study here for brevity called *Resolutions,* of the partition proposals in Resolution 181(II) of November 29, 1947.[1]

What would have been the resolution's effects on sovereign title in the territories concerned if the Arab states had not rejected it, and, in the words of the General Assembly Soviet delegate at the time, had not committed aggression against it and against Israel—aggression that completely aborted the resolution?

What residue (if any) of this potential binding effect of the resolution survived this destruction by the Arab aggression?

Assuming—*arguendo*—that some final residue of that legal effect did survive that rejection and abortion in 1948, what would be the effect of that final residue in the context of the international rights, obligations, and delinquencies arising from subsequent events from 1948 to date?

All these questions, assuredly, are part of what the authors call "the context of international law" in which they claim to be examining the U.N. resolutions concerned.[2] The legal relations of states cannot be frozen at a point of time a quarter of a century and more ago, even at the behest of these authors. In the lives of states, no less than individuals, legal rights and obligations move with acts and events in time. And for that reason we shall have to refer again under the third head to the analysis of the prevailing international law principles examined in Chapter 3 above.

The present section deals with the first of those questions, and with the other two thereafter. First, then, what would have been the binding effects on sovereign title of the Partition Resolution (181[II]) if its operation had not been aborted by Arab state rejection and related aggression against Israel?

On this matter the authors display a rather tortured struggle. They do not, on the one hand, dissociate themselves from Arab claims, which they cite at length,[3] that the Partition Resolution was invalid *ab initio,* as violative (in their view) of the mandate for Palestine, as interpreted by protagonists of the Arab cause.[4] This would obviously assist the authors' thesis as justifying the Arab states' rejection of the Partition Resolution, and ease the discomfort with which, in their so-called "background to the Partition Resolution," they do not refer at all to the resort by the Arab states to armed aggression against Israel, which aborted it. On the other hand, however, writing now in 1979, after failure of that aggression to destroy the state of Israel, the authors wish (for rather obvious reasons) to attach great value to certain provisions of the Partition Resolution that would, on their interpretation, be legally embarrassing to the state of Israel.[5] In this schizophrenic posture, their analysis succeeds in suggesting that the General Assembly's role in 1947 was both as a legitimate U.N. successor to the League mandates system, and as a usurping authority acting *ultra vires.* The schizophrenia of simultaneous validity and invalidity that they suggest for the Partition Resolution thus infects their account of the role of the General Assembly.

If we distinguish as we should, however, the three diverse aspects above identified of the rolled-up question concerning the legally binding effect of the Partition Resolution, and address ourselves to the first aspect—its potential legal effects on sovereign title if it had not been aborted by Arab aggression—the answer is not complicated. The validity side of the authors' schizophrenia then falls neatly into this slot.

It is clear that Great Britain as the mandatory power on April 2, 1947, gave formal notice to the United Nations and authorized the General Assembly to attempt a settlement for which that body summoned a special session in April 1947.[6] Since the charter itself refers to the mandates system, the United Kingdom request was certainly a "question or . . . matter within the scope" of the charter, for purposes of General Assembly discussion under Article 10.

No less clearly, however, the powers of the General Assembly acting on a matter within Article 10, seem limited to the nonbinding mode of "recommendations." Indeed, apart from a few specific matters, such as budget under Article 17, this is true of all General Assembly action.[7] The language of the partition resolution, moreover, is scarcely such as to convey titles instanter,[8] nor is it easy to see that the General Assembly had any territorial title in Palestine to cede.[9] Elihu Lauterpacht concludes, correctly, that the 1947 partition resolution had no such legislative character as to vest territorial rights in either Jews or Arabs. Any binding force of it would have had to arise from the principle *pacta sunt servanda,* that is, from the agreement of the parties concerned to the proposed plan. Such agreement, however, was frustrated *ab initio* by the Arab rejection,[10] a rejection underlined by armed invasion of Palestine by the forces of Egypt, Iraq, Lebanon, Syria, and Saudi Arabia, timed for the British withdrawal on May 14, 1948, and aimed at destroying Israel and at ending even the merely hortatory value of the plan.[11]

The state of Israel is thus not legally derived from the partition plan, but rests (as do most other states in the world) on assertion of independence by its people and government, on the vindication of that independence by arms against assault by other states, and on the establishment of orderly government within territory under its stable control. At most, as Israel's Declaration of Independence expressed it, the General Assembly resolution was a "recognition" of the "natural and historic right" of the Jewish people in Palestine. The immediate recognition of Israel by the United States and other states was in no way predicated on its creation by the partition resolution, nor was its admission in 1949 to membership in the United Nations.

The State of Israel's Declaration of Independence of May 14, 1948, made under the immediate shadow of armed attack from the Arab states, recited as its grounds for independence the following facts:

That Palestine was the birthplace of the Jewish people, where "their spiritual, religious and national identity was formed," where they achieved independence and created a culture of national and universal significance and wrote and gave the Bible to the world.

That Jews in exile had never ceased to pray and hope for their return to national freedom in this Land of Israel.

That efforts to return to the land had continued throughout the centuries, and in recent decades had become a mass movement, bringing a revival of the land, of the Hebrew language, and progress for all inhabitants.

That the historic connection of the Jewish people with Palestine and the right of the Jewish people to return there was internationally recognized by the Balfour Declaration of November 2, 1917, and by the League of Nations mandate.

That the contribution of the Jewish people to the victory of the freedom-loving nations over the Nazi evil entitled them to rank with the nations that founded the United Nations.

It will be noted that all these bases of Israel's title to self-determination (summed up in a concluding affirmation in the declaration that "it is the natural right of the Jewish people to lead, as do all other nations, an independent existence in its sovereign State") were independent of the United Nations. The bases refer, indeed, to facts existing before the United Nations itself came into existence. The preamble of the declaration did also refer to the Partition Resolution, but in terms that belie what, as we shall shortly show, the Mallisons draw from this reference. After the above enumeration, the preamble recited that the General Assembly had, on November 29, 1947, adopted the Partition Resolution *"calling for"* the establishment of a Jewish state in Palestine, and that "This *recognition* of the right of the Jewish people to establish their State is *irrevocable"* (emphasis supplied).[12]

I have italicized certain of the exact words used in the proclamation, because these words in the version that the authors of *Resolutions* purportedly have quoted have been altered in ways that seem to support the authors' otherwise untenable assertion "that the State of Israel has placed heavy reliance upon the Partition Resolution as providing legal authority" and that that resolution "is the preeminent juridical basis for the State of Israel." The authors change the verb "call for" to "authorise," which in context it cannot mean, for the words "call for" rather refer forward to the operative paragraph in which the proclamation states the readiness of the new state to cooperate in implementing Resolution 181(II). They also take liberties with the above-quoted words, which state that the United Nations "recognition" of Israel is "irrevocable." This in context means that the preceding five titles to self-determination justify "this recognition" by the United Nations. The authors under examination (still within quotation marks) substitute for the word "recognition" the word "resolution." Thus, the whole purport is changed to one that supports their claim (shortly to be examined) that the Partition Resolution must bind Israel forever, even though it never came into legal operation at all due to the Arab states' rejection of it and armed aggression against it, and against the State of Israel. They inject, without warrant, into the proclamation the statement that "This *resolution* by the United Nations . . . is *irrevocable,"*[13] (emphasis supplied), an injection, perhaps accidental, but still obviously helpful to their attempt to say that Israel remained and still remains bound by the Partition Resolution despite the fact that the Arab states and other authorities concerned rejected it, and aborted it by the war of aggression they launched against Israel.

We return then to the question to which this section is devoted, namely, what would have been the legal binding effect of the Partition Resolution if its coming into operation had not been aborted by the Arab state rejection and related aggression against Israel? The answer is that the Plan of Partition with Economic Union there set out would, if accepted, have bound the state of Israel and the Arab states, including the new Arab state once it was established, on the basis of the rule *pacta sunt servanda.* The effect of the agreement would have been to allocate sovereign titles *inter alia* to Israel, the proposed new Arab state, and the proposed *corpus separatum.* This also, as already indicated, was the view expressed by the state of Israel. On the other hand, as even these authors had to admit, the Arab states rejected it, and of course (though these authors do not mention the highly relevant fact) they also used armed aggression to destroy the plan.[14] There was in fact no such agreement, no such effect in vesting and delimiting titles, and no such entities as the proposed Arab state and *corpus separatum* came into being in fact or in law.

ABORTION BY ARAB REJECTION AND AGGRESSION

The chronology of events is vital in assessing whether Resolution 181(II) could affect sovereign titles in the territories involved. That resolution recommended to the mandatory power the adoption and implementation of the majority UNSCOP plan as revised, requested the Security Council to "take measures" to implement it, called upon the inhabitants of Palestine to take necessary steps to put the plan into effect, and appealed to all governments and all people to refrain from any action that might hamper or delay it. The plan attached envisaged termination of the mandate and withdrawal of British forces not later than August 1, 1948, and that the Arab and Jewish states and the "Special International Regime for the City of Jerusalem" should come into existence not later than October 1, 1948. It described future boundaries for these in parts 1-3 of the plan therein attached. It also included chapters on holy places, religious buildings and sites (Ch. 1), religious and minority rights (Ch. 2), and citizenship, international conventions, and financial obligations (Ch. 3).

The Jewish Agency for Palestine reluctantly accepted this resolution on the understanding that despite the negative attitudes of the Arab states in the General Assembly, they would accept the appeal of that body not to oppose its implementation by violent means—an understanding implicit in the reciprocity of international legal relations founded on consent. The Arab states, however, rejected the resolution as infringing Arab rights, and as ultra vires of the General Assembly; and they proceeded in May 1948 to attempt to seize the whole of Palestine by armed aggression. Consequently, all basis for bringing the plan into legal operation was destroyed by the Arab states in May, months before the date set for the four proposed territorial dispositions.

In the contemporary words of the U.S. representative in the Security Council in May 1948,[15] referring to Jordan's admission of her armed invasion of Palestine and occupation of the West Bank, "we have here the highest type of evidence of the international violation of the law: the admission by those who are committing this violation." A little earlier in the same debate the Soviet representative, Mr. Gromyko—now the Foreign Minister—expressed surprise that Arab states "have resorted to such action as sending their troops into Palestine and carrying out military operations aimed at the suppression of the national liberation movement in Palestine."[16] The national liberation movement he referred to was, of course, that which led to the establishment of the State of Israel. In Mr. Gromyko's words a few days later at the 309th meeting on May 29, 1948, "what is happening in

Palestine can only be described as military operations organised by a group of States against the Jewish State."

The authors of *Resolutions* pay little attention to these dates and events so critical for vesting titles in international law. After their opening vacillation as to whether the Partition Resolution was not "invalid" *ab initio*, they confuse matters further by vigorously asserting (without any further ceremony about its initial "validity") that the resolution is certainly of continuing validity today, that is, thirty years after it was prevented from coming into operation by the aborting action of the Arab states.[17] And it is perhaps no coincidence that their positions on this closely parallel the positions taken by the Arab states, which the authors report as follows:[18]

The Arab States not only voted against partition, but they initially took the position that it was invalid. It is, therefore, significant [*sic*!] that they have subsequently relied upon it in presenting legal arguments on behalf of the Palestinians. The Arab States are now not only [*sic*] supporting the basic principles of the Partition Resolution, but [*sic*] subsequent General Assembly resolutions which are consistent with those principles as well. The Arab States were deeply disturbed[19] by what they initially regarded as the violation of the right of self-determination by the Partition Resolution.[20]

Hence the miracle to be wrought by the Arab states, and by the Mallisons in their wake, is much more impressive than a mere revival of the dead. It is an attempt to resuscitate a resolution whose abortion the Arab states had themselves procured over a quarter of a century ago.

Whether this Resolution 181(II) would have been legally binding had it been allowed to come into operation is one question that I have answered in the last Section. But the present (second) question of which (if any) of these potential legal effects would come into being after rejection and aggression had destroyed the Plan—as it were in utero, before it could enter the world of legal effectiveness—is quite a different question. The answer to this question seems to be that in terms of its binding nature, none of these potential legal effects ever came into being.[21] Consequently, they cannot, as the Mallisons maintain,[22] have "continuing validity."

It has already been seen that their submission faces the difficulty of the authors' ambivalence as to whether, even *ab initio*, the Partition Resolution was "valid" or "invalid." A further difficulty is that they seem to mean by "validity" only the question whether that resolution violated what they claim to be preexisting rights of Arabs, for instance under the mandate. Because of their strangely exclusive preoccupation with "validity" in that *ultra vires* kind of sense, they do not appear to direct their minds at all to the second more important question here under discussion. This is whether, in view of the situation brought about by the Arab states' rejection and armed aggression openly aimed at thwarting the resolution and destroying the state of Israel, it ever reached the stage of entering into legal operation.[23]

The negative answer is decisively embedded in the facts of chronology rehearsed in the opening of this section. And this negative answer rests on no mere technicality. Rather is it the case that the opposite view pressed by the Mallisons is grossly repugnant to elementary considerations of justice and equity common to most legal systems, including international law. I venture to spell out some of these considerations.

The present submission is that the rejection of partition and the armed aggression by the Arab states constituted an anticipatory repudiation and frustration of the resolution and plan, the protracted use of force by these states against the latter effectively preventing them from coming into legal effect.[24] But there are also certain other legal grounds, rooted in basic notions of justice and equity, on which the Arab states (and the Palestinians whom they represented in these matters) should not, in any case, be permitted, after so lawless a resort to violence against the plan, to turn around, decades later, and claim legal entitlements under it. More than one of "the general principles of law" acknowledged in Article 38(1)(c) of the Statute of the International Court of Justice seem to forbid it. Such claimants do not come with "clean hands" to seek equity; their hands indeed are mired by their lawlessly violent bid to destroy the very resolution and plan from which they now seek equity. They may also be thought by their representations concerning these documents, to have led others to act to their own detriment, and thus to be debarred by their own conduct from espousing, in pursuit of present expediencies, positions they formerly so strongly denounced. They may also be thought to be in breach of the general principle of good faith in two other respects. Their position resembles that of a party to a transaction who has unlawfully repudiated the transaction, and comes to court years later claiming that selected provisions of it should be meticulously enforced against the wronged party. It also resembles that of a party who has by unlawful violence wilfully destroyed the subject-matter that is "the fundamental basis" on which consent rested, and now clamors to have the original terms enforced against the other party. These are grounds that reinforce the pithy view of U.S. Legal Adviser Herbert Hansell that the 1947 partition was never effectuated.[25]

On any of these grounds the answer to the second question must be that the Partition Resolution and Plan, since they were prevented by Arab rejection and armed aggression from entering into legal operation, could not thereafter carry any legal effects binding on Israel.

By what appears to be an afterthought, the authors of *Resolutions* seek to salvage some continuing binding effect for the Partition Resolution by suggesting that the gist of some later General Assembly resolutions, especially those concerning Palestinian peoplehood (those, I presume, adopted after 1973, as the oil weapon took hold) somehow gave new legal life retrospectively to the still-born Partition Resolution and Plan, since these later resolutions now "constitute a worldwide consensus and support."[26] I have already submitted in Chapter 2 that these authors have not adequately examined the limits within which votes in international bodies can be translated into rules of international law, and that, in particular, their arguments such as the above concerning recent resolutions of the General Assembly on Palestine are question-begging. That deficiency also affects this final basis of their claim that the provisions of the abortive Partition Plan of 1947 constitute binding norms of international law in 1979.

5

. . . . .

International Law
and Israel-Arab Relations
Since 1948

It was pointed out in Chapter 3 above that even if the authors had established (which they have not) a basis on which the aborted Partition Resolution and Plan could have "continuing" legal effects in 1979, these effects would in any case have to operate within the context of international law. That context must obviously include the consequences in international law of acts and events occurring in the intervening years. It was seen in adequate detail in Chapter 3 that unquestionable rules of international law entitle Israel to remain in Judea and Samaria (the West Bank) and in Gaza until a territorial settlement is agreed upon. The lawfulness of her entry, and unlawfulness of the Jordanian and Egyptian presence thus displaced, the unquestioned rule of *uti possidetis* applicable to this situation, all require that secure and recognized boundaries, possibly with ancillary territorial regimes such as demilitarized zones between herself and her neighbors, be negotiated between Israel and the neighboring Arab states.

THE "RIGHT OF RETURN"

In this light we may first proceed to examine the General Assembly resolutions on the right of return or compensation of Palestinian refugees, on which the authors of *Resolutions* so heavily rely.[1]

The first point, which never apparently occurs to the authors at all, is that any rule of international law requiring rights of return or compensation would have to apply equally to Jewish refugees from Arab countries, and to Arab refugees from Palestine, and that all claims to such rights should properly be dealt with together as a part of the peace negotiation. This also accords with principles implicit in the recognition (Chapter 1 above) that the overall distribution between the Jewish and Arab peoples after World War I was itself founded on the application of the self-determination principle.

Second, the authors themselves observe upon the fact that General Assembly Resolution 194(III) of December 11, 1948, which they properly recognize as the starting-point and very basis of their own argument, did not even purport to be in mandatory terms, but was merely part of the terms of reference of the Palestine Conciliation Commission.[2] A recital in Resolution 273(III) of May 11, 1949, admitting Israel to the United Nations, "recalled" that Resolution 194(III) provided an option for refugees to return to their homes, and compensation if they opted not to return, but it immediately, in the same recital, "noted" the declarations and explanations made by Israel before the ad hoc committee in respect of implementation of that resolution. Since Israel's declarations and explanations did not unqualifiedly accept the resolution, this can in no way be regarded as creating a legal obligation.[3] As E. Lauterpacht well observes, the General Assembly phrase "could not by its resolution give the Jews and Arabs in Palestine rights which they did not otherwise possess: nor, correspondingly, could it take away such rights as they did possess."[4]

It is clear that the next resolution they invoke, General Assembly Resolution 513(VI),[5] was designed to facilitate the resettlement of the refugees in place of the virtual confinement in refugee camps on Arab territory upon which some Arab states insisted. Resettlement, as observed in Chapter 1, had been the effective solution for the far greater and more complex refugee problems in Europe after World War II. It is a melancholy fact that this more humane course came to so little in the Middle East over so long a time, that some have concluded that, for the Arab states concerned, the refugee problem was more useful than its solution. Resolutions 2452(XXIII), 2535(XXIV), 2963(XXVII), and 3089(XXVIII), concerned with refugees fleeing in the aftermath of the Arab aggressions of both 1947-48 and 1967, are also directed to support activities of the Commissioner-General of the United Nations Relief and Rehabilitation Agency for Palestine Refugees in the Middle East in negotiations with the various parties. Though they contain calls to Israel, and expressions of regret on the matter of repatriation and compensation are included, the peremptory assertions that are vital for the theses of all these pamphlets, including *Resolutions,* only finally mature in Resolution 3236(XXIX) of November 22, 1974. In the era of the oil weapon, which then opened, the *Resolutions* "study" correctly points out, General Assembly resolutions begin regularly to insert the adjective "inalienable" before the words "right to return."

Even if we take these resolutions to be declaratory of principles of international law, the question would still have to be answered why the right of "return or compensation" must not be applied equally to Jewish refugees from Arab lands, as well as to Arab refugees, all being victims of the same complex conflict. Security Council Resolution 242, as already seen, makes no such arbitrary discrimination. In their doggedly meticulous analysis of these resolutions, the authors of *Resolutions* nowhere refer to Jewish refugees, nor do they even seek to explain why the general juridical principles on this matter from the Magna Carta of 1215 to the International Covenant on Civil and Political Rights of 1968, which they eloquently invoke, should apply to Arab refugees and not to Jewish refugees.[6] The point is none the less pertinent because the misfortunes of both categories arose from unsuccessful ventures in aggressive use of armed force in defiance of United Nations resolutions and of the charter by Arab states and not by Israel.

In this connection there are many strange reticences. Among these none is more remarkable than the short shrift they give to Security Council resolutions, especially the basic resolutions after the close respectively of the Arab-state-initiated wars of 1967 and 1973, namely, Resolution 242, of November 22, 1967, and Resolution 338, of October 22, 1973. After all, the full title of *Resolutions* concerns "Major United Nations Resolutions," not merely major General Assembly resolutions. Amid the tangled web of doctrine about "the right of return" of Palestinian refugees, the authors decline to pay any regard to the fact that the Security Council in 1967 did not feel that it could invoke any such black-letter rules of international law as the authors assert for the unilateral benefit of the Arab side. International lawyers should surely be curious about such incongruities. Nor do the authors deign to notice the fact that the formula of Resolution 242 calling for "a just settlement of the refugee question," lacks the deformity of their own one-sidedness in ignoring Jewish refugees from Arab lands, while insisting on redress to Arab refugees from Palestine. They might of course say in answer that the law developed after 1967. Yet, even then, they fail to notice that, as late as 1973, the Security Council reaffirmed in Resolution 338 all the provisions of Resolution 242, and called for urgent negotiation on their basis. This means (though the authors prefer not to notice it) that even in 1973 the resolutions of the Security Council, which is also a principal organ of the United Nations, had not conformed themselves to the version of international law presented by the authors of *Resolutions* or even these authors' version of United Nations resolutions.

SELF-DETERMINATION PRINCIPLE

The thesis presented by *Resolutions* and by *Self-Determination,* which precedes it,[7] requires an argument involving several steps that those authors do not adequately distinguish. Three issues must be identified, and kept distinct.

General Nature of Self-Determination Claims. Is the self-determination doctrine, whatever be its specific content, to be regarded as a precept of international law itself, or only as a consideration of policy or justice to be weighed as one among other facts and values in the interpretation and application of legal rules?

The authors of *Self-Determination* ask whether the doctrine is a principle or a right,[8] a rather obscure question that they answer even more obscurely by saying that, while the answer to it is not within their ambit, they will proceed "on the axiom" that "the right of self-determination exists as a crucial element in contemporary international life and is recognised as such by the political world community."[9] This supposed axiom is in itself ambiguous. It studiously avoids any juridical reference, and might be unexceptionable only in a textbook on the sociology of the international community. A careful lawyer knows that its central notion of a "right" may or may not refer to a legal right. It may, as Indian representative R. Rao observed in 1969, be more a function or consequence of geography than a legal right.[10] The grave weaknesses of the process by which these authors commissioned by the U.N. Secretariat seek to demonstrate the transmogrification of this sociological observation into a precept of international law at present in force, have been exposed in Chapter 2. The legal value of their major conclusions depends *inter alia* on the adequacy of that demonstration, whatever the supposed content of the right of self-determination. The evidence of state attitudes contradicting the central drive of those conclusions will be presented in Chapter 6, especially under "The 1974 Definition: Defeat . . ."

Assuming a Legal Precept as to Self-Determination, What Are Its Contents? If there is already an international legal precept concerning self-determination, what it prescribes for particular situations still also depends on its contents, and on what implications can be drawn from these. These U.N. "studies" properly treat the relevant provisions of the Declaration on Principles of International Law Concerning Friendly Relations and Co-operation Among States, of 1970, as central to this question. They do not, however, appear to give any attention at all to the later and far more illuminating discussions and conclusions on this matter that led up to the relevant provisions of the Resolution A/9890 A/Res/3314(XXIX) of December 14, 1974. These will show that, even if the right of self-determination be acknowledged as now enshrined in a rule or principle of international law, what this rule or principle directs and what implications flow from this still have to be determined on vital matters. And it will be shown that these include matters bearing closely on the claims of Palestinian Arabs, which are quite overlooked by the authors of these pamphlets.[11]

Among these is the confident assertion of both *Resolutions* and *Self-Determination* that various General Assembly resolutions (exemplified of course in the notorious P.L.O. resolution 3236[XXIX] of November 22, 1974) have produced a state of international law that authorizes the use of armed force by Palestinians or states who support these against the state of Israel. That the General Assembly adopted resolutions of this tenor is unquestionable; yet the present analysis will show, in Chapter 6 under "The 1974 Definition: Defeat . . .," that there is very convincing evidence, contemporaneous with the above P.L.O. resolution, that the votes of such resolutions emphatically do not represent any such consensus of states as is capable of changing the prevailing rules of international law, or creating new rules of such law. This evidence, as will be seen, lies in the proceedings of the General Assembly's own 1967 Special Committee on . . . Defining Aggression.

Temporal Context of Application.   Third, assuming that a legal precept concerning self-determination has come into existence, and that its contents are fixed, the date when this occurred becomes also of critical importance. For, like any other legal precept, this precept predicates certain facts for its operation at the relevant time. It will only operate if those facts exist at that time.

In order, therefore, to determine what legal effects such a precept can be said to produce in relation to the claims of Palestinian Arabs, two crucial questions still have to be answered. One is as to the intertemporal operation of the law. If, as these pamphlets sometimes suggest, for example, that date is somewhere around 1970, the new legal precept of 1970 cannot be applied retroactively to disturb territorial allocations made more than half a century before in satisfaction of the respective claims of self-determination of the nation of Israel and the "Arab Nation" (including Palestinian Arabs) in the post-World War I settlement of that time. It has already been shown, in Chapter 1, that on this temporal ground alone, it is erroneous to conceive the claims of Palestinian Arabs as claims against Israel, and that the proper targets of these claims should include all Arab states of the Middle East as cobeneficiaries of the initial post-World War I allocation. And the *Self-Determination* pamphlet, perhaps unwittingly, reinforces this by its emphatic conclusion (to be later further discussed) that the recognition of the national identity of the Palestinian people did not emerge onto the international scene until 1970, almost half a century after that basic post-World War I allocation according to the self-determination principle.

The other question still to be answered, even assuming that a legal principle concerning self-determination exists and that Palestinian Arabs now qualify for "national" rights, is whether it is a fact that this national group lacks a national home. As already pointed out in Chapter 1, under "Displaced Palestinian Arabs," there already exists in Palestine a state, the State of Jordan, a majority of whose population are Palestinian Arabs, constituting indeed a majority of all Palestinian Arabs. What stands in the

way of fuller Palestinian enjoyment of this ample national endowment is
the continued refusal of Jordan (which is part of Palestine) to heed the
basic precepts of international law prescribing negotiations of peace and
delimitation of "secure and recognised boundaries" between Jordan and
Israel. Palestinian self-determination has already in fact and in law been
largely realized in the area of Jordan; and the negotiation of peace with
Israel would extend the ambit for self-determination even further. (See
Map 3 in the Appendixes [Britain and the Jewish National Home: Pledges
and Border Changes, 1917-1923].)

In order to establish claims in respect of the "national rights" of Palestinian Arabs as against the state of Israel to the validation of which most of
both of these pamphlets seem to be directed, all of the above questions
would have to be answered in the affirmative. Yet a number of these
questions are not even noticed, let alone answered, in these "studies." It
will be shown in subsequent sections that a number of them cannot be
answered in the affirmative.

IS SELF-DETERMINATION PRESCRIBED BY INTERNATIONAL LAW?

The *Self-Determination* pamphlet, as well as a main section of the
Resolutions pamphlet, seems directed to answering the first question above
in the affirmative. The former opens, however, with a seeming self-contradiction. It declares it to be beyond its scope to decide between the "various
arguments," "academic" and "juridical" as to whether the self-determination
concept is a "principle" or a "right"; and declares in the same breath that it
will proceed on the axiom that "the right [*sic*] of self-determination" is a
crucial element of contemporary international life, recognized as such by
the political world community. It proceeds, in short, on an axiom that begs
the question that at the outset it declares to be beyond its scope, and that at
the end (as we shall see) it claims to have established as law.

The demonstration proceeds by culling the views of publicists who have
asserted "the right of self-determination as a principle of international
law."[12] Some of these are experts whose distinction is certainly not in the
field of international law;[13] but as a token of objectivity it also mentions
(though scarcely exhaustively) one or two publicists who hold the opposed
view. For the anonymous writers have perforce to admit that, even today,
there is a "variety of opinions on the issue of the juridical position in
international law of the right of self-determination."[14] Yet this, too, in no
way prevents them from assuming that the right of self-determination *is* "an
established principle of international law," because this is "the consistent
stand of the General Assembly" and this stand "reflects the will of the
international community."[15] This seems to return them to their opening
axiom, unless indeed they were expecting the necessary demonstration to

be made by the Mallisons in the later pamphlet, *Resolutions*. But it was seen in Chapter 2 above that though *Resolutions* opens with laborious effort to show that the "stand" of the General Assembly on a matter becomes international law, the authors of that pamphlet did not succeed in this. So that the assertion of "law" is but a premise of which proof has not even been attempted, or one whose proof has been attempted and failed.

It is thus on faith (or prejudice), rather than any juristic demonstration, that the anonymous writers of *Self-Determination* perform the extraordinary tour de force of elevating the self-determination principle to the level of *ius cogens*, which under the Vienna Convention on Treaties, Article 53, will make void any inconsistent treaty provision.[16] It is to be observed that no treaty nor any serious scholar has yet given to the *ius cogens* any function other than the negative one of making void a treaty provision that conflicts with it. And the major study by Aureliu Cristescu in the same series states flatly that "no United Nations instrument confers such a peremptory character on the right of peoples to self-determination."[17] It should perhaps also be added that even if they had better succeeded in raising the self-determination principle to *ius cogens* status within Article 53 of the Vienna Convention on Treaties of 1969, and even if the *ius cogens* doctrine had some function beyond annulling contrary treaty provisions (neither of which conditions is fulfilled), the principle would in no way impeach Israel's standing and rights under international law. For the only authoritative version of *ius cogens* in Article 53 is very precise that any taint of a treaty provision arising from conflict with *ius cogens* is limited to a provision that *"at the time of its conclusion . . .* conflicts with a peremptory norm of international law" (emphasis supplied). Insofar as the establishment of the Jewish national home leading to the state of Israel was itself based on the self-determination principle, and insofar also as a Palestinian nation was neither in existence nor recognized at the relevant times, the state of Israel is doubly invulnerable to any impact of Article 53 by dint of that limitation.

Both in *Self-Determination* and in *Resolutions*, therefore, the legal nature of the right of self-determination in general is only asserted, not demonstrated. Within this hazardous frame, however, the authors produce a collage of documents critical of the Balfour Declaration, of the mandate incorporating it, and of the Jewish self-determination movement, which at latest was already institutionalized by the time of the first Zionist Congress in 1897.[18] They similarly rehearse selectively the history of the British administration in Palestine,[19] and the first phase of U.N. involvement up to the abortion of Resolution 181(II) by what the authors delicately call "the sending" by "the Arab States" of "forces" into Palestine. In this presentation they nowhere give any reason why self-determination as the legal right they claim it to be, did not spread its blessings over the Jewish people as well as other peoples. And this is entirely parallel, as already seen, to their treatment of the rights of return and compensation. As many Jews as Arabs, if not more, were displaced from their homes in Arab lands during the lamentable struggles initiated by Arab state aggression in 1948. But it was observed, above under "The 'Right of Return,'" that only the Arab refugees are worth the authors' sympathy or even mention.[20] The fact that Israel defended its statehood by repelling the Arab states' aggression in 1948, is relevant for these authors only as an occasion for chiding the 1948 boundaries thus established. Equally irrelevant for them is the unlawful occupation and annexation by Jordan of the West Bank, and Jordan's failure from 1948 to 1967 to accord the slightest degree of autonomy, let alone self-determination, to the Palestinians living there. But this is of a piece with other strange neglects of these productions of the Special Unit on Palestinian Rights of the U.N. Secretariat, to which attention has been drawn above.[21]

INTERTEMPORAL LAW AND SELF-DETERMINATION

Self-Determination concludes with a section entitled "The Affirmation by the United Nations of the Right of Self-Determination of the Palestinian People."[22] This section, largely duplicated in *Resolutions,* stresses the series of General Assembly resolutions from 1970 onwards, but accelerating after the use of the oil weapon in 1973.[23] In terms of correct analysis of the legal effects of General Assembly resolutions on issues between the state of Israel and the Palestinian Arabs, it has a triple importance.

First, while the *Resolutions* pamphlet rather blurs the precise time of full recognition by the General Assembly of the claim of Palestinians as a national group, the *Self-Determination* "study" is here crystal clear and accurate. The anonymous authors of *Self-Determination* point out that the General Assembly's assertion and reassertion of Palestinian qualification as a nation does not begin until Resolution 2672C(XXV) of December 8, 1970.[24] They even stress, with perspicacity, but without mentioning the oil weapon, that it was with the Arab war of aggression of October 1973 that the cause of self-determination for the Palestinian people began a rapid advance".[25] They also stress the close time relation between Rabat affirmations by Arab heads of state of the right of self-determination of the Palestinians and the status of the P.L.O., and the General Assembly's adoption of the notorious P.L.O. Resolution 3236(XXIX) on November 22, 1974. All this leads inexorably to the admission that the General Assembly's action was taken under pressure of the Arab states, including those now flexing their muscles in the Organization of Arab Petroleum Exporting Countries. The authors of *Self-Determination* admirably summarize the main point as to national claims of the Palestinian people in this striking way: "Thus it will be seen that the right of self-determination of the Palestinian people, denied for three decades during the Mandate, ignored for two decades in the United Nations, have over almost the last decade received consistent recognition and strong assertion by a preponderant majority of Member States of the United Nations . . ."[26] It is ironic that this eloquence underscores the intertemporal dimension as a most critical fact relevant to the application of the self-determination concept. Applied to Palestinian Arabs it also admits (indeed, insists) that that date is placed around 1970, and certainly not a half-century before in 1917. The consequences of this have already been analyzed in Chapter 1.

The International Court of Justice (I.C.J.) has been insistent, not least as regards questions of territorial title, that the rules and concepts of international law have to be interpreted "by reference to the law in force" and "the State practice" at the relevant period. (Majority Opinion in the *Western Sahara* case, I.C.J. Reports, 1975, p. 12, esp. at 38-39). Judge de Castro in his Separate Opinion (ibid., 127, at 168 ff.) declared the principle *tempus regit factum* as a recognized principle of international law. He continued (p. 169): "Consequently, the creation of ties with or titles to a territory must be determined according to the law in force at the time. . . . The rule *tempus regit factum* must also be applied to ascertain the legal force of new facts and their impact on the existing situation." He went on to illustrate this influence of "new facts and new law" by reference to the impact on the supersession of the colonial status of Western Sahara by the principles concerning non-self-governing territories emanating from the United Nations Charter and the later application to them of the principle of self-determination (pp. 169-71). This limiting rider has reference to the appearance of new principles of international law, overriding the different principles on which earlier titles are based. But, of course, it can have no application to vested titles based, as was the very territorial allocation between the Jewish and Arab peoples, on the principle of self-determination itself.

Judge Petrén, in his Separate Opinion in the *Western Sahara* case, voiced apprehensions as to even initial applications of the self-determination principle, in this "as yet inadequately explored area of contemporary international law" (I.C.J. Reports, 1975, p. 104 at 111-12). The ground for such apprehensions would no doubt become *a fortiori* much graver if past self-determination decisions of the formal organs of the international community could be repeatedly brought into question and reopened at the whim of coalitions of states for the time being commanding majorities in the General Assembly. And it accords with this that Indian Representative R. Rao, chairman of the Special Committee on the Principles of International Law Concerning Friendly Relations and Cooperation between States, denied that the right has any application to independent states. This was even though he also thought that this "right" was "more a function and consequence of geography than a legal right."[27]

6

$\cdots\cdots$

General Assembly: Dismantler
of Sovereignties?

The authors of *Resolutions* obviously regard as their central mission the establishment of the self-determination claims of Palestinian Arabs at the expense of the state of Israel.[1] This solicitude is astutely woven through section 1,[2] in which they beg the capital question by offering the General Assembly resolutions on the rights of the Palestinians[3] as proof that General Assembly resolutions as such make international law. It even persists through section 2,[4] where they all but say that Resolution 181(II) of 1947 was void *ab initio* since, by affording some recognition to national rights of the Jewish people, it violated the "national rights" of the Palestinians. But they finally conclude,[5] with some apparent pain, that that 1947 resolution was not necessarily void *ab initio* merely because it recognized the "national rights" of the Jewish people as well as of the Arabs of Palestine. The self-determination issue (they say) may have been resolved in an unusual manner, but it is not possible to conclude as a matter of law that the particular method of self-determination in two States was invalid per se.

Given these writers' premises, this does indeed have an air of major concession. They head the title of their relevant section "The National Rights of the People of Palestine," which seems to imply that there is only one "people of Palestine" entitled to self-determination. And it is clear from all they have written, as from all the exercises of "The Committee on . . . Rights of the Palestinian People," that as there is only one people of Palestine, the Arabs are the one. This logical inference from that title would have conformed openly to the claims of Article 6 of the 1968 Palestine National Covenant, that all Jews who were not living permanently in Palestine before 1917 should be barred from citizenship in the "Palestinian State" and presumably should be expelled. It would also match both the Arab states' threats and their use of military force to drive the Jews into the sea.

So there is an air of magnanimity in the admission that the Jewish people, as well as the Arabs of Palestine, might be entitled to self-determination. Yet, as these authors expatiate on this admission, it is clear that there is little reality in the air.

Proceeding throughout as if any resolution of the General Assembly is now law (despite their failure, as noted in Chapter 2 above, to provide any foundation for this), they review the assertions of Palestinian national identity in the resolutions since 1970, especially the era of the oil weapon since 1973.[6]

They then try to make precise the geographical area, presumably within "Palestine," "to which Palestinian self-determination applies,"[7] and struggle to show how, despite the title of the section in which they do so, there may be two states in Palestine warranted by the self-determination principle, despite the fact that the self-determination these authors are vindicating is that of "the people of Palestine." Their solution is regrettably of little comfort either to international law as hitherto understood, or to the state of Israel.

What they seriously assert is that the General Assembly now has the legal authority, under General Assembly Resolution 2625(XXV), commonly known as "The Declaration on Principles of International Law Concerning Friendly Relations and Cooperation among States," whenever any group hitherto connected with a state asserts a right to self-determination against it, to redraw the frontiers of that state in accordance with that same body's view (expressed no doubt through stacked majorities) of how far the government of that target State "represents" the whole people of its territory.

This extraordinary power of the General Assembly the authors infer from the proviso in Resolution 2625(XXV) protecting "the territorial integrity and political unity" of sovereign and independent states, which follows the paragraphs of the cited declaration dealing with equal rights and self-determination of peoples, as follows:

Nothing in the foregoing paragraphs shall be construed as authorizing or encouraging any action which would dismember or impair, totally or in part, the territorial integrity or political unity of sovereign and independent States conducting themselves in compliance with the principle of equal rights and self-determination of peoples as described above and thus possessed of a government representing the whole people belonging to the territory without distinction as to race, creed or colour.

Every State shall refrain from any action aimed at the partial or total disruption of the national unity and territorial integrity of any other State or country [emphasis supplied].

It is not proposed to canvass the question whether, assuming that the General Assembly could by resolution create for itself so drastic a legal power of cutting up or even dismantling United Nations member states, the quoted words of the declaration would base such a usurpation. For that assumption itself transcends the bounds of credulity to be expected from either international lawyers or national political leaders.

The threat thus posed to the territorial integrity and political unity and independence of all states by a General Assembly attempt to usurp such power does not need much elaboration.

The self-determination principle is now increasingly invoked not merely as against Western excolonial powers, but also within and between the populations of new states that have come to independence since World War II. Consequently, those states, too, would become subject to any such pretended and unprecedented General Assembly powers of making and unmaking states and their boundaries.

The authors themselves show some awareness of the dangers that all states may apprehend from their extraordinary proposal. They try to quiet or neutralize these by arguing that the case of Israel is a special one. The boundaries of Israel, they say, are only de facto existing "at a particular time as a result of military conquest and of illegal annexation."[8] This egregiously false assertion of both fact and law is lifted almost literally from the first report of the Committee on . . . Rights of the Palestinian People,[9] which sponsored the authors' researches. It ignores the considered opinions to the contrary of many reputable international lawyers, as well as the rejection of any such finding by repeated actions of the General Assembly and the Security Council, as already seen in Chapter 3 above.

It is quite clear, as there set out at length, that Israel's standing within her territorial domains is in no sense violative of international law. This is so also as to the territories occupied in the course of self-defense against the renewed Arab states' aggression of 1967. Israel stands ready, as international law requires, to negotiate treaties of peace with the former aggressor Arab states, including their territorial claims. It is these other states that flout the processes of international law. International law itself provides the rule to govern such a situation, namely, *uti possidetis*—that the state in lawful possession is entitled to stay in the territory until peace is negotiated. It follows that the resort of *Resolutions* to a patently untenable ground for usurpation and use by the General Assembly of this extraordinary pretense of power against Israel in no way protects other states from similar resorts. The argument in *Resolutions* imports no less a threat to all other states in the international community, in the lawful courses of these states within their lawful territorial domains. Whenever these other law-abiding states have neighbors who have predatory designs against them, neighbors who can find or promote, and then manipulate General Assembly majorities and self-determination claims against them, they will be vulnerable to similar machinations. The sinister game in which the committee sponsoring these international law "researches" is engaged, is a deep and wide-ranging threat to the whole international legal order, and to the United Nations itself.

In a pamphlet issued late in 1979, following *Resolutions,* the Committee on . . . Rights of the Palestinian People made this threat patent. That Committee asks, somewhat disingenuously: "If a series of General Assembly resolutions on the right of self-determination in general has the effect of creating a principle of international law, then do not a series of resolutions on the specific right of self-determination of a particular people create obligations on the part of the international community?"[10] Chapter 2, under "Standing of Resolutions," has already shown the neglect by the committee's lawyers of the limits imposed by international law on the creation of obligations for states by resolutions that have no such effect under the charter. This makes the premise of the above argument simply false, and the conclusion (as to resolutions on the specific rights "of a particular people") is correspondingly vitiated.

The significant point, however, is that the committee here reveals so frankly its intent to invest General Assembly majorities with binding power to disrupt, dismember, or even destroy the life of sovereign independent states, members of the United Nations, under pretext of self-determination claims of dissident groups favored for the time being by those majorities. The fact that the states-victims of this Draconian power would be disposed of one by one in no way softens the threat to them all. The travesty of international law thus proposed matches the travesty of the charter involved. For, under the charter, this kind of power can only be exercised (if at all) by the Security Council under Chapter 7, and subject to the safeguards provided by Article 27.

The authors of *Resolutions* themselves, indeed, have finally and grudgingly to admit that Israel's pre-1967 boundaries "may [*sic*] have received some [*sic*] international assent."[11] At least here they dare not ignore Security Council Resolution 242 of November 22, 1967, which clearly indicates that withdrawal of Israel armed forces was to be only from "territories occupied in the recent conflict," and also states the principle of "the sovereignty, territorial integrity and political independence of every state in the area." Since these provisions of Resolution 242 are there laid down as bases for the negotiations that the secretary-general is instructed to promote between the states concerned, they are in exact accord with the principles of international law that I have recalled in the preceding paragraph and examined in Chapter 3 above. Under those principles it is both wrong, and pathetically naive, to assert that the General Assembly has any power under international law to determine the boundaries of Israel that would not also expose numerous other law-abiding states to equally extravagant and unwarranted intrusions.

IS FORCE LAWFUL AGAINST SOVEREIGN STATES
IN SELF-DETERMINATION STRUGGLES?

Numerous questions have been raised in what has gone before as to the adequacy and objectivity on particular matters of the "research" embodied in these pamphlets, ostensibly directed to fixing the rights and duties of states under international law. It was also shown in Chapter 2 above that on the general matter, central for that argument, of the criteria for attributing legal binding force to resolutions adopted by the General Assembly, the researchers have begged questions rather than provided answers.

It is now proposed to display in depth, and in relation to two key and related matters on which many of the researchers' conclusions rest, the falsity of the simplistic assumption that insofar as General Assembly resolutions can be said to manifest a consensus among states, they also manifest sufficient evidence of new binding rules of international law. The related matters chosen for this display concern the supposed legal right of self-determination as giving rise, also under international law, to the legal license of any people claiming self-determination, and of third states supporting it, to use armed force against a sovereign state in vindication of the people claiming self-determination.[12]

At the time when this supposed legal liberty to use force in liberation struggles was being thus asserted against the state of Israel in 1974 in the General Assembly, this body's Fourth Special Committee on the Question of Defining Aggression was concluding its seven years of labor, a good deal of this period having been devoted to examining that supposed liberty. No question was more debated at the 109 plenary sessions and other group meetings than the question whether such use of force in liberation struggles was lawful, notwithstanding the prohibitions of the charter. Thirty-five member states of the United Nations participated in these deliberations and I have not heard it suggested that they were not a fair representation of the membership of the United Nations. The basic questions as to the legal standing of assertions in General Assembly resolutions are how far the voting behavior of states toward particular assertions manifests either the *opinio iuris sive necessitatis* of states necessary for reformation of a rule of customary law, or the kind of consent that can be assimilated to consent to be found by a treaty between states. This being so, the exchanges and confrontations in the above Special Committee represented a rare, indispensable, and decisive body of research material. This is the more so, since the General Assembly received and accepted the outcome of this committee's work, and these authors hold in such high esteem other emanations of the General Assembly.

Yet among much esoteric material that the authors, named or anonymous, commissioned by the Unit on Palestinian Rights invoke against Israel, there is no sign that any of these writers has the slightest interest in the proceedings that so closely touched their intellectual concerns. Had they not thus shunned this extraordinary opportunity, they might have made a major contribution to knowledge. Had they gone to the records of the work of the 1967 Special Committee, or even only to those of the Sixth Committee, or even only to Resolution 3314(XXIX) of December 14, 1974, they would certainly have been more guarded in leaping to simplistic conclusions. They would have found that the assertion that international law now permits armed force to be used by peoples and third states in support of liberation struggles was emphatically not accepted as international law by states, at the very time when General Assembly resolutions offered as evidence of it were being adopted.

The examination that follows will call for the reader's close attention to the complex uncertainties and divisions of state attitudes towards assertions of this proposed new license to use force in General Assembly resolutions, which the authors of these United Nations "studies" declare to have already become clear rules of international law. The very uncertainties and divisions of state attitudes, resisting acceptance of such resolutions as international law, are worth review precisely because they manifest rejection by states of theses that are central to the conclusions of these U.N. "studies." These rejected theses include not only the claim of a legal license of states to use force against other states in support of "liberation struggles," but also the thesis that repeated recitals or assertion by majorities in the General Assembly have legislative effect in international law.

It is the more necessary to examine this up-to-date evidence because the researchers for the Committee on . . . Rights of the Palestinian People have so neglected it. The fact that this review demands a degree of patience from both this author and his readers is itself an indictment of the superficiality of that committee's ill-researched studies. There are great dangers to international law, and to the international community, arising from the indulgence of simplistic, careless, and selective research supporting the contentions of some member states against others by organs whose constant duty should be to serve all members with impartiality. We proceed, therefore, in Chapter 6, before turning to the question of Jerusalem, to examine in some depth the views of states on the critical matter of the limits on the use of force in "liberation" or self-determination struggles, as expressed through their specially designated representatives on the 1967 Special Committee on the Question of Defining Aggression. The importance of the issues demand that we confront the complexities involved, which are inherent in the present state of international law in this crucial area.

FORCE AND SELF-DETERMINATION: CONTEXT

A General Assembly increasingly dominated by the newer states and their political allies has certainly initiated moves—for example, by the Declaration on Principles of International Law Concerning Friendly Relations and Cooperation among States, 1970 (Resol. 2625[XXV])—to invest the doctrine of "wars of liberation" with some kind of legal standing. The outcome of these moves became a main focus of contention of the Special Committee on the Question of Defining Aggression appointed in 1967, which reported in 1974. The legal position of nonstate entities, such as insurgent groups or peoples, struggling to break away from the state under whose sovereignty they live, and the lawfulness of the use of force in their support, were not even a major issue for the General Assembly's first two special committees on the Question of Defining Aggression in the fifties.

One possible rationale for legitimation of the use of force by peoples struggling for independence, and by third states supporting them, rests on an ingenious reading of Article 51 of the charter. The "target" state, insofar as it resists the self-determination demand, is said not to be a "target" state at all, but an "aggressor" in a continuing state of "armed attack" against the people concerned. That people, and third states giving armed support to such a people, may thus be said to be acting lawfully in individual and collective self-defense under Article 51 as "a right of self-defence of peoples and nations against colonial domination."[13] Some such analogical use or abuse of the scope of Article 51 seems to underlie various cumulative declarations of the General Assembly onwards from the 1960 Resolution 1514(XV) on the Granting of Independence to Colonial Countries. This declared in paragraph 4 that "all armed action . . . against dependent peoples" should cease. Resolution 2131(XX) of 1965 declared in paragraph 3 that "the use of force to deprive peoples of their national identity constitutes a violation of their inalienable rights and of the principles of non-intervention." And Resolution 2625(XXV) of 1970 on Principles of International Law Concerning Friendly Relations and Cooperation among States affirmed the applicability of such self-determination within existing States (paras. 3, 5, and 7 read together). We have shown in Chapter 1, under "Parallel Liberations: 'Arab Asia' and Jewish Palestine," that even in Resolution 2625(XXV) affirmations of rights to struggle or assist in struggles for self-determination are hedged by prohibitions against intervention by states and against use of force to dismantle or impair the integrity of other states. Insofar as the Republic of India offered any legal basis for its armed attack on the Portuguese colony of Goa, on the Indian subcontinent in 1961, it was an analogy of the present kind. "There can be no question of aggression against your own frontier, against your own people, whom you want to liberate . . ." (Security Council Official Records, 987th Meeting, Dec. 18, 1961). A majority of the Security Council, however, rejected this reasoning in a resolution calling for withdrawal that was defeated by a Soviet veto. Despite later resolutions that clearly forbid acquisition of territory by unlawful force, this Indian seizure of territory has remained as a *fait accompli.*[14]

How far does the definition[15] presented by the 1967 Special Committee, and accepted by the General Assembly in 1974, in some way commit the states who shared in its adoption by consensus, to some form of the above thesis? How far does it treat a "people" engaged in armed struggle for self-determination, and third states assisting them, against the parent state, as engaged in collective self-defense justified under some extension of Article 51? The arguments involved, often tenuous and tedious, rest on a plurality of textual points in the Definition, as well as on various preceding resolutions of the General Assembly. The more important of these textual points and resolutions need to be recalled as a preliminary to analysis.

(1) Paragraph 6 of the preamble to the 1974 Definition refers to the duty of states not to use armed force to deprive peoples of their right of self-determination, freedom, and independence, and not to disrupt "territorial integrity." (The last phrase, as will be seen, seems directed less to advancing struggles for independence than to protecting existing sovereign states against them.)

(2) Paragraph 7 of the preamble "reaffirms" that territory should neither be occupied nor be "the object of acquisition" by force, etc. "in contravention of the Charter."

(3) Paragraph 8 of the preamble "reaffirms" in general terms the Declaration of Principles of International Law Concerning Friendly Relations and Cooperation among States of 1970.[16] This declaration contains the following possibly relevant though sometimes mutually neutralizing paragraphs, some of which have already been considered in the special context of Chapter 1, above, under "Self-Determination and the International Court."

(a) The preamble recited the obligation of states not to intervene in the internal or external affairs of any other state.

(b) It expressed the conviction that alien subjugation, domination, and exploitation of peoples are a major obstacle to international peace and security, and that the equal rights and self-determination principles are a significant contribution to contemporary international law.

(c) It expressed the conviction that any attempt aimed at partial or total disruption of the national unity, territorial integrity, or independence of a state or country is incompatible with the purposes and principles of the charter, and that these principles are worthy of progressive development.

(d) The body of the 1970 declaration condemned as unlawful armed intervention and all other interference or threats against the personality of the state or against its political, economic, and cultural elements.

(e) It similarly forbad states to "use or encourage the use of economic, political or any other type of measures to coerce another State in order to obtain from it the subordination of the exercise of its sovereign rights and to secure from it advantages of any kind. Also, States were forbidden to organize, assist, foment, finance, incite or tolerate subversive, terrorist, or armed activities directed towards the violent overthrow of the regime of another State, or interfere in civil strife in another State."

(f) The declaration then, again with Olympian ambivalence, forbad the use of force to deprive peoples of their national identity, thus violating their "inalienable rights and . . . *the principle of non-intervention"* (emphasis supplied).

(g) A section of the Declaration headed "The Principle of Equal Rights and Self-Determination of Peoples," then proceeded as follows:

By virtue of the principle of equal rights and self-determination of peoples enshrined in the Charter of the United Nations, all peoples have the right freely to determine, without external interference, their political status and to pursue their economic, social and cultural development, and every state has the duty to respect this right in accordance with the provisions of the Charter. . . .

Every state has the duty to promote, through joint and separate action, realization of the principle of equal rights and self-determination of peoples. . . .

Every state has the duty to refrain from any forcible action which deprives peoples referred to above . . . of their right to self-determination and freedom and independence. In their actions against, and resistance to, such forcible action in pursuit of the exercise of their right to self-determination, such peoples are entitled to seek and to receive support *in accordance with the purposes and principles of the Charter [emphasis supplied]*.

The territory of a colony or other non-self-governing territory has, under the Charter, a status separate and distinct from the territory of the state administering it; and such separate and distinct status under the Charter shall exist until the people of the colony or non-self-governing territory have exercised their right of self-determination in accordance with the Charter, and particularly its purposes and principles.

Nothing in the foregoing paragraphs shall be construed as authorizing or encouraging any action which would dismember or impair, totally or in part, the territorial integrity or political unity of sovereign and independent states conducting themselves in compliance with the principle of equal rights and self-determination of peoples as described above and thus possessed of a government representing the whole people belonging to the territory without distinction as to race, creed or color.

Every state shall refrain from any action aimed at the partial or total disruption of the national unity and territorial integrity of any other state or country.

(h) Each of the above and all other principles of this 1970 declaration were (according to its terms) to be construed in the context of the others. None of them could prejudice the provisions of the charter or the rights and duties of members thereunder or the rights of peoples under the charter, taking into account the elaboration of these rights in this declaration, and that the charter principles embodied in the declaration were basic principles of international law.

(4) The Declaration on the Strengthening of International Security (1970), reciting *inter alia* the above 1970 declaration, reaffirmed the principle that

states "desist from any forcible or other action which deprives peoples, in particular those still under colonial or any other form of external domination, of their inalienable right to self-determination, freedom and independence and refrain from measures aimed at preventing the attainment of independence of all dependent peoples . . . and render assistance . . . to the oppressed peoples in their legitimate struggle in order to bring about the speedy elimination of colonialism or any other form of external domination."[17]

(5) Explanatory Note (a) attached to Article 1 of the 1974 definition stipulates: "In this Definition the term State—(a) is used without prejudice to questions of recognition or to whether a State is a Member of the United Nations."

(6) Article 7 of the definition provides:

Nothing in this Definition, and in particular Article 3, could in any way prejudice the right to self-determination, freedom and independence, as derived from the Charter, of peoples forcibly deprived of that right and referred to in the Declaration on Principles of International Law concerning Friendly Relations and Co-operation among States in accordance with the Charter of the United Nations, particularly peoples under colonial and racist regimes or other forms of alien domination; nor the right of these peoples to struggle to that end and to seek and receive support, in accordance with the principles of the Charter and in conformity with the above-mentioned Declaration.

(7) The "armed bands" item in the list of acts of aggression, as stigmatized by Article 3(g) of the Consensus Definition, covers: "The sending by or on behalf of a State of armed bands, groups, irregulars or mercenaries, which carry out acts of armed force against another State of such gravity as to amount to the acts listed above, or its substantial involvement therein."

Under the preceding Article 3(f) there is also stigmatized the action of a state "in allowing its territory, which it has placed at the disposal of another State, to be used by that other State for perpetrating an act of aggression against a third State."

The answer to the question what is the legal status of armed force used by or in support of a people "struggling" for self-determination must be some net result of interaction of these provisions. This is a legal question, however, and it therefore depends not only on the textual contents of the above items, but also on the extent to which the text concerned, and any resolution into which it is incorporated, have legal binding force. Starkly conflicting and mutually blocking positions on all this were apparent right up to the emergence of the final text of the 1974 definition from the Special Committee. But the following section will show that, on the central question here of force in self-determination struggles, the states that prevailed exhibited attitudes that denied the lawfulness of such use.

THE 1974 DEFINITION OF AGGRESSION:
PEOPLES AND STATES AS AGENTS AND TARGETS

At the outset there was stark conflict as to whether the entities restrained or protected by the international law precepts involving use of force are limited to states. Is aggression, in short, only a state-to-state relation? United Kingdom delegate Steel pointed to one focus of the complexly interrelated issues touching armed force and self-determination when he asserted that the aggression that the Special Committee sought to define was concerned only with the acts of one State against another State. On this basis, he insisted that the saving of self-determination struggles in Article 7 was not strictly relevant to the definition; so that the clause, if included, did no more than preserve the legitimacy of struggles by means other than use of force.[18] Surprisingly, at first sight, M. Ustor of Hungary[19] also asserted that Article 1 deals only with state-to-state armed force. But he removed the cause of surprise by explaining (with Soviet bloc overtones about internal dissent and the Brezhnev Doctrine) that "ordinary police action" of a state to suppress disorder within it could not possibly be caught by the definition. With no sign of awareness of inconsistency, he then went on, now in flat contrast to Mr. Steel, to say that neither the state-to-state context, nor even the armed bands provision of Article 3(g), could bring into doubt the legitimacy of armed struggles by national liberation movements, since these were "not included in the notion of aggression but [were] considered a lawful form of the use of force."[20]

To reach this latter point, Mr. Khan of Bangladesh had to proceed from a denial of the state-to-state limitation, and a claim that the acts of aggression enumerated in Article 3 are such whether committed against peoples or against States.[21] This would, of course, if consistently followed, make serious inroads on the Soviet reservation of liberty to take "police action" against peoples, e.g., Lithuanians, Estonians, Latvians, Ukrainians, or Jews (not to speak of Hungarians and Czechs), held in subjection to its sovereignty. So also Mr. Elias of Spain,[22] carrying the point to explicit extremes, thought that Article 7 not only allowed a people struggling for self-determination to invade the "territorial integrity" of a state, but also gave each people its own right of "territorial integrity," and protected this right against the sovereign of that territory.

A barely conceivable basis for giving any "people," as such, the rights of a state (though even then only with great strain) might be found in Explanatory Note (a) to Article 1. This provides that the term "State" is used in the definition "without prejudice to questions of recognition or to whether a State is a member of the United Nations." That note seems related in origin to the provision in paragraph 2 of the Six-Power Draft that if the territory of a state is delimited by international boundaries, or internationally agreed lines of demarcation, it could be an aggressor or a victim of aggression within the definition, despite nonrecognition of it as a state (or of its government) by other states.[23] In that meaning, Note (a) would be directed to situations such as that between Israel and the Arab states, of special significance here. A central controversy has been whether the U.N. Charter obligations of the Arab states not to resort to armed force bound them vis-à-vis Israel, in view of their refusal to recognize Israel's statehood. In this context, the note would confirm that despite their nonrecognition of Israel, their first use of armed force against her would constitute aggression. It would also confirm that their respect for their charter obligations would not imply recognition of Israel.

Another plausible meaning of Note (a) offered by the New Zealand delegate, Mr. Quentin Baxter,[24] referred to the case of hostilities across disputed boundaries, which by this very nature are intractable to criteria of aggression turning on the armed crossing of boundaries. He thought that the effect of Explanatory Note (a) was that the Consensus Definition would not be applicable to such cases. Since the Explanatory Note, as it were, bars any prejudice to "questions of recognition" of either state's boundaries, to apply the definition to such cases would violate this by prerequiring recognition of some particular boundary.

The kind of view that simply assimilates "people" to a "state" lacks any such plausible basis in Explanatory Note (a). For it would require the reference to "recognition" in that note to be understood as requiring that every aspiration to self-determination of a "people" living under sovereignty of an existing state be immediately treated, as soon as it emerges, as equivalent to a separate new statehood displacing or breaking away from the old state. No proponent of the assimilation of "a people" to "a state" was prepared to make such an argument explicit, nor was any prepared to accept the consequence that (under Explanatory Note [a]) such a people would have to be treated as a possible aggressor, as well as a possible victim of aggression.

THE 1974 DEFINITION: DEFEAT OF PROPOSALS TO LEGALIZE FORCE

The acts qualifying as acts of aggression under Article 3 of the 1974 Definition include: "(g) The sending by or on behalf of a State of armed bands, groups, irregular or mercenaries, which carry out acts of armed force against another State of such gravity as to amount to the acts listed above, or its substantial involvement therein." An Indonesian view[25] would have extended the stigmata to cover "supporting and organising" as well as "sending" and (in the final phrase) "active participation" even without "substantial involvement."

The history of this element of aggression definition goes back to an addition made to the Soviet proposals of February 6, 1933, on the definition of aggression to the League of Nations Committee on Security Questions, as follows: "Provision of support to armed bands formed in its territory which have invaded the territory of another State, or refusal, notwithstanding the request of the invaded State to take in its own territory all the measures in its power to deprive those bands of all assistance or protection." This exact text appeared in later Soviet proposals to the United Nations, for instance in the drafts of 1953, presented to the first Special Committee on the Question of Defining Aggression (Para. 1[f]).[26]

The crucial point for present purposes is the relation between Article 3(g) and the self-determination reservation of Article 7, which it may be recalled reads as follows:

Nothing in this Definition, and in particular Article 3, could in any way prejudice the right to self-determination, freedom and independence, as derived from the Charter, of peoples forcibly deprived of that right and referred to in the Declaration on Principles of International Law concerning Friendly Relations and Co-operation among States in accordance with the Charter of the United Nations, particularly peoples under colonial and racist regimes or other forms of alien domination; nor the right of these peoples to struggle to that end and to seek and receive support, in accordance with the principles of the Charter and in conformity with the above-mentioned Declaration.

As late as 1972 when Mr. Ferencz[27] and Professor Schwebel[28] discussed the deliberations about "indirect aggression," the full antinomy between the self-determination saving clause (Soviet Draft, Para. 5; Thirteen-Power Draft, para. 10) and the indirect aggression armed bands provision (Art. 3[g] of the Consolidated Text) had not emerged.[29] The Soviet draft, paragraph 6, did not save struggle for self-determination in merely vague terms, but unambiguously specified the lawfulness of its use by dependent peoples in exercising their inherent right of self-determination in accordance with General Assembly Resolution 1514(XV). The Thirteen-Power Draft, paragraph 10, contrarily, saved the charter's provisions as to "the right of peoples to self-determination, sovereignty and territorial integrity," but did not make express whether armed force could be used by them. And the Six-Power (Western) Draft was careful in paragraph 2 to make an exception to its treatment of a nonrecognized "political entity" with internationally demarcated boundaries as a state that can be the victim of aggression, precisely for cases where the political entity concerned is "subject to the authority" of the state alleged to be committing aggression against it. Some committee members resisted even this degree of concession for nonstate political entities, and thought the definition should be limited to aggression between states.

At this stage Professor Schwebel was able to speculate about the problem of nonstate entities in some abstraction from the political issues burning fiercely in the background. He wrote, by way of example, of "an entity which sought to break away from an African State," and "in the course of its rebellion attacks a neighbouring State sympathetic to the cause of the

Central Government," the aggressor against the breakaway entity. And conversely, of a European state attacking a neighboring entity that (because of its supposed revanchism) is not recognized as a state. Would not the entity be a victim of aggression? Except for the hypothetical breakaway from an African state, Professor Schwebel is obviously thinking of an entity of stable governmental authority over defined territory such as was contemplated in paragraph 2 of the Six-Power Draft above referred to. The singular case of Rhodesia (a technically nonstate identity deemed "illegal") being condemned as an aggressor by the Security Council seems to be within these parameters. To think that this precedent shows that aggression is proscribed from any quarter merely covers over, without dissolving, the central issue whether a "people struggling for self-determination" can be an "aggressor."

Professor Schwebel thinks that the whole problem is solved by the formula "without prejudice to questions of recognition" in Explanatory Note (a). And he even finds it "difficult to see why use of the concept of nonstate entities would be confusing." Such words from so perceptive a scholar as late as 1972 provide an intriguing measure of the treacherous layerings of the *arrière-pensées* of political warfare surrounding these matters. The words show obliviousness to the complex and often dangerous possibilities of proposals to license "peoples" who might have neither ostensible control of territory nor any stable government, and third states who choose from whatever motive to support them, to use armed force against any selected target state. It is no less intriguing, in view of the problems that the following sections will reveal, that Professor Schwebel thought at that time that the question of nonstate entities "may be readily solved."

Against this background of the failure of the Thirteen-State Draft to free the use of armed bands and other modes of indirect aggression from the stigma of aggression, there appeared in draft Article 5 of the Consolidated Text the saving clause about self-determination, which, with notable changes, later became Article 7. In draft Article 5 (as to which the Contact Group was careful to say that there was at that stage "no general agreement") the bid to legitimize use of force by nonstate groups and by states assisting them is quite explicit, following in this respect the above paragraph of the Soviet Draft. Nothing in the definition (it ran) was to prevent "peoples . . . from using force and seeking or receiving support and assistance" in exercise of "their inherent right to self-determination in accordance with the principles of the Charter."

If those quoted words in draft Article 5 had survived through to the final Article 7, this would have compensated the proponents of wars of liberation for the failure (seen in the last section) of their bid to free the sending, etc. of armed bands from the stigma of aggression. The quoted words, however, did not survive. In the final Article 7, the range of conduct saved from inculpation was narrowed in various respects. The special inclusion of "peoples under military occupation" disappeared, a matter specially relevant to the problems of the Middle East here under discussion. Not "foreign domination" as such, but only "forcible deprivation" of the charter right of self-determination was the basis of the right to "struggle." Above all, it was stripped of any express reference to a right to use force in the "struggle," and of third states to use force to assist. What remains in Article 7 is the blander formula of "the right of these people to struggle to that end and to seek and receive support."[30] As between the states utterly opposed to extending the freedom to use armed bands or other indirect aggression under the banner of "wars of self-determination" or "liberation," and those resolved to extend this freedom and legalize (as it were) such "wars," the latter again (and finally) failed to establish their position.

This failure is no less apparent as to Article 3(f).[31] That paragraph qualifies as aggression a host state's allowing forces of a foreign state to use its territory for committing an act of aggression against third states. Suppose, however, the action of these guest forces is by way of assistance to a "national liberation movement" against the third state? Mr. Omar of Libya was critical of Article 3(f), apparently because he thought it should have explicitly made an exception for such a case.[32] If, however, such an exception were necessary to subject Article 3(f) to the qualification of the legality of armed "struggle" for self-determination, it would also be necessary (and was similarly absent) for so qualifying Article 3(g). (The saving clause in Article 7 refers without distinction to the whole of Article 3.)

If, furthermore, the provision of Explanatory Note (a) to Article 1 that the term "State" is used "without prejudice to questions of recognition," is taken to mean that "State" includes a people that has not yet achieved statehood, Article 3(f) would be an even more serious obstacle to any license to use force in self-determination struggles. It would stigmatize as aggression not only a host state's allowing another state to use its territory for perpetrating aggression against a third state, but also so allowing any armed elements of "a people" operating from its territory against third states, as for instance Lebanon in regard to Palestinian bands operating against Israel. The stigmatization as "aggression" might be a more severe rule than that under customary international law. This has hitherto been thought only to require a host state to abate the depredations, and on its default authorizing the victim state after due notice to enter the host territory and itself abate it. For Explanatory Note (a) to have been agreed to on the basis that it produces this more extreme result would have been most extraordinary.

In relation to Article 3(f), it was also urged that the conduct of the host state could not be stigmatized as aggression unless the aggressive hostilities against the third state[33] were carried on with its consent. If "allowing" in Article 3(f) refers to grant of consent, this would be self-evidently correct. If that word is taken, however, to mean merely "not preventing," doubts would persist as to the imputation of aggression in cases where, for example, the host state is genuinely ignorant of the hostilities, or impotent to end them. Such doubts as to when to attach the stigma of "aggression" do not, of course, affect the clear customary rules mentioned above imposing on the host state the duty to abate the activities and, if the host state defaults in its obligations, conferring on the victim state the liberty of taking measures of abatement.[34] With Article 3(f), as with self-defense against armed bands under Article 3(g) discussed above, the efforts of the Thirteen-Power Draft to deny to the victim state the usual right of self-defense against aggression were thus (in one of the rare moments of clarity of drafting) rejected by the 1974 Definition. This decisively supports the present writer's rejection of a contrary speculative thesis in Chapter 3, above, under "Aggression by Attacks by Armed Bands."

Important questions have been raised as to the limits of the right of lawful response accorded to the victim state in these and related situations. It has been argued, for example, that forceful retaliation may further weaken the host state's control over its own territory, may strengthen the insurgents, and even lead the host state to overt support of them. Such prudential considerations cannot, of course, dispose of the established rights of states to abate organized violence directed against them from private or insurgent groups organized, supported, or tolerated by the host state, and to take necessary measures across the frontiers of the host state that willfully or by other default fails, after due notice, to abate them.[35]

To say that standards of proportionality ought to be worked out for both self-defense and other forceful measures taken by a state for what customary law termed its self-preservation is, however, only to state the problem, not to solve it, nor, indeed, to imply that it can be solved. The Soviet view was that such a requirement would unreasonably hamper the victim of aggression and favor the aggressor, who in the nature of things already had the advantage of surprise as to timing, weapons, and the like. The effect of such a requirement in shifting the ex post facto burden of proof as to justification from the aggressor to his victim was also resisted. And it was argued that the drafting history of Article 51 and its designation of self-defense as an "inherent right" excluded such a requirement. The British and United States views were close to that of the Soviet Union. Most delegations, for one reason or another, thought that a proportionality requirement was in any case irrelevant to or unnecessary for the definition of aggression, or that its existence and meaning were too uncertain and required further study.[36]

THE 1974 DEFINITION: LIMITS ON SELF-DETERMINATION RIGHTS

Even the attitudes of states discussed up to this point expose two major deficiencies in the research "studies" sponsored by the Committee on . . .

Rights of the Palestinian People. Firstly, these attitudes, manifested by states, contradict the simplistic assumption of the "studies" that prior General Assembly resolutions had established new rules of international law licensing the use of force in self-determination struggles. Secondly, these attitudes show the complexities of the legal arguments involved, quite glossed over by these "studies."

The final stages in the drafting of the 1974 Definition now to be addressed give this exposure a resounding emphasis. For the prefinal ("consolidated") text draft of the relevant article had proposed to save the right of self-determination of peoples in terms in three respects exceeding what was finally to be included in Article 7 of the Consensus Definition. First, the draft had explicitly reserved a people's right to use force in such struggles. Second, it had implied that these people had a right to receive assistance of third states in this use of force. Third, this right to use force had been proposed to extend also to "peoples under military occupation." The license of "peoples" to use force against states under whose sovereignty they lived, and of third states to support them in this, was strongly denied by many states. In respect of the above three points, especially the first two, these proposals were adamantly resisted, and not only by Western states. The Soviet Union and other Soviet bloc states were, for example, zealous, even while predictably supporting self-determination claims, to deny that anything in the definition could affect a state's right to take "police action" against "dissident" movements.

On this matter "there was no general agreement as to the text to be adopted,"[37] as the Drafting Committee carefully reported.

In Article 7 of the 1974 Definition as finally adopted, all express reference to use of force by peoples under military occupations was excised. Paragraph 6 of the preamble, reaffirming the duty of states not to use force to "deprive" peoples of self-determination had also had added to it a similar duty not to use force "to disrupt territorial integrity." Whether the right of peoples to "struggle" includes the right to use armed force against the parent state, and the corresponding question as to the right of third states to support such struggles by force, were answered in the negative. The addition of a duty not to "disrupt territorial integrity" to paragraph 6 highlighted those negative answers since territorial integrity is an attribute of sovereign states rather than peoples "struggling" for self-determination, which may, indeed, often have no defined territorial base. The addition thus corroborates the exclusion of any license to use of force in support of a "struggle" for self-determination against the target state. The refusal of the Working Group to attribute "sovereignty" and "territorial integrity" as rights of peoples parallel to their right of self-determination, marches with this conclusion.[38] A central thesis of the research sponsored and disseminated by the Committee on . . . Rights of the Palestinian People asserting the right of states to use armed force in support of struggles for self-determination, is thus exposed as departing grossly from the positions of United Nations members as manifest in the latest Committee on . . . Defining Aggression, in the Sixth Committee on legal questions of the General Assembly, and in the General Assembly itself, as recently as 1974.

PROBLEMATICS OF SELF-DETERMINATION

The attitudes of states manifested during the preparation and adoption of the General Assembly's 1974 Definition of Aggression thus contrast starkly with the international law as to the use of force in self-determination struggles, attributed by these research "studies" to the General Assembly's "lawmaking" activity. These attitudes afford thus a notable object lesson in the risks of attribution of lawmaking effect to General Assembly resolutions, with inadequate regard to the established criteria for the emergence of international law. It should also alert us to the problematical content, so far as international law is concerned, of the right of self-determination itself, about which the researchers of the Committee on . . . Rights of the Palestinian People have also presented a very simplistic account. That right, whatever its nature, is hemmed in by a whole series of legal limits and uncertainties, on some or other of which judgment in a particular case must depend.[39] These the committee's researchers have appeared quite to ignore. I conclude by commending some of these to their future attention.

At the threshold the question of which peoples are the beneficiaries of the saving clause in Article 7 is even more at large than is suggested by the vagueness of such complementary terms as "colonialist," "racist," or "imperialist." If, indeed, the references to "self-determination" in the charter and in General Assembly declarations have established some legal (as distinct from political) principle, the legal marks for identifying a "people" having this entitlement—the "self" entitled to "determine" itself—remain highly speculative. Those who do not recognize this as a problem will do well to recall the continuing stream of violence arising from it, of which the affairs concerning Katanga, Biafra, Cyprus and Angola, Lebanon, Bougainville, and now Zaire, Western Sahara, Eritrea, are only a few of the contemporary warnings.

This threshold issue is a critical one, moreover, for some of the oldest and most powerful states, as well as for newborn and young ones. Thus, in the form proposed in the preamble, paragraph 6 and Article 7 of the 1974 Definition, that document would strictly raise questions concerning the legal rights of the Baltic peoples overrun by the Soviet Union at the opening of World War II, not to speak of the Ukrainian people or of the Soviet Union's armed actions against the Hungarian and Czechoslovak peoples in 1956 and 1968. And such rights might even at some time be invoked by the Welsh and Scots in the United Kingdom, not to speak of the Indians and blacks of the United States, the aborigines of Australia, and the Chinese of Malaysia, the French in Canada, the Walloons in Belgium, the Bretons in France, Basques and Castilians in Spain, the Kurds in Iraq and Iran, and many other identified peoples in Europe, Asia, and the Americas. The qualifying phrase "peoples under colonial and racist regimes or other forms of alien domination" in Article 7 is itself so subject to diverse interpretations or political perceptions as to leave such claims open now or in the future. Thus the specification "colonial and racist" will only protect the Soviet adventures as long as it commands Third World majorities in the General Assembly. The persistent Chinese charges of Soviet "imperialism," as well as the insistence of the Soviet and its satellites that the 1974 Definition does not bar "police" action by a state within its own territory, signal awareness that such issues are not finally closed. Nor, despite the surrounding rhetoric, has any finality been brought to such issues by the Helsinki Declaration of 1975.[40]

It aggravates this problem of vagueness, as well as the problem of competing claims to self-determination to be discussed shortly, that what delimits (if it does not actually create) the "self" that demands "self-determination," not to speak of the "self" that succeeds, is often the subversive or direct armed action of third states. Neither the definition of aggression, nor generalities about self-determination, makes much contribution to the solution of such problems.

Approaching now the situation in which claims of two or more peoples for self-determination compete with regard to the same territory, it is to be noted that Article 7 of the 1974 Definition is directed solely to peoples oppressed by states and ignores struggles of people against people. The rights of the Katangan and Biafran peoples are mostly water under the international bridge, whatever the merits of those outcomes. But the bloody struggle in Lebanon in 1975-76 involving local insurgency by Lebanese leftist forces allied with Palestine Liberation Organization (P.L.O.) forces localized in Lebanon, opposed by the Christian rightists and also by other Palestinian forces trained in and dispatched from Syria, then by regular Syrian forces, later renamed Arab "peacekeeping forces," signals again the increasing intimacy between civil strife, wars of liberation or self-determination, and international aggression. So does the claim of the P.L.O. to dismantle and replace the state of Israel. Here again, the 1974 Definition says little that is pertinent and plain. The controverted doctrine of the legitimacy of "wars of liberation" only adds to the confusion where, as in Israel and Lebanon, the "inalienable right of self-determination" can be invoked by both peoples engaged in a "struggle" to vindicate it.

There is no neater example of the uncertainties than the France-Comoros affair of 1976.[41] The fact that the island of Mayotte alone did not join in the overwhelming vote of the people of the Comoros four-island archipelago of December 12, 1974, in favor of independence, led France to hold a special referendum on Mayotte on February 8, 1976. No less than 99.4% of the Mayotte people then voted to remain an integral part of France. On February 6, 1976, two days before the above referendum, Comoros, which had meanwhile been admitted to the United Nations, and other states, sought in the Security Council to have this French action declared an interference in Comoros's internal affairs, from which France must desist. Comoros even declared that it was a "flagrant aggression." The draft resolution to the above effect, sponsored by Benin, Guyana, Libya, Panama, and Tanzania—defeated naturally by a French veto—received 11 votes, with Italy, the United Kingdom, and the United States abstaining.

It was not seriously challenged that while "the people" of the other three islands overwhelmingly wanted independence, the people of Mayotte overwhelmingly wanted to remain integral with France. "Self"-determination, therefore, pointed both ways, according to which "self" was regarded as entitled to this right. What was the bearing on this question of the facts that (1) all four islands were, under a French law of 1912, a single administrative unit? or (2) that after the vote of December 12, 1974, Comoros unilaterally proclaimed its independence on July 5, 1975? and (3) that thereafter, on December 31, 1975, the French parliament (under its exclusive constitutional power to that end) recognized the independence of the three islands, but provided for a referendum on Mayotte's future to be held in Mayotte on February 8, 1976? or (4) that the General Assembly, by Resolution 3385 (XXX) of 1975, admitted Comoros (embracing all four islands) to U.N. Membership? or (5) that France by abstaining rather than vetoing allowed the corresponding Security Council resolution concerning Comoros's admission to pass?

Did the "self" entitled to self-determination consist only of the four islands together, either because they were while under French rule a single administrative unit, or because the General Assembly had admitted them *qua* single entity to Membership? Or were the people of Mayotte entitled also to this right? Neither the charter references nor the plethora of assembly declarations and recitals of the self-determination principle offer much guidance for such a problem, any more than they do for Middle East problems, as I have shown. Indeed, paragraph 4 of the section on self-determination in the 1970 Declaration on Principles . . . Concerning Friendly Relations . . . among States (Resol. 2625[XXV]) seems to support the French argument rather than that of Comoros. It provides: "The establishment of a sovereign and independent State, *the free association or integration with an independent State* or the emergence into any other political status freely determined by a people constitute modes of implementing the right to self-determination by that people." (Emphasis supplied.) Yet precisely the contrary view can be inferred from the wide affirmation of the 1960 Declaration on the Granting of Independence to Colonial Countries and Peoples (Resol. 15.5[XV]) of the principle of territorial integrity of territories destined for independence. Paragraph 6 of the above section of the 1970 Declaration, while it requires that the territory concerned maintain its separate and distinct status until its people exercises self-determination, is silent as to status after such an exercise.

The self-determination principle as it applies to rival peoples both claiming self-determination, in relation to a particular territory, is somewhat analogous to the impasse that faces the notion of aggression when the aggression charged is intrusion across disputed boundaries into territory of which the invader claims that it is sovereign. If the latter (the intrusion) be regarded as a legal impasse caused by legally undetermined entitlements in the dimension of space, the former (the rival peoples) might be regarded as an impasse created by legally undetermined entitlements in the dimension of time.[42] The answer in the *Comoros* case depended on whether France's prior (and still unrenounced) claim of sovereignty could support the Mayotte claim to self-determination, or whether Comoros's later assumption of independence for all four islands precluded the Mayotte claim.

The problem of competing self-determination becomes, indeed, even more difficult, whether for purposes of determining aggression or for other purposes, where the competing claims and accompanying military activities, punctuated by actual wars, armistices, and cease-fire agreements, have been made over protracted historical periods. The test of priority of resort to armed force in Article 2 of the 1974 Definition presupposes a fixed point in time from which priority is to be calculated. Does one fix the aggression in the Cyprus crisis of 1974 from the action of the Greek officers who led the coup d'état, or the Turkish response by invasion, even assuming that the 1974 crisis can be severed from earlier struggles? Is the critical date of the Middle East crisis 1973 or 1967, or the first Arab states' attack on Israel in 1948, or is it at the Balfour Declaration in 1917, or at the Arab invasions and conquest of the seventh century A.D., or even perhaps at the initial Israelite conquest of the thirteenth century B.C.? The priority question, as well as the self-determination question, are difficult enough. They become quite baffling when, in the course of such a long span of time, a later developing claim of self-determination like that of the Palestinian people in the 1960s, arises, and claims to override retrospectively the sovereign statehood of another nation, here the Jewish people, already attained by right of self-determination.

Finally, though without seeking to exhaust the matter, the phrase "forcibly deprived" of "the right of self-determination" (in Article 7) and the phrase "the duty of States not to use armed force to deprive peoples of their self-determination" (paragraph 6 of the preamble) raise questions to which there is no obvious answer. Does "forcibly deprived" refer only to future or at least contemporary acts? Or does it embrace all such deprivations that have occurred, at however remote a time, in the establishment of a state now existing? Considering that most, if not all, well-established states have been founded by armed force, if not by conquest, common sense indicates the need for some kind of statute of limitations, the precise terms of which remain shrouded in doubt. Conversely, does a peaceable settlement in a territory, decades or even centuries ago, become forcible deprivation of the self-determination of the original inhabitants when these latter, at a later time, come to a group consciousness that regards the presence of the long-settled community as an oppression or even demands exclusive repossession of the whole territory for itself? How would this be applied to the problems of Chinese in Southeast Asia? the European settlers of the American continent, North and South, and of Australia? the English in Scotland and Wales? the Indians in Fiji? and the rich variety of peoples in India? The list could be vastly extended.

The continuous millennial connection of the Jewish people with the territory of Palestine, the conquest of the territory by Arab arms in the seventh century,[43] the solemn recognition of Jewish self-determination rights in respect of the territory after World War I, and the establishment of the state of Israel, followed half a century later by self-recognition of a Palestinian Arab nation as such, and as claimants to self-determination on the same territory, create a focus for these and other problems to which the self-determination principle offers no unambiguous directives. Yet it has to be observed that the self-styled "research studies" disseminated by the Committee on . . . Rights of the Palestinian People scarcely address these unsolved problems in reaching their rather dogmatic conclusions favoring the claims of the Palestinian people as asserted by the P.L.O.

7

· · · · ·

Sovereignty in
Jerusalem: The International
Concern

The Committee on the Exercise of the Inalienable Rights of the Palestinian People has now, after the publication in 1978 and 1979 of two "studies" relating *inter alia* to Jerusalem,[1] published still another pamphlet entitled *The Status of Jerusalem.*[2] We can now perhaps assess the standing in international law of the committee's rather dogmatic and tendentious position on the status of Jerusalem.

The committee's first step concerns, of course, the legal effect they wish to attribute to the General Assembly's Resolution 181(II) of November 29, 1947 (the Plan of Partition with Economic Union, which also proposed as part of the Economic Union the creation of the *corpus separatum* under U.N. control), and certain other resolutions of that period. These are Resolution 194(III) of December 11, 1948 (which in the terms of reference for the Palestine Conciliation Commission referred to "special and separate treatment" for Jerusalem, under U.N. control), and Resolution 303(IV) of December 9, 1949. This referred to "a permanent international regime" including "guarantees for the protection of the Holy Places," purportedly confirmed the proposal in Resolution 181(II) for the creation of a *corpus separatum,* and instructed the Trusteeship Council to prepare a Statute of Jerusalem and immediately proceed with its implementation.

From this series of resolutions both the committee in its *Jerusalem* pamphlet and their legal experts in the *Resolutions* "study" seek to reach the conclusion that "the legal status of Jerusalem is that of a *corpus separatum* under an international regime."[3] Insofar as this conclusion is finally anchored to some assumed legal effects of vesting territorial title of the basic Palestine Partition Resolution 181(II), I have already shown in Chapter 4, above, that it cannot be sustained. This is a cardinal point that controls all discussion of territorial entitlements, whether in Jerusalem or elsewhere in Palestine.

The fact that the resolution did not, for these many reasons, operate to change title in the territories concerned is even clearer, if possible, in relation to Jerusalem. The fighting there began almost immediately after the Partition Resolution of November 29, 1947, was adopted. Once the resolution had become fully frustrated by the Arab states' aggression, the General Assembly asked the Palestine Conciliation Commission to present "proposals" for a permanent international regime for the Jerusalem area. That commission acted on the principle that "acceptance by Israel and the several Arab States" was a prerequisite even for formulating proposals.[4] The commission limited itself to trying to design a functional regime for the holy places. Even as the Trusteeship Council was drafting the abortive Draft Statute for an internationalized Jerusalem, the fate of Jerusalem was being determined "by force of arms rather than international compact."[5] In later developments, the Assembly itself sheered away from claims for a territorial disposition of the whole of Jerusalem to discuss the Swedish and Belgian proposals, which I shall describe below under "Holy Places: The Functional Concern."[6] Conversely, and more obviously, the legal standing of Jordan and Egypt in the West Bank (including East Jerusalem) and Gaza occupied by them in the course of their aggressive invasion in 1948, can receive neither legal nor moral warrant from the Partition Resolution. As even Soviet-bloc states as well as others then viewed the matter, Transjordan, Egypt, Syria, and Lebanon "had invaded the territory earmarked for the Arab State of Palestine. This State had not been established, as provided for in the 1947 Resolution. On the other hand, the State of Israel had been set up."[7]

The committee's researchers perforce, therefore, have to make a rather more complex argument in relation to Jerusalem, which I must in fairness outline before I proceed to evaluate it. As I understand it, the essential steps in the committee's exposé are two:

(1) That Resolution 181(II) adopted by the General Assembly on November 29, 1947, provided that "the City of Jerusalem shall be established as a *corpus separatum* under a special international regime and shall be administered by the United Nations." Under this plan a Statute of the City was to be elaborated and approved by the Trusteeship Council, which should also appoint a governor to organize an adequate "special police force." There should also be an independent judiciary and a Legislative Council of the city, elected by adult residents irrespective of nationality by universal secret suffrage. Existing rights in respect of the holy places and religious

buildings and sites were to be respected, and free access in conformity therewith assured.[8] It was also (says this argument) part of the terms of reference of the Palestine Conciliation Commission, established under Resolution 194(III) of December 11, 1948, to discuss with the parties the future of Jerusalem, now divided between Israel and Jordan following on the Arab states' armed aggression of that time.[9] And the Trusteeship Council, on April 4, 1950, approved a Draft Statute for an internationalized Jerusalem in compliance with its reference under the Partition Resolution.

(2) That a series of resolutions of the General Assembly and the Security Council since the 1967 War (enumerated and discussed in the next section) have referred to "the status" of Jerusalem, called for the maintenance of this status and censured measures by Israel allegedly altering this status.

These resolutions after 1967, the committee seems to be arguing, prove that "despite the international acquiescence in the division of the City of Jerusalem," and the failure of the United Nations to seek to resurrect the *corpus separatum* plan from 1950 to 1967, that plan remained somehow in legal force and remains so today.[10]

The *Jerusalem* pamphlet also suggests, rather deviously, but with clear intent to persuade, that the diplomatic record shows some kind of contractual undertaking by Israel to give effect to the *corpus separatum*. They refer vaguely to "Israel's assurances in regard of [*sic*] the implementation of Resolutions 181(II) and 194(III)."[11] This suggestion can be disposed of briefly before examining the above two main grounds. For the alleged assurances as recited by the *Jerusalem* pamphlet itself (pp. 9-10) were not as to the territorial *corpus separatum* but as to a regime "concerned exclusively with the control and protection of Holy Places" including holy places outside of Jerusalem. Prime Minister Ben Gurion in fact was reported by the Palestine Conciliation Commission as explicitly rejecting the territorial *corpus separatum,* and the representative of Israel was careful to explain this in terms of Israel's readiness to cooperate with a regime for the protection of the holy places, and the claim of Israel to "sovereign authority in Jerusalem."[12] So that when this pamphlet in the above passage refers to Israel's assurances concerning the partition resolution mentioned in General Assembly Resolution 273(III) of May 11, 1949, admitting Israel, it seems to be suggesting what by its own account is grossly false. Israel's "assurances" were only as to a regime for the holy places and not as to a territorial regime that excluded her sovereignty in Jerusalem.

The weakness of the two main steps of this argument is as striking as their apparent simplicity. I propose, in the next section, first to examine their cogency in international law within the proponents' own terms. This demonstration, however, that the committee has presented no basis in international law for its conclusion is only the beginning. For, here again, the more serious vice of these international law researchers is their simplistic neglect of the capital and settled doctrines, principles, and rules of international law applicable to the subject matters of the "research." I shall, therefore, have to proceed in subsequent sections to a full-scale examination of the international law framework in which alone the present legal status of Jerusalem can be described. This will show, as was also seen at length in Chapter 6, that the research on self-determination and the use of force sponsored by the Committee on . . . Rights of the Palestinian People has too often resorted to simplistic *parti-pris* assertions that trivialize and distort the processes of international law.

LEGAL EVALUATION OF CLAIMS

Lapse of **Corpus Separatum** *Proposals 1947-50.* The claim that bases the committee's first step in argument that the Plan of Partition with Economic Union proposed in Resolution 181(II) came into legal operation in 1947, and continues so, was seen in Chapter 4 to be simply wrong. As a mere resolution of the General Assembly, Resolution 181(II) lacked binding force *ab initio.* It would have acquired this force under the principle *pacta sunt servanda* if the parties at variance had accepted it. While the state of Israel did for her part express willingness to accept it, the other states concerned both rejected it and took up arms unlawfully against it. Quite contrary therefore to the thesis under examination the Partition Resolution never became operative either in law or in fact, either as to the proposed Jerusalem *corpus separatum* or other territorial dispositions in Palestine.

In the legal study, *Resolutions,* the authors seek to put life into the partition proposals by stressing that between 1947 and 1950 the General Assembly referred back to the Partition Plan in Resolution 194(III) of December 11, 1948, in the course of setting terms of reference for the Palestine Conciliation Commission, and in requesting the Trusteeship Council to draw up a statute for Jerusalem and proceed immediately to implement it. But the same facts that aborted the Partition Plan as a whole *ab initio* vitiated these subordinate delegated proceedings.

The Palestine Conciliation Commission itself obviously took this view, for its proposals, far from treating the Partition Resolution as legally operative as to Jerusalem, made proposals closer to the position of Israel for international control "limited only to the Holy Places," rather than a *corpus separatum.*[13] The committee's researchers are obviously unhappy that the commission took this view, but it in no way deters them from the conclusion that such a *corpus separatum* remained in 1950, and for that matter remained in 1979, an entity somehow already existing in international law and limiting the territorial entitlements of Israel under that same law. I shall show in a moment that their own account of the outcome of the request to the Trusteeship Council concerning a statute for this phantom-like legal entity is also unpalatable to them. But they are ready, on that point also, to ignore the effect of that outcome in undermining their basic conclusions.

While the *corpus separatum* was thus still-born *ab initio* with the rest of the Partition Resolution, it may still be necessary to inquire whether later events or actions of the United Nations or the parties with specific reference to Jerusalem, between 1947 and 1950, might somehow have breathed life into it. On this, the authors of *Jerusalem*, perhaps inadvertently, give the first of several independent reasons for a negative answer. They themselves observe[14] that when the draft statute approved by the Trusteeship Council on April 4, 1950, conforming to the Partition Resolution, was not accepted by Jordan, and (in the changed circumstances of the Arab states' rejection and aggression) was agreed to by Israel only so far as concerned an international regime for the holy places within the Walled City and its environs, "the Trusteeship Council proposals lapsed for all practical purposes." At that time, of course, in 1950, Jordan had seized East Jerusalem in the course of its armed attack on Israel, and the latter state had maintained its position in West Jerusalem in the course of self-defense. And another ground of censure by these researchers against the Palestine Conciliation Commission is that the commission's report gave "the appearance of conforming to the *fait accompli* of a divided Jerusalem."[15] They note, again without perceiving its effect in undermining their conclusion, that the commission's proposals were not even debated in the General Assembly.

The **Corpus Separatum** *in Limbo.*   The authors of *Resolutions* could have hadded, if their frankness had been greater, that from 1950 to 1967, during the continued unlawful occupation by Jordan of East Jerusalem, no further resolutions calling for (or even recalling) the *corpus separatum* entity were adopted by the General Assembly. It would appear, therefore, not only that the entity never came into legal existence, but also that even the General Assembly, for seventeen long years, was not visited by any nostalgic vision of it. The authors of *Jerusalem* implicitly acknowledge these facts, for they speak of "the international acquiescence in the division of the City of Jerusalem during the period 1950-1967" as a fact;[16] but they do not explain how their main conclusion can stand in the light of it.

The authors give the impression, indeed, in that very context, that during this same period the General Assembly had nevertheless continued to uphold the *corpus separatum* as a legal entity. This is simply not so. And the Mallisons, as lawyers somewhat more careful with documents, follow another tack. Their account[17] glosses over the significance of the General Assembly's loss of concern with the *corpus separatum* after its abortion by Arab rejection and aggression, from 1950 to 1967, by taking a sudden very long jump. They move swiftly without ceremony, from what their colleagues in the *Jerusalem* pamphlet admit to be the "lapse" for all practical purposes of the proposals for the *corpus separatum* in 1950, to the series of General Assembly resolutions following the 1967 War. Seventeen years from one line to the next, sandwiched between two pages on resolutions of the years 1948-50, and four pages on the years 1967-71![18]

Apparently neither the General Assembly nor the Security Council shared to any degree the views of the present Committee on . . . Rights of the Palestinian People that the *corpus separatum* was an existing legal entity, restricting either the legal position of Israel in West Jerusalem, or that of Jordan in East Jerusalem. And this is even more striking as regards East Jerusalem, since (as seen in Chapter 3) the Jordanian entry and occupation there were based on aggression and were unlawful, and were the more vulnerable to any legal emanations from the *corpus separatum*. Even attempted annexation[19] and gross violations by Jordan of the more modest design for free access to the holy places through refusal of access to Jews stirred no U.N. action in defense of the stillborn *corpus separatum*. Even this committee's researchers have to admit that "United Nations efforts to secure the internationalisation of Jerusalem faded after 1950,"[20] and they do not seek to give this any less significance vis-à-vis Israel's clearly lawful position at that time in West Jerusalem.

Post-1967 Resolutions and the **Corpus Separatum.** The researchers, thus, in the first step of their argument, have been unable to demonstrate that the *corpus separatum* ever came to legal life. They have also had to admit unhappily that both the General Assembly and the Security Council from 1950 to 1967 showed an inactivity and indeed indifference only explicable (though this they do not admit) on the basis that it never did so come to legal life. They are thus driven to the second step in their argument, by which they seek to breathe legal life retrospectively into this *corpus*. It is now necessary to examine this second step.

This second step in the argument of both the *Jerusalem* pamphlet and the *Resolutions* study consists of a string of quotations of General Assembly and Security Council resolutions adopted in the aftermath of the 1967 War, in which, it is to be recalled, the state of Israel again succeeded in its lawful self-defense against Arab state aggression. In the particular context here relevant, it defeated Jordanian aggression from East Jerusalem and came thus to control the whole of Jerusalem. Clearly this produced a lawful territorial standing of some kind of Israel in East Jerusalem. I shall later have to examine whether this standing is merely as a military occupant, or (as some eminent international lawyers think) a closer approximation to sovereignty. For the moment, however, we are concerned only to test the assertion that certain U.N. resolutions passed after 1967 gave legal life to the *corpus separatum* as a territorial entity, this *corpus separatum* being that proposed and discussed but which never entered into legal operation during the period of conflict, 1947-50.

The two publications are agreed as to the U.N. resolutions and phrases in the resolutions that the publications claim to have this vivifying (or, from the point of view of the publications, resurrecting) effect.[21] They are resolutions 2253, Emergency Session Five (ES-V), of July 4, 1967, and 2254 (ES-V) of July 14, 1967, expressing concern as to, declaring "invalid," and calling upon Israel to rescind, "all measures [unspecified] already taken and to desist . . . from taking any action which would alter the status of Jerusalem." At this point we are only concerned with the question whether these post-1967 resolutions somehow establish that the *corpus separatum* plan for Jerusalem as proposed in General Assembly Partition Resolution 181(II) and Resolution 194(III), of 1947 and 1948 respectively, was after two decades brought into legal life and made binding on states under international law.

The first point, the virtual decisiveness of which all the committee's researchers meticulously overlook in examining these later resolutions, is that none of the later resolutions refer by way of preamble or otherwise to any of the earlier resolutions proposing the *corpus separatum*—neither to the initial 1947 resolution itself nor to the later ones of 1948 and 1949. Other resolutions relating to the situation in the Middle East adopted since 1967 regularly accumulate in their recitals details of prior resolutions, noncompliance with which is deplored or censured or the like. In such circumstances, it would be grotesque to assume that draftsmen who intended to assert that Israel was bound by the *corpus separatum* proposals for Jerusalem of the period 1947-49 would so consistently refrain from referring to these resolutions.

In face of this rather decisive fact, the argument that these post-1967 resolutions bring the *corpus separatum* to legal life is understandably obscure and weak. What the authors of that *Resolutions* study seek to argue is that whenever the resolutions refer to "the status of the City" or "the status of "Jerusalem" or "the legal status of Jerusalem," the word "status" must be read as meaning "the *corpus separatum* proposed in the Resolution, 181(II) of 1947, and now existing in international law."[22] They are particularly happy with the single use of the phrase *"legal* status" (emphasis supplied) in Security Council Resolution 252, paragraph 2, as necessarily (in their view) referring to the *corpus separatum*.[23] (Yet they fail to attach any significance to the fact that the adjective "legal" does not appear in the prior General Assembly resolutions of 1967, or in any other of the Security Council resolutions on which they rely. Nor, indeed, does even Security Council Resolution 252 use *"legal* status," as distinct from "status" in its own paragraph 3, which refers simply to "the status of Jerusalem" in an indistinguishable context.)

Only dire poverty of arguments could treat the distinction between "status" and "legal status" as in any way vital. The present writer proposes to ignore it for the purpose of examining the conclusions reached by these pamphlets. I will, accordingly, assume for this purpose that whereas the word "status" alone is used seven times, in the relevant resolutions, and "legal status" only once, all eight references were to "legal status." I thus give to these writers' arguments, by way of hypothesis only, the benefits of all doubt. In my view they still remain untenable.

This second step of their argument then becomes, in the words of the *Jerusalem* pamphlet, that the "references to 'the legal status of Jerusalem' . . . could mean only the status of the internationalised *corpus separatum* defined in the Partition Resolution."[24] Or, in the words of the authors of *Resolutions,*[25] "the only legal status that has been provided for Jerusalem is the one establishing it as a *corpus separatum.*"

The first answer to the vehemence of these conclusions has already been stated. They are, of course, grotesquely at odds with the fact that if this were what was meant by the relevant resolutions, it is quite inexplicable that both the General Assembly and the Security Council failed in every one of them to refer to the General Assembly's Resolution 181(II) or its later resolutions of that period. Nor do these writers attempt any explanation for this failure. Moreover, a meaning flying even less than this in the face of the text should only be attributed to the passage if no more plausible meaning is available. This leads immediately to the second answer to the assertion that all references to "the status of Jerusalem" must embody implicit reference to the *corpus separatum* of the Partition Resolution.

This second answer, it might be thought, would have been evident to students of international law. All the post-1967 resolutions involved were passed in the aftermath of the 1967 War. In that war Israel, the target of armed aggression, had defeated the aggressor states, and the cease-fire and the international law of *uti possidetis* had left the Israel forces in lawful control of various areas, including East Jerusalem. And in its aftermath the kingdom of Jordan, with the other defeated states, rejected the normal and orderly courses provided by international law for postwar pacification, namely, the negotiation of treaties of peace.

Even if no notion of a *corpus separatum* had ever been floated on the international seas, serious questions about "the legal status of Jerusalem" would have arisen after the 1967 War. Did it have the status of territory that came under belligerent occupation in the course of active hostilities, for which international law prescribes a detailed regime of powers granted to the occupying power—or withheld from him in the interests of the ousted reversionary sovereign? Or was this status qualified in Israel's favor by virtue of the fact that the ousted power, in this case, Jordan, itself had occupied the city in the course of unlawful aggression and therefore could not, under the principle of *ex iniuria non oritur ius,* be regarded as an ousted reversioner?[26] Or was Jerusalem, as we will see that a distinguished authority thought at the time, in the legal status of *res nullius modo juridico?* That is, was it a territory to which by reason of the complex of international instruments, and their lacunae, together with the above vice in the Jordanian title, no other state than Israel could have sovereign title? The consequence of this could be to make "the legal status of Jerusalem" that of subjection to Israel sovereignty. Other possible aspects of the uncertainty of "the legal status of East Jerusalem" could be added, but it is not necessary to exhaust them. They will be further examined below under "Bases of Sovereignty under International Law." The question which of the above constituted "the legal status of Jerusalem" after the 1967 War is obviously sufficient to give meaning to this phrase in the post-1967 resolutions, without the rather obscure reasonings by which the Mallisons and their colleagues vainly seek to identify it with the abortive *corpus separatum.*

What the various enjoinders and admonishments to Israel against changing "the status of Jerusalem" would mean is also, on this basis of international law as usually understood, clear enough. The U.N. organ concerned was presumably intent on limiting any powers that Israel was asserting (or might in future assert) to those appertaining to "the legal status" of the territory that came under Israel's occupation in the circumstances already described. All the measures frowned on by these resolutions, such as those as to expropriation of properties, are consistent with this ordinary meaning in international law of the terms used.

Conversely, the conclusion to which both these overlapping bodies of research of the Committee on . . . Rights of the Palestinian People are directed is revealed as unsound. Not only do the post-1967 resolutions exclude any explicit reference to the Partition Resolution, 181(II), and its abortive *corpus separatum.* Any implicit reference to that corpus is also excluded by the ready meaning attributable to "the legal status of Jerusalem" under everyday rules of international law relevant to the actual situation, without far-fetched invocations of proposals that never matured into legal existence.

Indeed, despite their pertinacious resolve to breathe legal life into the legally stillborn, Professor Mallison and Research Associate Mallison are themselves compelled to make certain admissions that support my above criticisms and undermine their own conclusion. They are obviously puzzled (as the anonymous authors of *Jerusalem* are not) by the failure of all the post-1967 resolutions, already observed, to invoke any resolution directly relevant to partition or the *corpus separatum.*[27] They also admit that there is "an apparent ambiguity" in General Assembly resolutions 2253 (ES-V) and 2254 (ES-V), so basic to their argument. These resolutions (they admit) could conceivably refer, by "the status of Jerusalem," to the *corpus separatum* proposals; but the resolutions could also refer merely to "the status of the city as it existed under partial Jordanian and partial Israel control prior to the intense hostilities of June 1967."[28] These writers could scarcely mean by this latter that the resolution might be requiring the Israelis to hand back immediately the control of East Jerusalem to Jordan. They must mean that the Israelis were to be limited to the powers of a belligerent occupant in terms of the well-known categories of of international law. In any case, the second alternative of the ambiguity they admit in the meaning of "legal status of Jerusalem" would rule out any reference whatsoever to a *corpus separatum.*

That the second alternative is, indeed, a more likely meaning is surely placed beyond serious doubt by the preamble to the Security Council's Resolution 298 of September 25, 1971. This recites all the preceding General Assembly and Security Council resolutions adopted since 1969, describing them as referring to "measures and actions by Israel designed to change the status of the Israeli-occupied section of Jerusalem." All the resolutions concerned are thus here securely attached, as regards their references to "the status of Jerusalem," to the law of belligerent or similar military occupation; and any reference to the *corpus separatum* of the partition proposals is clearly excluded.[29]

For these reasons we venture to agree with the results of the careful examination of the *corpus separatum* proposal by E. Lauterpacht in his monograph *Jerusalem and the Holy Places:*

(i) During the critical period of the changeover of power in Palestine from British to Israeli and Arab hands, the U.N. did nothing effectively to implement the idea of the internationalization of Jerusalem.

(ii) In the five years 1948-1952 inclusive, the U.N. sought to develop the concept as a theoretical exercise in the face of a gradual realization that it was acceptable neither to Israel nor to Jordan and could never be enforced. Eventually the idea was allowed quietly to drop.

(iii) In the meantime, both Israel and Jordan demonstrated that each was capable of ensuring the security of the Holy Places and of maintaining access to and free worship at them—with the exception, on the part of Jordan, that Jews were not allowed access to Jewish Holy Places in the area of Jordanian control.

(iv) The U.N. by its unconcern with the idea of territorial internationalization, as demonstrated from 1952 to the present date [1968] effectively acquiesced in the demise of the concept. The events of 1967 and 1968 have not led to its revival.

(v) Nonetheless, there began to emerge, as long ago as 1950, the idea of 'functional' internationalization of the Holy Places in contradistinction to the "territorial" internationalization of Jerusalem. This means that there should be no element of international government of the City, but only a measure of international interest in and concern with the Holy Places. This idea has been propounded by Israel and has been said to be acceptable to her. Jordan has not subscribed to it.[30]

At this final juncture, even the international law researchers of *Resolutions* have to part company from the anonymous authors of *Jerusalem.* The latter still in 1979 embrace the *corpus separatum* declaring it vibrant with legal life. But the Mallisons draw back from such ghoulish dallying. They still confess in their concluding paragraph to finding the ambiguity in all the post-1967 General Assembly and Security Council resolutions between an implied reference to maintaining a supposedly continuing *corpus separatum*, and a mere reference to maintaining "the factual status of the pre-June 1967 divided city."[31] I have already given ample reasons why the former alternative is really not open, either, to international lawyers.

It may be observed that even Security Council resolution 465 (1980) of March 1, 1980, the unanimous adoption of which was the occasion of a declaration by the United States government that its representative had voted for it by a mistake arising from faulty communication among its representatives, negatives by its omissions any continuing validity of the *corpus separatum* proposals. References in that resolution to Jerusalem were a main focus of bitter controversy surrounding the attitude to it of the United States government and its representative. Yet paragraphs 5, 6, and 7 of that resolution, in purporting to deny "legal validity" to measures taken by Israel to change the status quo, expressly attribute to Jerusalem the same territorial status as to other "Arab territories occupied since 1967." The same is to be said of the fourth paragraph of the preamble; while the eighth paragraph limits its explanation of the "specific" status of Jerusalem, to a general "need for protection and preservation of the unique spiritual and religious dimension of the Holy Places in the city."

HOLY PLACES: THE FUNCTIONAL CONCERN

The two preceding sections have shown that there is no basis in international law for the thesis of the Committee on . . . Rights of the Palestinian People that Jerusalem is under international law a *corpus separatum* that cannot be subject to Israel's sovereignty. The bearing of international law on the future of Jerusalem, however, is far richer than the committee indicated. This richer aspect now remains to be examined in this and the succeeding section.

It is common knowledge in an arena where so little is common, that about thirty holy places, revered by adherents of the Christian, Jewish, or Moslem faiths, are located in Jerusalem or its vicinity. The fact that these adherents are spread throughout the world, often engaging patronage and even commitments of governments, makes the security of the holy places, and freedom of access to them, a matter of real international concern. The proposal in 1947 for a *corpus separatum* was one way of expressing this international concern; but it certainly is not the only way and probably not the best, nor even a practicable one.

We have seen in Chapter 4, and in the previous two sections of the present chapter that there is no basis for treating the *corpus separatum* proposals as setting any international law limits on the territorial future of Jerusalem. Under that law, *de lege lata,* it is difficult to differentiate Jerusalem from the rest of the West Bank. What differentiates Jerusalem is, on the one hand, the incalculable spiritual significance for communities of the three great faiths mentioned above, communities widely dispersed among the 150 members of the United Nations; and, on the other hand, its historic role, political, cultural, and social, throughout more than three millennia of the recorded history of the Jewish people, joined now to its strategic importance for the survival of the state of Israel.

The spiritual significance of Jerusalem to Christianity, Islam and Judaism undoubtedly calls for devising appropriate structural forms on the level of the religious institutions involved, appropriate to the specific functions of maintaining and protecting the holy places, and guaranteeing freedom of access and of worship to members of the faiths involved. On the importance of these functions, and the machinery apt for their fulfillment, Israel agreed as long ago as 1950. Its "primary purpose," in the words of the government of Israel on November 25, 1949, was "to ensure protection of the Holy Places in Jerusalem . . . in view of the special character of Jerusalem whose soil is consecrated by the prayers and pilgrimages of the adherents of three religious faiths." Its proposals would have given assurances for the free exercise of all forms of worship then existing (Art. 2 [sect. 3]), for preservation and nonimpairment of the sacred character of the holy places, and their amenities and precincts (Art. 3 [sects. 4-5]). It would have guaranteed free access, visit, and transit without distinction of race, religion, or nationality, except where the Faith concerned requires exclusion of nonadherents during rites and ceremonies (Art. 4 [sects. 6-7]), police protection against disturbances (Art. 5 [sect. 10]), and provided for public services and utilities (Art. 7 [sects. 12-13]). It also would have provided for the same tax immunity as hitherto (Art.8[sect.14]).[32] There have been great changes, no doubt, in both the local and regional situations, as well as in the constitution and operation of the U.N. organs, which may affect the applicability of these and other proposals of 1949, to the circumstances of today.

An alternative plan of a similarly functional apolitical nature was submitted by Sweden on December 5, 1950,[33] for application also to East Jerusalem then recently seized by Transjordan (now Jordan). Its main additional provisions expressly preserved the existing rights, immunities, and privileges of religious denominations with respect to monasteries and missionary education and welfare establishments (Art. 1). As under the Israel proposals, jurisdiction and control over the area of Jerusalem concerned was generally to be exercised by the states concerned (Art. 8), but these were to "gradually reduce their armed forces" down to "normal peace-time requirements" within three months after a peace settlement (Art. 8).[34]

Such proposals for protecting the holy places and securing access of religious adherents to them are part of the essential agenda for settlement of the Middle East conflict. And this is so even though Resolution 242 (1967) does not mention any need for a special regime for the holy places among its "principles" or "necessities" for a just and lasting peace. A reasonable argument could, indeed, be made for giving to a representative body of each religious faith involved somewhat more substantial functions in regard to the holy places than contemplated in 1949-50. Those early proposals, in any case, were finally shelved in 1950. The committee of the General Assembly rather adopted a Belgian proposal calling for further study of the problem of the holy places, but in the General Assembly itself this failed to marshal the required two-thirds majority, leaving the question in limbo.[35]

Rejectionist Arab states, including those that had joined in the attempt to destroy Israel in 1948-49, continue to make wider political demands for full territorial "internationalisation" of Jerusalem, going well beyond any legitimate concern for the holy places and their relation to the three great religious faiths. Such political demands are understandable enough as a means of depriving Israel of control of the city from which the Arab states had failed to oust her by military means.[36] This political objective has had some revival in the seventies as part of Arab demands after the defeat of Jordan's attack from East Jerusalem and Israel's entry there, and is now supported by the Arab states' oil weapon. The ending of the illegal Jordanian presence in East Jerusalem naturally increases Arab state support of such political objectives, not least by Jordan, which during its occupation was cold towards them. King Feisal of Saudi Arabia rather stripped such demands of the cloak of universal religious concern when, in late 1973, he joined his use of the oil embargo with the demand that East Jerusalem become an "Arab" city.[37] We are not here immediately concerned with such political designs. The internationalization proposal, as has been seen in the first two sections above, is even today sometimes pressed as if it were an arrangement that somehow went into legally binding and operative force after the termination of the British mandate. This view has also there been shown to be untenable.

POST-1967 RESOLUTIONS AND "THE STATUS OF JERUSALEM"

It was seen above under "Legal Evaluation of Claims" that admonitions to Israel in General Assembly and Security Council resolutions adopted after 1967 concerning the maintenance of "the status of Jerusalem" cannot be interpreted as referring to a supposed legally existent international territorial *corpus separatum.* This is dramatically reinforced by recalling the story of Jordan's presence in East Jerusalem.

From the unlawful military occupation by Jordan of East Jerusalem as a result of her armed aggression of 1948, right until the Jordanian forces were ousted after her renewed aggression from that territory in 1967, no U.N.

resolution censured her for measures tending to change the status of Jerusalem, even when she purported formally to annex the city. This stands in puzzling contrast to the flurry of admonitory and censuring activity of the bodies concerned after she was ousted.[38]

Immediately following the 1967 War a number of urgent measures were taken by Israel to deal with the plight of the inhabitants of East Jerusalem in the aftermath of the Jordanian-initiated hostilities. These measures were primarily designed to meet responsibilities that then suddenly fell on the authorities of the Israel Municipality of Jerusalem, by the additional needs of 60,000 inhabitants of the Old City, with services originally inadequate, and now collapsed under war conditions. Fulfillment of these responsibilities was hampered by blockages of communication resulting from the grotesque walls of division between East and West Jerusalem thrown up after Jordan seized East Jerusalem in 1948. The only authorities in a position to assume these responsibilities were those of the city of Jerusalem, which for this purpose had to reestablish lines of communication and extend an orderly chain of municipal authority, along with substantial means, to the Old City. The necessary preliminary to providing the means for all this was to bring East Jerusalem within the boundaries of the municipality of Jerusalem subject to Israel law and jurisdiction. A municipal authority, be it in Israel or elsewhere, must act *intra vires* of the municipality, and certainly cannot use its budget to maintain services in foreign parts.

All substantial measures taken in East Jerusalem before the first admonitory General Assembly resolution consisted (apart from measures to ensure free and safe access to holy places and their protection) of extensions of the water, public health (and especially child health), and epidemic-prevention, fire-fighting, and other emergency services to the Arab citizens of East Jerusalem. These various steps were basically not concerned with the legal status of Jerusalem under international law, but with the provision of a framework within Israel law to allow the only available municipal and other authorities to restore, maintain, and improve the services and welfare entitlements of the local inhabitants. The United Nations secretary-general's personal representative, Ernesto Thalemann, indeed, reported to the secretary-general that the Israel measures were directed to equalizing the legal and administrative status of all residents in the city.[39]

On June 27, 1967, the Knesset passed three laws, the Law and Administration Ordinance (Amendment no. 11) Law, the Municipalities Ordinance (Amendment no. 6) Law, and the Protection of the Holy Places Law.[40] The first added a new section II B to a 1948 law, stating that the law, jurisdiction, and administration of the state should extend to any area of Eretz Israel designated by the government by order. The second empowered the minister of the interior by proclamation to enlarge the area of a particular municipality. The third, which requires no discussion here, imposed a maximum penalty of seven years imprisonment for desecration or violation of a holy place, and of five years imprisonment for anyone doing anything likely to violate the freedom of access of members of the different religions to places sacred to them or their feeling with regard to those places. On the basis of the first of these two laws, an order and a proclamation were issued the next day,[41] the effect of which was to enlarge the area of the Jerusalem Municipality to include what had previously been known as East Jerusalem, or the area of the municipality formerly functioning under the Jordanian occupation.[42] The term "Eretz Israel," as distinct from the term "Medinat Israel," refers in a historicogeographical sense to the area that during the period of the mandate was administered by the government of Palestine. A semantic confusion arising from this terminology may, nevertheless, have raised undue apprehension among some members of the General Assembly.

For proper understanding of the import of this law, we must return to the policies stated at the foundation of the state of Israel, when, on May 14, 1948—two hours before independence was proclaimed—the future prime minister said that specification of boundaries was *deliberately* omitted from the proclamation for two reasons. First, because the United Nations had "done nothing" to give effect to its resolutions, or to "preserve the peace" and "this burden has fallen on us." "We have not said: 'no U.N. boundaries'; we have not said the opposite either. *We have left the matter open for future developments.*"[43] The invasion of Palestine by the armies of the surrounding states was already impending at that moment, and showed its full proportions within ten hours of this statement; so that it is obvious that it was the uncertainties of the future that lay behind this basic stand.

In this light, it is clear that it was the necessities of ensuring a stable legal order in the face of these and other wartime uncertainties that underlay section 1 of the Area of Jurisdiction and Powers Ordinance 5708-1948, of September 22, 1948, that "any law applying to the whole of the State of Israel shall be deemed to apply . . . to both the area of the State of Israel and any part of Palestine [in the Hebrew: "Eretz Yisrael"] which the Minister of Defence has defined by proclamation as being held by the Defence Army of Israel."[44] The question whether a particular territory was or was not controlled by the army after the 1948 War was obviously a question of fact to be determined in the light of the evolving military and political situation, which then still rested on a fragile truce until the Armistice Regime of 1949 became effective.[45] And it is this openness towards the uncertainties affecting the future boundaries that would seem to inspire section 1 of the law of June 27, 1967, above cited, which allowed "law, jurisdiction and administration" to extend to any "area of Eretz Israel" designated by the government by order. It was under this law and amendment no. 6 to the Municipalities Ordinance that an order was made on June 28, 1967, proclaiming new boundaries for the municipality of Jerusalem, to include East Jerusalem. The explanations of the bill for that

June 27, 1967, act given by the Minister of Justice Shapira to the Knesset are consistent with this.[46]

Clearly, by the proclamation of June 28, 1967, Israel asserted some powers in relation to East Jerusalem that she did not assert for Judea and Samaria (the West Bank). In the latter areas, subject to military security requirements, the general rule is that the existing law continued in force. But this does not affect the basic point as to both, namely that final territorial entitlements will have to be determined according to the applicable principles of international law. Eminent authorities, as will shortly be seen, are of the view that Israel's entitlements under these principles go well beyond that of mere belligerent occupation, for both East Jerusalem and Judea and Samaria (the West Bank), as well as Gaza.

Yet the immediate differentiation in June 1967 did not go beyond what is readily explained by urgent practical exigencies. The health, security, and well-being of 60,000 Arab inhabitants of East Jerusalem amid the collapse of the Jordanian administration became enmeshed with those of West Jerusalem. The two "cities" are, after all, nearer to each other than Silver Spring, Maryland, or Alexandria, Virginia, to Washington, D.C. The municipality of Jerusalem was the only authority in a position to act, and yet could only act if its lawful authority, jurisdiction, and authorized budget were extended to embrace East Jerusalem. Virtually every step taken before the first General Assembly resolution of July 4, 1967, consisted of measures to protect the holy places, extend the water supply (under Jordanian administration not continuously available), collect garbage, and provide other sanitary, educational, banking, transport, telephone, and public and child health services and epidemic control safeguards, to the inhabitants of the congested Old City.[47] It was basically these exigencies, in such close proximity to West Jerusalem, that account for the apparently special measures in East Jerusalem. At the same time, it would also be unrealistic to overlook the sentiments stirred by the profound and enduring religious and historical associations of the City of David and the Western Wall, from which Jews had been unlawfully barred by Jordan in flagrant breach of the Armistice Agreement.[48] The resolve that Jerusalem should never again be divided was an inevitable reaction to that wrong, even while Israel limited her measures elsewhere to the minimum indicated by the law of military occupation, precisely in order to keep the way open for a territorial settlement with Jordan.

The admonitory and censuring contents of Resolution 2253 (ES-V) of July 4, 1967, and subsequent General Assembly and Security Council resolutions have been indicated in Chapter 5 and above under "Legal Evaluation of Claims." Insofar as any clear line emerges from the general vagueness of these resolutions, it is one of apprehension that Israel intended to foreclose by her actions whatever might be the territorial "status of

Jerusalem" under international law. The resulting controversies focused on the question whether Israel's action constituted "annexation." Mr. Eban stated immediately during the debates that the question of annexation was not involved. Prime Minister Eshkol stated that the term "annexation" used to support the General Assembly's Jerusalem Resolution, was "out of place." "The measures adopted," said Mr. Eban, related to "the integration of Jerusalem in the administrative and municipal spheres and furnish a legal basis for the protection of the Holy Places."[49]

These resolutions represent accordingly the reservation of their positions by these bodies as to the effects of any post-1967 actions taken by Israel that might differ from whatever the status of Jerusalem might be under existing international law. They in effect refer the status to the operation of the general principles of international law and of the charter as they affect the course of events touching control and title of Jerusalem and other territories involved. These principles had unfortunately been somewhat obscured when the General Assembly and the Security Council remained inactive in face of Jordan's open claim to annex East Jerusalem (and the West Bank),[50] especially since this was in spite of the fact that even her status as a belligerent occupant was tainted by the unlawfulness of her entry into a war of aggression. We may, on the other hand, have to conclude that international law accords to Israel, because of the lawfulness of her entry, grounds of legal territorial title other than those of a mere belligerent occupant.

Even, indeed, on the merely political and commonsense level, there was also ground for some greater tolerance towards Israel's position, not only because of the historic centrality of Jerusalem to Judaism for 3,000 years, but also because in modern times Jews have always exceeded Arabs in Jerusalem. In 1844 there were 7,000 Jews to 5,000 Moslems; in 1876, 12,000 Jews to 7,500 Moslems; in 1896, 28,112 Jews to 8,560 Moslems; in 1910, 47,000 Jews to 9,800 Moslems; in 1931, 51,222 Jews to 19,894 Moslems; in 1948, 100,000 Jews to 40,000 Moslems; in 1967, 200,000 Jews to 54,902 Moslems. Statistics for Christian inhabitants are footnoted.[51]

This study, however, is concerned rather with grounds of legal title. On this I have already excluded, above under "Legal Evaluation of Claims," any possibility that international law imposes any territorial status of *corpus separatum* on Jerusalem. I still have to examine the wider question, to which these post-1967 resolutions refer when they insist on maintenance of "the status of Jerusalem"—namely what is the territorial status of the region under the relevant principles of international law and the charter, as applied to the events since the renunciation by Turkey of sovereignty over this whole area in the Treaty of Lausanne of 1923.

This examination must take account of powerful arguments of a number of outstanding international lawyers, who envisage a sovereign title to East

Jerusalem vested in Israel, some on grounds of possible lawful annexation, some on other grounds of international law,[52] for instance, on an analysis of the sovereignty-title movement since the Turkish renunciation of 1923, or on the basis of the law pertaining to lawful and unlawful military occupation.[53]

BASES OF SOVEREIGNTY UNDER INTERNATIONAL LAW

There is not now, nor has there ever been, any consensus in international law or state practice as to where sovereign title over territories placed under League of Nations mandate was vested. In the case of former Mandated Palestine the matter was even more complicated by the language of Article 16 of the Treaty of Lausanne, 1923, which did not indicate any transferee in favor of whom renunciation was made.

Among the theories agitated concerning the location of sovereign title, four repositories in particular were canvassed: (1) the Principal Allied and Associated Powers; (2) the League of Nations or possibly the Council of the League (which its Covenant authorized to "confer" the mandate in respect of each territory); (3) the peoples concerned (on whose behalf the particular territory was to be administered by the mandatory power);[54] and (4) the mandatory power (to which the particular territory was thus entrusted). To these bewildering possibilities have to be added two further complicating factors. One is the fact that though, as already seen, Jews have been in the majority in Jerusalem for a century, when the mandate incorporating in itself the object of "the establishment of a Jewish National Home" in Palestine was conferred, part of the wider Arab people was a majority in the whole country, which included then Transjordan. The mandate clearly envisaged the continued entry of Jews from the wider Jewish people scattered the world over.[55] The second complicating factor, as shown in the first section of our opening chapter, is that the original allocation after World War I of Palestine for a Jewish National Home, and of the rest of the Middle East for "the Arab Nation" (including the Arabs in Palestine), was itself the application of the principle of self-determination to the facts that existed. If this framework were not complicated enough, the action of the United Kingdom in referring the future government of Mandated Palestine to the General Assembly on April 2, 1947, was notice of its intention to abandon all further interest and authority over territory, an intention that it proceeded to carry out.

Even if, as examination has revealed, the relevant post-1967 General Assembly and Security Council resolutions are directed to reserving questions of sovereignty in East Jerusalem, it may still turn out to be the case that international law already accords that sovereignty, or the right to assume it, to Israel. For what those resolutions did, as already seen, was to reserve whatever might be the territorial juridical status of Jerusalem under international law. It is to the examination of that status that attention must now turn.[56]

West Jerusalem. As to West Jerusalem, the state of Israel, since she maintained control by her self-defensive struggle in 1948-49, has claimed full sovereignty, as she has over the rest of the territory she controlled after the 1948 aggression against her by the Arab states.[57] Under well-settled rules of international law the claim of Israel seems difficult to challenge. For not only was her entry lawful, being in self-defense, but the history of the territory to that time reveals no other claimant state with any legal title at all—let alone better title or full sovereignty. Conversely, since the Arab states' attack of 1948-49 was thus unlawful, the maxim *ex iniuria non oritur ius* prevented Jordan from acquiring any titles whether in Jerusalem or elsewhere even if we adopt the view, propounded by some authorities, that there was a sovereignty vacuum at the time. Whether in terms of that view, or of the more conventional view that the better lawful title prevails, the effect of international law is that Israel acquired sovereignty over the territory that she controlled at her independence on May 14, 1948, as well as over any other territory in Palestine that came under her control in the course of her lawful self-defense. And West Jerusalem was certainly within these areas. And, as I have shown in Chapter 2, the legally abortive partition proposals did not operate as a matter of law either to enable this, or to prevent it.

East Jerusalem. It is not in dispute that at the very least Israel's standing in East Jerusalem, as on the West Bank and in Gaza, derives from what was initially a situation of belligerent occupation during active hostilities. Nor is it seriously in dispute that her entry there was lawful, because it occurred in the course of self-defense. That matter has been examined in Chapter 3. The present inquiry is whether the principles of international law and the charter, to which by its admonitions after 1967 the General Assembly correctly referred the future territorial status of East Jerusalem, give any guidance as to this future.

At least four differing views have been offered by international lawyers leading to the conclusion that Israel's standing in East Jerusalem, as well as in Judea and Samaria (the West Bank) and Gaza, goes beyond that of a merely lawful belligerent occupant to territorial sovereignty either already vested or *in posse*. Two of these views conclude that under international law, sovereignty is already at present vested in Israel. A third view leads to the conclusion that although sovereignty may not at present be so vested, it requires only a formal act of annexation by Israel for it so to vest. A fourth view asserts that even if it were impossible to attribute sovereignty in these areas to any state, the residual territory concerned would remain subject to the central obligation of the Palestine mandate, namely, the obligation to permit access of Jews to this territory.

Lawful Presence Filling a "Sovereignty Vacuum" (E. Lauterpacht). Elihu Lauterpacht has offered a cogent legal analysis leading to the conclusion that sovereignty over Jerusalem has already vested in Israel. His view is that when the partition proposals were immediately rejected and then aborted by Arab armed aggression, those proposals could not, both because of their inherent nature and because of the terms in which they were framed, operate as an effective legal redisposition of the sovereign title. They might (he thinks) have been transformed by agreement of the parties concerned into a consensual root of title, but this never happened. And he points out that the idea that some kind of title remained in the United Nations is quite at odds, both with the absence of any evidence of vesting, and with "complete United Nations silence on this aspect of the matter" from 1950 to 1967.

In these circumstances, that writer is led to the view that there was, following the British withdrawal and the abortion of the partition proposals, a "lapse" or "vacancy" or "vacuum" of sovereignty.[58] In this situation of sovereignty vacuum, he thinks, sovereignty could be forthwith acquired by any state that was in a position to assert effective and stable control without resort to unlawful means. The presence in Palestine of the authorities that declared the independence of the state of Israel on May 14, 1948, was perfectly lawful. No doubt, its territorial limits still had to be legally defined, but this problem (and much else) was settled, so far as international law is concerned, by the war initiated, on the very day of that declaration, by the invasion of Palestine by the forces of Egypt, Transjordan, and other Arab states. For that invasion was in clear violation of Article 2(4) of the charter, even without the recommendation in advance by the General Assembly that such a use of force be treated by the Security Council as a violation of Article 39 of the charter. Neither in intention nor in fact (as the event showed), nor in law, could it be justified as a way of merely taking possession of the territory on behalf of the yet unborn Arab state. Nor could that use of force against Israel be regarded as justified on the ground that the attackers did not recognize the statehood of Israel. There is no such qualification to the prohibition of force in Article 2(4) of the charter.[59] States cannot opt out of the obligation not to resort to force by simply not recognizing their victim. Nor could the absurdity be mitigated by arguing that the victim (in this case Israel) was not entitled to exist, so that its very continued existence invites attack by way of "self-defense."

This analysis, based on the sovereignty vacuum, moreover, affords a common legal frame for the legal positions of both West and East Jerusalem after both the 1948-49 and the 1967 wars. In 1967, Israel's entry into East Jerusalem was again by way of lawful self-defense, confirmed in the Security Council and General Assembly by the defeat of Soviet- and Arab-sponsored resolutions demanding her withdrawal, or branding her action as aggressive. When Jordanian forces attacked from East Jerusalem, therefore, and were then ousted from there, the legal effects were as follows.

Before the attack, Jordan was an unlawful belligerent occupant, the unlawfulness of whose entry in 1948 had prevented her from acquiring any lawful title, despite her purported annexation. The ouster of her forces by Israel in course of lawful self-defense in 1967 then had three legal effects.

One was the loss of *any* continued Jordanian territorial standing at all in relation to Jerusalem: for clearly an occupation (even if lawful, as was not here the case) does not outlast the occupant's effective control.[60] Second, the Jordanian attack operated as a completely unjustifiable repudiation of the Israel-Jordan General Armistice Agreement of April 3, 1949, the core of which was the prohibition of "resort to military force," "aggressive action," and "warlike or hostile acts" by any "land, sea or air forces." This repudiation released Israel from the restraints of the agreement.[61] Third, no less important, is that the entry of Israel into East Jerusalem, and indeed the whole West Bank, was a lawful entry in course of self-defense. In the context of the sovereignty vacuum in East Jerusalem, her lawful presence entitled her to assert full sovereignty. Dr. Lauterpacht, indeed, believes that the effect of these legal principles was to clear Israel of any reproaches made in the post-1967 resolutions against some measures taken by her. For, he observes, if "the larger measures would be justifiable, then the lesser" (actually taken by Israel) "certainly are."[62]

The phenomenon of a sovereignty vacuum on this juridical level is obviously rare and unfamiliar. But the circumstances of Great Britain's abandonment of the mandate and the abortion by simultaneous Arab aggression of any orderly proposals for the future were no less so. The analysis based on it certainly affords a well-based self-consistent and objectively grounded account of the territorial outcome of the course of legal events in historic Palestine.

Strongest Relative Title and Absence of "Sovereign Reversioner." It is interesting and important that substantially similar results, both as to East Jerusalem and the West Bank, are reached independently, even when we limit the analysis to more traditional categories of the rights of military occupants, and sovereign reversioners of the occupied territories.

Here, again, the starting point is the plain illegality of the hostilities opened up by Jordan against Israel, and the lawfulness of Israel's self-defense. Both characterizations, as observed, were clearly endorsed by the defeat in the Security Council and the General Assembly of the Arab and Soviet demands that Israel be declared an aggressor and ordered to withdraw.[63]

It follows from this initial position that Israel's standing in the territories is that of a lawful occupant, entitled to stay under the rule *uti possidetis* until a peace agreement is concluded. Furthermore, insofar as Jordan on the West Bank and in East Jerusalem was itself a belligerent occupant, following its attack of 1948, even that level of control was itself unlawful. But the rights of eventual restoration of the ousted sovereign in the law of belligerent occupation derive from ultimate de jure title—territorial sovereignty. They do not inure to a merely de facto belligerent occupant, much less such an occupant whose entry was unlawful. *Ex iniuria non oritur ius.*

In short, because the Jordanian entry onto the West Bank and East Jerusalem in 1948 was an "unlawful invasion"[64] and an aggression,[65] the principle *ex iniuria non oritur ius* beclouded even Jordan's limited status of belligerent occupant.[66] Her purported annexation was invalid on that account, as well as because it violated the "freezing" provisions of the Armistice Agreement.[67] Conversely, Israel's standing in East Jerusalem after her lawful entry in the course of self-defense certainly displaced Jordan's unlawful possession, and placed Israel in the position (at the least) of lawful belligerent occupant.

The application of the settled principles of the international law of belligerent occupation to this state of the facts, and in particular those underlying the rights of the ousted sovereign (or reversioner state), results in a dramatic transformation of Israel's territorial standing, beyond that of a mere military occupant.

One main objective of the law of belligerent occupation is to accord protection to the local population while enabling the occupant to maintain the security of his forces and their operation during his administration. Another is concerned with the relations between the occupant and the ousted lawful sovereign. In other words, the law of military occupation proceeds on the double assumption, first, that it was a legitimate sovereign that was ousted from the territory by the occupant; second, that the ousting power qualifies as a lawful belligerent occupant of it.[68] The assumption that there are these two legal standings simultaneously present in the same territory underlies this whole body of law. Its rules here are designed to sanction the occupant's administration ad interim as limited by the future reversionary rights of the ousted lawful sovereign.

It follows from this that where the ousted state was never even in lawful occupation, much less the sovereign, the rules to assure the reversion of the legitimate sovereign cannot operate in its favor.[69]

Once this position is reached, and it is remembered that neither Jordan nor any other state is a sovereign reversioner entitled to reenter the West Bank, the legal standing of Israel takes on new aspects. She becomes then a state in lawful control of territory in respect of which no other state can show a better (or, indeed, any) legal title. The general principles of international law applicable to such a situation, moreover, are well-established. The International Court of Justice, when called upon to adjudicate in territorial disputes, for instance in the *Minquiers and Echrehos* case between the United Kingdom and France, proceeded "to appraise the relative strength of the opposing claims to sovereignty."[70] Since title to territory is thus based on a claim not of *absolute* but only of *relative* validity, the result seems decisive in East Jerusalem. No other state having a legal claim even equal to that of Israel under the unconditional cease-fire agreement of 1967 and the rule of *uti possidetis,* this relative superiority of title would seem to assimilate Israel's possession under international law to an absolute title, valid *erga omnes.*[71]

Right of Annexation on Refusal to Negotiate Peace. The preceding two international law grounds would base the conclusion that sovereignty in (*inter alia*) East Jerusalem is already vested in the state of Israel. No less important is the third ground advanced by international law authorities, under which only a unilateral formal act of annexation is required to vest that sovereignty in herself.

The most succinct statement of this position is in Professor Stephen Schwebel's "What Weight to Conquest?"[72] published in 1970, before he entered U.S. government service. He points out that the answer to that question in terms of international law, after the charter's prohibitions of the use of force, makes necessary a vital distinction "between aggressive conquest and defensive conquest, between the taking of territory legally held and the taking of territory illegally held."

Those distinctions may be summarized as follows: (a) A state acting in lawful exercise of its right of self-defense may seize and occupy foreign territory as long as such seizure and occupation are necessary to its self-defense. (b) As a condition of its withdrawal from such territory, that state may require the institution of security measures reasonably designed to ensure that that territory shall not again be used to mount a threat or use of force against it of such a nature as to justify exercise of self-defense. (c) Where the prior holder of territory had seized that territory unlawfully, the state which subsequently takes that territory in the lawful exercise of self-defense has, against that prior holder, better title.

Applying this analysis to the territorial issues in Palestine he relates the facts as to the earlier hostilities of 1948 that lead him to conclude that "Egypt's seizure of the Gaza Strip, and Jordan's seizure and subsequent annexation of the West Bank and the Old City of Jerusalem, were unlawful." They "could not vest in Egypt and Jordan lawful, indefinite control, whether as occupying power or sovereign: *ex iniuria non oritur ius.*" Correspondingly, he concludes that the unlawful attacks by these states, "both within and as necessary without the boundaries allotted to her [as in West Jerusalem] under the partition plan," justified Israel's defensive action. He states:

[H]aving regard to the consideration that, as between Israel, acting defensively in 1948 and 1967, on the one hand, and her Arab neighbors, acting aggressively in 1948 and 1967, on the other, Israel has better title in the territory of what was Palestine, including the whole of Jerusalem, than do Jordan and Egypt (the U.A.R.

indeed has, unlike Jordan, not asserted sovereign title), it follows that modifications of the 1949 armistice lines among those states within former Palestinian territory are lawful. . . . In the second place, as regards territory bordering Palestine, and under unquestioned Arab sovereignty in 1949 and thereafter, such as Sinai and the Golan Heights, it follows not that no weight shall be given to conquest, but that such weight shall be given to defensive action as is reasonably required to ensure that such Arab territory will not again be used for aggressive purposes against Israel. For example free navigation through the Straits of Tiran shall be effectively guaranteed and demilitarized zones shall be established.

So also the present writer might add, with the contemporary example of the Israel-Egypt Treaty of Peace under which, while the whole of Sinai is to be restored to Egypt, the future of Gaza, in its more proximate relation to past aggressions against Israel, has been left open. The quoted article continued:

The foregoing analysis accords not only with the terms of the United Nations Charter, notably Article 2, paragraph 4, and Article 51, but law and practice as they have developed since the Charter's conclusion. In point of practice, it is instructive to recall that the Republic of Korea and indeed the United Nations itself have given considerable weight to conquest in Korea, to the extent of that substantial territory north of the 38th parallel from which the aggressor was driven and remains excluded — a territory which, if the full will of the United Nations has prevailed, would have been much larger (indeed, perhaps the whole of North Korea).

Continuing Obligations of the Mandate. The fourth of the various independent bases of Israel's rights under international law in East Jerusalem, Judea and Samaria (the West Bank), and Gaza, going beyond those of a belligerent occupant, rests on the terms of the Palestine mandate under which these territories were held by the United Kingdom until her withdrawal from the mandatory role in 1947. On this view, when the territories now constituting the sovereign states of Israel (within its 1967 borders) and Jordan (within its 1947 borders) have been extracted from the historic Palestine that was subject to the Palestine mandate, certain residual areas remain still subject to the mandate. These residual areas include East Jerusalem, Judea and Samaria (the West Bank), and Gaza. They remain subject to the mandate, this view submits, for reasons analogous to those given by the International Court of Justice (I.C.J.) for its early advisory opinion on South West Africa (1950 I.C.J. Reports 128, 131 ff.) in which the court held that the substantive obligations of the mandate over that territory continued in force despite the dissolution of the League of Nations.

The court's opinion in that case, after rehearsing obligations arising in respect of the territory from the terms of the mandate for South-West Africa, held that these obligations remained the essence of the "sacred trust of civilisation" despite the dissolution of the League. They were the *raison d'être* and original objective of the whole mandatory arrangement.

They did not depend for fulfillment on the continued existence of the League of Nations, nor did they come to an end merely because the League's supervisory organs ceased to exist. Even the two dissenting judges (Judges McNair and Read) substantially agreed with the majority on this main point. The twelve majority judges also held that insofar as organs of supervision existed in the United Nations, similar to those of the now defunct League of Nations, the supervisory functions could be exercised cy pres, as it were, by those organs.

On the above foundation, Professor Eugene Rostow has argued[73] that the fact that the United Kingdom abandoned its mandatory role in Palestine in 1947, and no longer claims, nor can claim, any related powers in respect of Palestine, still leaves in force the international obligations affecting the residual territories of former historic Palestine. There is no reason why the withdrawal of the original mandatory power should have any greater influence on the continuance of the "sacred trust of civilisation" to which the territory has been solemnly dedicated, than the disappearance of the former supervisory organs of the League of Nations. On this view, therefore, the status of these residual territories is not merely, as is too often assumed, that of territories under belligerent occupation; it is rather that of continuing dedication to the objectives of the mandate. Central among these is "the establishment of the Jewish National Home" in Palestine for the benefit of the Jews of Israel, and of any Jews elsewhere who wish to go there to live. This, in leading contemporary pronouncements, was "the very soul of the Mandate," its "primary purpose."[74]

Security Council Resolution 242 of November 22, 1967, should accordingly be viewed, in this light, as calling on Israel and Jordan (both of which states came into existence on territory formerly within the Palestine mandate) to agree on a regime for the residual territories, which accords with these objectives of the mandate. It would follow, in the meanwhile, that the right of Jews to enter and settle in these territories, subject only to the "civil and religious rights" of the other inhabitants reserved by the terms of the mandate, must remain as a central element of its territorial status.

This *aperçu* affords a number of insights, some of which reflect with almost poetic justice on the intransigencies of today. In the days of the League of Nations, as already observed, no conclusion emerged, despite herculean labors, as to the location of territorial sovereignty in Mandated Palestine. Perhaps the time has come when that negative outcome of the search for a traditional sovereign may be turned into a positive foundation for the future of the residual territories. The essential task should cease to be the location of sovereignty, and become the achievement of agreement between Israel and the de facto Palestinian Arab State of Jordan, on a regime accommodating the political, economic, and strategic concerns of both states, the rights of entry of Jews under the mandate, as well as the entitlement of the inhabitants under the Camp David Agreement to "full autonomy."

It is, above all, the rival claims to territorial sovereignty that have blocked the search for such a functional regime in the residual territories. Not only the period of the mandate, but nearly fourteen years of virtually open frontiers between Israel, the residual territories, and the state of Jordan since 1967, testify to the irrelevance of the attribution of sovereignty to the fulfillment of the tasks of government involved. The regime suggested by Eugene Rostow's analysis, romantically archaic as it at first sight appears in its discarding of the sovereignty issue, may for that very reason be functionally harmonious with the latest testimony of history for this area.

This analysis also displays the negative contribution to workable solutions of simple assertions of the "illegality" of settlement by Jews in the residual areas of the mandate, mentioned in Chapter 3 (at n. 22) above. Such assertions are generally based on the assumption that the only international law relevant is that of belligerent occupation. Even if these assertions were correct conclusions from the law of belligerent occupation (which is very questionable), they would, in Professor Rostow's view, be beside the point. For the basic territorial regime in the residual areas is, in this view, that of the mandate for Palestine. That regime, far from forbidding the settlement of Jews, contemplates such settlement as a principal objective. The accommodation of this right of settlement by Jews with the claims of Palestinian Arabs in these areas to "full autonomy" has to proceed by practical specification of the volume of permissible entry and settlement, in relation to the range of Palestinian Arab autonomy. Any blanket prohibition of Jewish entry would violate the central principle of the Palestine mandate. It would also set back the clock to the arbitrary design, during Jordan's illegal presence in 1948 to 1967, of seeking to render *judenrein* territories inextricably interwoven with the history of Jews and Judaism.

A right of Jewish entry thus controlled by mutual agreement, moreover, would not be too drastic a break with current claims of Israel. Despite the stridency of controversy, Israel's settlement policy has only involved the admission of a quite negligible proportion of Jews, in relation to the whole population. Such settlements, moreover, have not been directed to changing the demographic complexion of the whole area, but to certain limited goals of military security, goals that will, in any case, have to be taken into account in the autonomy regime to be agreed for the area.[75]

8

. . . . .

Conclusions:
Assault on Israel and
International Law

The preceding chapters have examined the principal issues of international law raised in the series of tendentious studies on the Arab-Israel conflict prepared and published under U.N. auspices in 1978 and 1979, for which the Committee on the Exercise of the Inalienable Rights of the Palestinian People apparently accepts responsibility. *An International Law Analysis of the Major United Nations Resolutions Concerning the Palestine Question* (1979) (which has here been referred to as *"Resolutions"*), by W. T. Mallison and Sally B. Mallison is, indeed, stated to have been prepared "at the request of the Committee," but to express only the views of the Mallisons. The three "studies" that preceded it do not disclose authorship. They are presumably the work of an anonymous "Special Unit" of the United Nations Secretariat referred to in the opening "study" on *The Origins and Evolution of the Palestine Problem* (1978), and are not accompanied by any disclaimer (Introduction). This concluding chapter will draw together, with references back to the preceding chapters, the results of the present examination of these ostensibly objective "studies," and make some concluding observations.

These studies present rather consistently anti-Israel positions on the central issues of the Arab-Israel conflict. They have, consequently, raised serious questions of the proper limits of the Secretariat's role, as well as of the substantive validity of the main positions they espouse. Even more serious are the questions they raise of the confrontation between the United Nations and the law of nations as hitherto understood, and the implications of this not only for the state of Israel, but for the stability of the international community and the United Nations as its focal institution.

Main Theses Examined. The main positions that these "studies" sought to establish are (1) that the General Assembly is an international "lawmaker"; (2) that the proposals in Resolution 181(II) of 1947 (often called "the Partition Plan") remain in 1980 as "law" created by the General Assembly; (3) that repeated recitals in General Assembly resolutions from Resolution 149(III) to Resolution 3236(XXIX) have established an international law "right of return" of Palestinian Arabs; (4) that similar repeated references in such resolutions after 1970 have established a legal "right to self-determination" of Palestinian Arabs empowering the General Assembly to remodel the boundaries of the state of Israel; (5) that the status of Jerusalem under international law remains today that of a *corpus separatum* under an international regime, as proposed in Resolution 181(II). The present chapter will state the findings of the present examination of these theses. For the reader's convenience, the fuller treatment in preceding chapters of the various matters will be pinpointed seriatim in the text.

Concurrence of Self-Determination Movements of Arab and Jewish Peoples. Claims made in the name of the right of self-determination obviously underlie most of the above thesis. However controversial the legal standing of that right, its basis in justice is agreed on all hands. And on both levels, of law as of justice, it is fatal to misidentify the claimants among whom distribution is to be made. A fundamental preliminary question, therefore, concerns the parallel claims to self-determination in the historical context out of which the Arab states and the state of Israel finally emerged. The modern self-determination movement of the Jewish people, known as the Zionist movement, antedates the first Zionist congress in 1897. Its claims to a share of the former Ottoman domains were adjusted with those of the Arab nation, including those Arabs living in Palestine, in the post-World War I settlement. Arabs living in Palestine did not then, nor indeed until half a century later, recognize themselves as a distinct people among the Arab people of this area.

The self-determination principle was correctly applied to the facts of Arab and Jewish peoplehoods as they then existed. The Arab leadership at Versailles applauded this application. The overwhelming share of territory and resources of the Middle East, "Arab Asia" to use the Peel Commission's term, was allocated to the Arab people, including Arabs living in Palestine, enough to accommodate later a dozen Arab independent states (Chapter 1, first section). A comparatively tiny allocation embracing Cisjordan and Transjordan was made to the Jewish people, reduced almost immediately by separating off four-fifths of it to establish Transjordan as a future Arab state in Palestine. The Hashemite Kingdom of Jordan is thus, by history as well as by predominance of Palestinians among its subjects, a living witness to the justice of the original post-World War I distribution (Chapter 1, second section).

The central thesis of these studies from the Secretariat that the Israel-Arab question arises from encroachment by the state of Israel on some international law right of self-determination of a *Palestinian Arab nation* is thus quite wrong. Examination has shown it to be a gross distortion of history and of law and justice, emerging from intervening decades of biased political operations inside and outside the United Nations. Any moral claim of Palestine Arabs by reason of their later self-identification as a distinct national group in the 1960s is a claim that should be directed against all the vast former Ottoman territories distributed after World War I, most of which is now the foundation of a dozen Arab states. The state of Israel, in its minute share, assumed responsibility for no less than 700,000 refugees from Arab lands; this provides a model for the corresponding duties of Jordan and other Arab states (Chapter 1, third section).

Legal Effects of General Assembly Resolutions.   Another preliminary matter erroneously treated as axiomatic, thus also undermining the conclusions of these U.N.-sponsored studies, concerns the lawmaking effect of General Assembly resolutions. The relation of such resolutions to international law is hemmed in by legal authorities with requirements that these studies quite neglect. In the words of the eminent former judge of the International Court of Justice, Sir Hersch Lauterpacht, where the charter does not otherwise provide (as in articles 4 and 17) such resolutions "are not legally binding on the members of the United Nations" even if framed as "decisions" (Chapter 2, second section). And as late as 1973 another learned former judge, Sir Gerald Fitzmaurice, rejected what he called the "illusion" that a General Assembly resolution can have "legislative effect" (Chapter 2, second section). As Professor Arangio-Ruiz concluded, in his notable lectures on this very matter to the Hague Academy of International Law in 1972, discussed at length in Chapter 2, fourth section, above: "It would be too easy if the 'shouting out' of rules through General Assembly resolutions were to be law making, simply as a matter of 'times' shouted and the size of the choir." The dangers referred to by Sir Gerald of indulging contrary illusions are seen in the many notorious taints that often affect General Assembly resolutions, including those of pressure and even duress.

The assumption of these "studies" that General Assembly resolutions as such create international law is thus erroneous. And this undermines their main submissions, virtually all of which rest on this error (Chapter 2, first and second sections).

It is of capital importance to prevent the consolidation of this error into a de facto amendment of international law and the charter. In a General Assembly in which a two-thirds majority is virtually always available for any cause that can momentarily marshal the 100-odd votes of the Third World, the oil power of the Organization of Arab Petroleum Exporting

Countries and the strategic objectives of the Soviet Union, the fate of a great number of nations, and of international law itself, would be at the mercy of duress concealed by double standards and double-talk (Chapter 2, first, fourth, and fifth sections).

Territorial Rights Under International Law. Such effects as General Assembly resolutions can have, can in any case operate only within the frame of rights and duties of the states concerned under international law, including the charter. By their armed attacks against the state of Israel in 1948, 1967, and 1973, and by various acts of belligerency throughout this period, these Arab states flouted their basic obligations as United Nations members to refrain from threat or use of force against Israel's territorial integrity and political independence. These acts were in flagrant violation *inter alia* of Article 2(4) and paragraphs (1), (2), and (3) of the same article.

The present territorial rights of Israel on the one hand, and of Jordan and Egypt on the other, rest on two undoubted international law principles, on the one hand, of *ex iniuria non oritur ius,* and on the other hand, *uti possidetis,* applicable to territorial rights on the termination of hostilities, as applied to the above facts (Chapter 3, first and second sections).

The claim that these established principles were abrogated by an ambiguous reference in the preamble to Security Council Resolution 242 of November 22, 1967, concerning "the acquisition of territory by war" does not survive legal examination (Chapter 3, the fourth section, esp. nn. 43, 44, and related text). Such claims of abrogation were clearly rejected in the formulation by the 1967 Committee on the Question of Defining Aggression, adopted by the General Assembly in 1974. The above two principles still stand as law (Chapter 6, esp. the fifth section).

Under the former principle Jordan acquired no rights in the West Bank by virtue of her illegal entry in 1947; nor did Egypt in Gaza in 1947 for the same reason. By contrast, Israel's presence there after 1967, in the course of self-defense, was lawful. Under the latter principle Israel is entitled to stay in those territories until peace and secure and mutually recognized boundaries are negotiated with Jordan and Egypt (Chapter 3, first and third sections; Chapter 7, fifth section).

In accordance with this legal position the state of Israel has steadily maintained its readiness to negotiate the comprehensive peace treaties envisaged by international law. The continuance of this intention and will to peace are manifest in the recently concluded Israel-Egypt Treaty of Peace.

Legal Standing and Effect of Resolution 181(II) ("Partition Plan" of 1947). The view urged by these studies that the General Assembly's Resolution 181(II) remains in legal force, ignores the stark historical reality that that resolution never came into legal force at all. That resolution would have come into force if the parties concerned had accepted it. But it is well known that the Arab states not only rejected it, but committed armed aggression against it and against Israel, and thus wholly aborted it. They deliberately destroyed it, as it were *in utero*, before it entered the world of legal effectiveness.

To attempt to show, as these studies do, that Resolution 181(II) "remains" in force in 1981 is thus an undertaking even more miraculous than would be the revival of the dead. It is an attempt to give life to an entity that the Arab states had themselves aborted before it came to maturity and birth. To propose that Resolution 181(II) can be treated as if it has binding force in 1981, for the benefit of the same Arab states, who by their aggression destroyed it *ab initio*, also violates "general principles of law," such as those requiring claimants to equity to come "with clean hands," and forbidding a party who has unlawfully repudiated a transaction from holding the other party to terms that suit the later expediencies of the repudiating party (Chapter 4).

Duties with Regard to Refugees: Right of Return or Compensation. Although these U.N. studies claim that rights of "return or compensation" are based on General Assembly resolutions establishing rules of international law, the resolutions mainly relied on are merely exhortations or directives aimed to support the activities of the commissioner-general of the United Nations Relief and Rehabilitation Agency for Palestine Refugees in the Middle East. The solutions found for the refugee problems of Europe after World War II, involving far greater numbers of refugees and states concerned, show that "return or compensation" is neither a necessary nor a feasible basis of solution. Its basis was rather international cooperation based on humane planning.

Moreover, even if such claims as to international law were less weak than they are, these studies do not explain how the claimed legal right of "return or compensation" could be applied to Arab refugees, without also applying for the benefit of the 700,000 Jewish refugees from Arab countries. They ignore the fact that the Security Council Resolution 242 of November 22, 1967, makes no such arbitrary distinction between Arab and Jewish refugees.

Finally, the attempt to place the whole burden of the refugee problem on the state of Israel ignores the responsibilities arising from the indubitable relation, direct and immediate, between Arab state aggression and the very creation of the refugee problem (Chapter 1, first section; Chapter 5, first section).

Right of Self-Determination. These "studies" admit that there is a "variety of opinion on the issue of the juridical position in international law of the right of self-determination." In the same breath they assert as axiomatic that this "right" is "an established principle of international law." Insofar as this "axiom" rests on declarations in General Assembly resolutions, the present examination has shown that no identification of such resolutions with international law is warranted. Some of the more notable authorities cited in support of these dogmatic assertions simply do not support them (Chapter 5, esp. the second section).

Moreover, as was shown in Chapter 1, the first section, the self-determination principle (whatever its nature) was properly applied after World War I to the respective claims of the Arab and Jewish peoples. There is no basis for undoing this proper application to the facts as they then existed, merely because half a century later a small segment of the Arab people came to have — or at any rate to claim — a separate identity as "a Palestinian Arab people" within the original Arab people or nation. It confirms this observation that even these Secretariat-sponsored publications have to admit that during the whole League of Nations period and two decades of United Nations these international organizations did not recognize any such separate identity of a "Palestinian Arab people" (Chapter 5, esp. fifth section).

Threats to the Integrity of All States from Usurpation of Power by the General Assembly. These publications also finally concede that the right of self-determination entitles the Jewish people, as well as others, to "national rights," and that the State of Israel embodies this entitlement. This apparent magnanimity is, however, deceptive, since they immediately proceed to claim for the General Assembly a power to redraw the frontiers of Israel in accordance with any political criteria that a majority in that body can be brought to support.

The threat from seizure of such power by the General Assembly, under cover of endorsing claims of particular ethnic, religious, linguistic, or other groups within particular established states, imperils the future security and integrity of most U.N. members. Few of these states are immune from the kinds of pretexts that those "studies" offer for such power seizures by the General Assembly. The fact that states that would be victims of these Draconian pretensions would be disposed of one by one should not conceal the direness of such perils.

Such pretensions illustrate well the ominous consequences of surrendering international law to the momentary alliances, expediencies, biases, and coercive pressures too often at play in U.N. procedures, and to which the Secretariat's duty of impartial service to members can also fall victim (Chapter 6, first through third sections).

Continuing Illegality of Use of Force Against Sovereign States in Self-Determination. Much of the argument of these studies, especially their extraordinary partisanship, rests on the assumption that international law licenses the use of force against sovereign states—including force by third states—in support of any "self-determination struggle" for which a majority of members of the General Assembly can be brought to vote. They even invoke General Assembly affirmations as establishing such a license.

The present examination has shown that such General Assembly affirmations do not as such make international law. And the weakness of these studies in matters of international law is nowhere more dramatic than in their assumptions concerning lawfulness of use of force in struggles for self-determination. At the very time that they were proceeding on these false assumptions, the General Assembly adopted, on the recommendation of its 1967 Committee on the Question of Defining Aggression, a definition of aggression that excludes any such license.

The *travaux préparatoires* of this definition make clear that the exclusion was not accidental. After substantial exchanges on Soviet proposals to include provisions explicitly authorizing use of force by peoples "struggling for self-determination," and by third states supporting them, all such provisions were dropped from the text adopted by consensus of the 1967 Special Committee, of the Sixth Committee of the General Assembly, and of the General Assembly itself, at its twenty-ninth session (Chapter 5, fifth and sixth sections).

Inadmissibility of the Rewriting of Law and History by the Secretariat's Special Unit and Its Consultants.   To the examples given of illicit rewriting of both history and law must be added certain regretful comments. First, the main international law authority chosen for citation by these studies on Arab-Israel issues, Mr. Henry Cattan, is a former member of the Palestine Higher Arab Committee led by the notorious Haj Amin al-Husseini, Mufti of Jerusalem, a self-declared collaborator in Hitler's design of genocide against the Jewish people. Second, the "consultant" selected to provide the "study" now offered as an "international law analysis," is Professor W. T. Mallison, one of whose qualifications in this area appears to be that he wrote an introduction to Mr. Cattan's book *Palestine and International Law* (1973) and was sometime consultant to the fanatically anti-Israel American Council for Judaism. Such handpicking may naturally be related to the biased outcomes of these research efforts and may even suggest that the selective rewriting of the relevant law and history is not by accident.

Third, in aid of these outcomes, the specifically juridical study *Resolutions* states rather astonishingly its intention to ignore the "negotiating history" of the materials of its research, a renunciation strange and alien to scholarship in international law. (A dramatic example is given above in Chapter 3, the final section, and n. 24.) Fourth, as has been shown at several points, the studies under examination manifest at least a serious misrepresentation of the positions of the authorities they cite (see, e.g., Chapter 5, the third section, at n. 16), or of facts (see, e.g., Chapter 1, the first section, the first subsection), or of the contents of legal documents (see, e.g., Chapter 4, the first section, text following n. 12).

Sovereignty in Jerusalem. The authors whose work is sponsored in the publications here under examination do not emphasize the importance for Jerusalem of the self-determination principle, an understandable restraint in view of the conclusions they seek to reach. One reason for this importance is the fact that, apart from the millennial role of that city in the history of the Jews since its foundation as the City of David in 1000 B.C., Jews have been a majority of the inhabitants as far back as reliable modern records can take us. A more legitimate and overt reason for the authors' restraint is, of course, the deep involvement of Jerusalem in the Islamic and Christian faiths as well as Judaism, derivative though this be from the Judaic origins.

The authors offer instead the thesis proposed in Resolution 181(II) of November 29, 1947, that Jerusalem should be a *corpus separatum* under a special international regime administered by the United Nations. They are unable to establish that such proposals ever matured into a binding legal regime. They have to admit that the U.N. organs abandoned efforts to pursue them in 1950, and did not even try to resurrect such proposals from 1950 to 1967, and "acquiesced" in the national control of the city by Israel and Jordan during that period. They fall back finally on two arguments.

One argument is that the proposals were, so to speak, revived and given some kind of legal force by general references in various U.N. resolutions following the 1967 War calling for "the status of Jerusalem" not to be altered under Israel's administration. They seek to read into the term "status" or "legal status" a reference to that of a *corpus separatum*, the proposal for which (as observed) failed and was abandoned in 1950. Even if that had been the intent of the post-1967 resolutions, there would have been difficulty in attributing binding legal force to them, for instance because the General Assembly does not have the "lawmaking" power that these writers (as seen above) erroneously take for granted. In fact it is clear, for at least two reasons, that the references to "status" in these post-1967 resolutions were not intended to revive the *corpus separatum* proposal.

In the first place, if it had been the intention to revive that proposal, these resolutions would certainly have referred by way of recital or otherwise to Resolution 181(II) of 1947 or related matters of the period 1947-50 that described that proposal. This they do not do. In the second place, the terms "status" and "legal status" in the post-1967 resolutions have ample other legal applications to problems in the aftermath of the 1967 War, without far-fetched implied references to proposals that never matured into legal existence. Was the status of East Jerusalem in Israel's hands that of land under mere belligerent occupation? Was it, in view of the illegality of the former Jordanian occupation, and the principle *ex iniuria non oritur ius,* subject or potentially subject to Israel sovereignty? Or was it, as some authorities argued, *res nullius modo juridico?* (Chapter 7, first and second sections, esp. the second subsection of the second section).

A further basis offered by *Resolutions* for asserting that the *corpus separatum* is binding under international law consists, it is alleged, of "Israel's assurances in regard of [*sic*] the implementation of Resolutions 181(II) and 194(III)." The present examination has shown that this allegation is factually incorrect, since the assurances given were not as to the territorial *corpus separatum,* but only as to a regime concerned with the control and protection of holy places whether in Jerusalem or elsewhere. The Palestine Conciliation Committee, indeed, reported that Prime Minister Ben-Gurion rejected the *corpus separatum* proposal, and the Israel representative later explained this in terms that Israel claimed "sovereign authority in Jerusalem," but would cooperate in a regime to protect the holy places (Chapter 7, first subsection of the second section).

It is basically the assurance of some regime of protection for the holy places in Jerusalem to which it can be said the states concerned and the United Nations have a degree of commitment. The Security Council Resolution 465 of March 1, 1980, referred to this as a "need for protection and preservation of the unique spiritual and religious dimension of the Holy Places in the city." This particular aspect as distinct from territorial status is not a major preoccupation in the work here under examination, but it is worthy of close attention as a part of a comprehensive peace settlement (Chapter 7, third section).

On the level of international law the present examination has to conclude that Israel's legal standing in East Jerusalem as well as in Judea and Samaria (the West Bank) and Gaza extend, at the least, well beyond that of belligerent occupant. There are two strong legal grounds, indeed, for thinking that on the level of international law Israel is already vested with territorial sovereignty, and a third ground that would require only a formal act of annexation by Israel for it to become so vested. Still a fourth legal ground, while it does not speak to the issue of territorial sovereignty, would regard Judea and Samaria (the West Bank) and Gaza as a residual area surviving from and under the former Palestine mandate. So that under well-known decisions of the International Court of Justice the area must continue—cy pres as it were—to be subject to the central obligations of that mandate, which certainly include the obligation to permit access of Jews there as of right (Chapter 7, fifth section).

The International Law Position and the Peace Process. The above are three independent bases in international law for concluding that Israel has actual or potential rights of sovereignty in East Jerusalem as well as the West Bank and Gaza; to which is added a fourth basis resting on the original mandate for Palestine, entitling Jews as of right to enter and remain in these areas. These bases are also, by the same token, part of the answer of international law to the question posed to it by the post-1967 General Assembly and Security Council resolutions reserving "the status of Jerusalem" for clarification under international law. They are, of course, only part of the answer of international law, since that law also provides for such situations the process of pacification by negotiations of peace, including appropriate territorial adjustments. The state of Israel has manifested in its Treaty of Peace with Egypt a readiness to enter this process, and there may be some hope that Jordan and even Syria may yet join it. In the absence of such wider participation in the peace process, it is nevertheless important to make clear, as a base-line from which negotiation may proceed, what modern international law at present prescribes. That a great deal of looseness has entered into general and even diplomatic discourse on these essentially legal matters should not conceal the cogency of the legal principles that support the territorial entitlements of Israel. These principles underscore how vital it is that agreed terms of settlement be reached and embodied in treaties of peace or other appropriate agreements between states so long and so tragically in conflict.

It was the aim of the present work to display the existing international legal framework within which it may be hoped that peace will be negotiated. It is not the aim to propose the terms of a just and lasting settlement, though obviously international law has some bearing on this. The very peace process prescribed by international law for such situations is to determine the respects in which legal entitlements ought to be adjusted as a basis for neighborly living or at least peaceable coexistence.

The respect in which one might hope for such an adjustment with regard to Jerusalem is the creation of appropriate functional institutions to express and reassure the legitimate concerns of the principal faiths of the world for the holy places that are there located. Experience since the Protection of the Holy Places Law, 1967, passed by Israel after the Six-Day War, suggests that good order, safety, and repair of the holy places and freedom of access to them, can be assured on the basis of national law. Indeed, historically, national law of one country or another has always been the basis of assurance since far back in the days of Ottoman rule. Yet a strong case can be made, if only the impulse to use claims to the holy places as instruments of political warfare is restrained, for creating a consultative body of high dignity, representing the principal faiths involved in terms of their local presence and even perhaps of their transnational associations.

Maps

· · · · ·

1. The Arab World, 1945-62   136
2. The Jews of Palestine before the Arab Conquest, 1000 B.C.-636 A.D.   137
3. Britain and the Jewish National Home: Pledges and Border Changes,
   1917-23   138
4. The Arab Invasion of the State of Israel, May 15, 1948   139
5. Jewish Refugees from Arab Lands, May 15, 1948-December 31, 1967   140
6. The Middle East Crisis, May 25-30, 1967   141
7. European Dependence on Arab Oil, January-June 1973   142
8. Arab Oil Pressure, September-November 1973   143

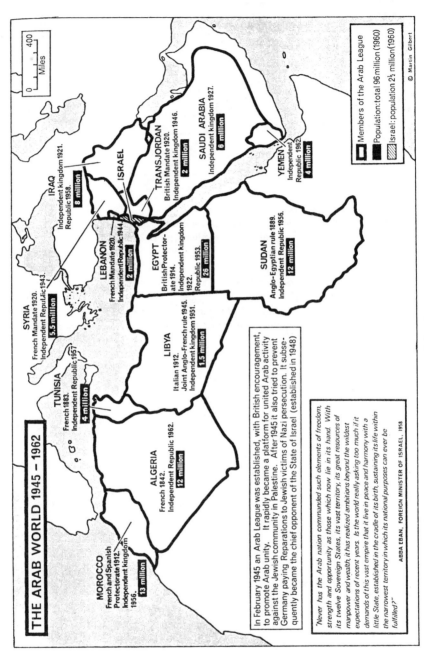

THE ARAB WORLD 1945 – 1962

Map 1

MOROCCO
French and Spanish
Protectorate 1912.
Independent kingdom
1956.
13 million

ALGERIA
French 1842.
Independent Republic 1962.
12 million

TUNISIA
French 1883.
Independent Republic 1957.
4 million

SYRIA
French Mandate 1920.
Independent Republic 1943.
5.5 million

LIBYA
Italian 1912.
Joint Anglo-French rule 1945.
Independent kingdom 1951.
1.5 million

IRAQ
Independent kingdom 1921.
Republic 1958.
8 million

LEBANON
French Mandate 1920.
Independent Republic 1944.
2 million

ISRAEL

EGYPT
British Protector-
ate 1914.
Independent kingdom
1922.
Republic 1953.
26 million

TRANSJORDAN
British Mandate 1920.
Independent kingdom 1946.
2 million

SAUDI ARABIA
Independent kingdom 1927.
6 million

SUDAN
Anglo-Egyptian rule 1889.
Independent Republic 1956.
12 million

YEMEN
Independent
Republic 1962.
4 million

0 — 400 Miles

□ Members of the Arab League
■ Population: total 96 million (1960)
▨ Israel: population 2½ million (1960)

© Martin Gilbert

In February 1945 an Arab League was established, with British encouragement, to promote Arab unity. It rapidly became a platform for united Arab activity against the Jewish community in Palestine. After 1945 it also tried to prevent Germany paying Reparations to Jewish victims of Nazi persecution. It subsequently became the chief opponent of the State of Israel (established in 1948)

"Never has the Arab nation commanded such elements of freedom, strength and opportunity as those which now lie in its hand. With its twelve Sovereign States, its vast territory, its great resources of manpower and wealth, it has realized ambitions beyond the wildest expectations of recent years. Is the world really asking too much if it demands of this vast empire that it live in peace and harmony with a little State, established in the cradle of its birth, sustaining its life within the narrowest territory in which its national purposes can ever be fulfilled?"

ABBA EBAN, FOREIGN MINISTER OF ISRAEL, 1958

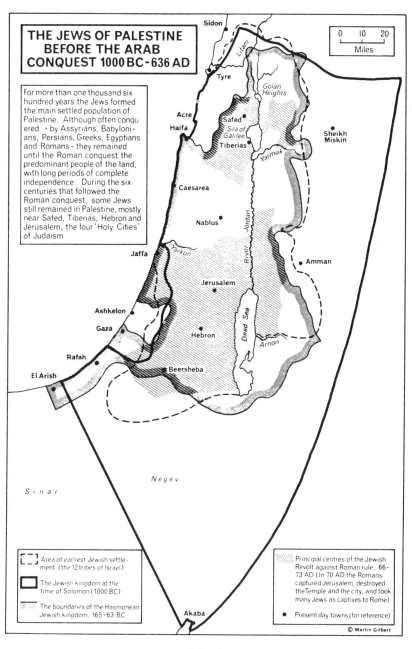

THE JEWS OF PALESTINE BEFORE THE ARAB CONQUEST 1000 BC - 636 AD

For more than one thousand six hundred years the Jews formed the main settled population of Palestine. Although often conqu ered - by Assyrians, Babyloni- ans, Persians, Greeks, Egyptians and Romans - they remained until the Roman conquest the predominant people of the land, with long periods of complete independence. During the six centuries that followed the Roman conquest, some Jews still remained in Palestine, mostly near Safed, Tiberias, Hebron and Jerusalem, the four 'Holy Cities' of Judaism

0   10   20
Miles

Sidon

Litani

Tyre

Golan Heights

Acre

Haifa

Safed
Sea of Galilee

Tiberias

Yarmuk

Sheikh Miskin

Caesarea

Nablus

River Jordan

Jaffa

Yarkon

Amman

Jerusalem

Ashkelon

Gaza

Hebron

Dead Sea

Arnon

Rafah

Beersheba

El Arish

Negev

Sinai

☐ Area of earliest Jewish settle - ment (the 12 tribes of Israel)

☐ The Jewish kingdom at the time of Solomon (1000 BC)

The boundaries of the Hasmonean Jewish kingdom, 165 - 63 BC

Akaba

Principal centres of the Jewish Revolt against Roman rule, 66 - 73 AD (In 70 AD the Romans captured Jerusalem, destroyed the Temple and the city, and took many Jews as captives to Rome)

● Present day towns (for reference)

© Martin Gilbert

Map 2

137

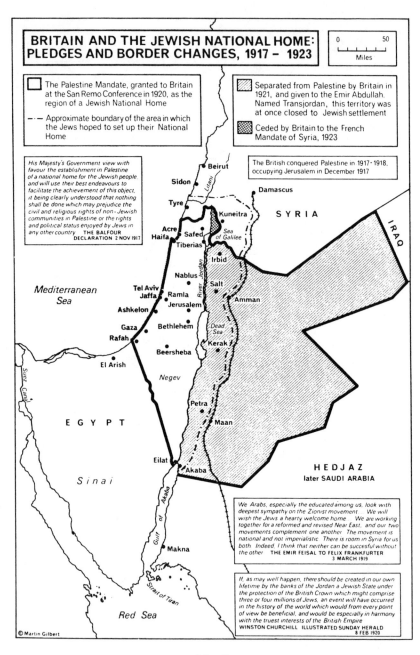

BRITAIN AND THE JEWISH NATIONAL HOME:
PLEDGES AND BORDER CHANGES, 1917 – 1923

0   50
Miles

☐ The Palestine Mandate, granted to Britain at the San Remo Conference in 1920, as the region of a Jewish National Home

—·— Approximate boundary of the area in which the Jews hoped to set up their National Home

▨ Separated from Palestine by Britain in 1921, and given to the Emir Abdullah. Named Transjordan, this territory was at once closed to Jewish settlement

▨ Ceded by Britain to the French Mandate of Syria, 1923

His Majesty's Government view with favour the establishment in Palestine of a national home for the Jewish people, and will use their best endeavours to facilitate the achievement of this object, it being clearly understood that nothing shall be done which may prejudice the civil and religious rights of non-Jewish communities in Palestine or the rights and political status enjoyed by Jews in any other country THE BALFOUR DECLARATION 2 NOV 1917

The British conquered Palestine in 1917-1918, occupying Jerusalem in December 1917

Beirut

Sidon

Tyre

Acre
Haifa · Safed
Tiberias

Kuneitra

Damascus

SYRIA

Sea of Galilee

IRAQ

Irbid

Nablus

Mediterranean Sea

Tel Aviv
Jaffa · Ramla

Ashkelon

Salt

Jerusalem

Amman

Gaza · Bethlehem
Rafah

Beersheba

Dead Sea

Kerak

El Arish

Negev

Petra

E G Y P T

Maan

Eilat

Akaba

H E D J A Z
later SAUDI ARABIA

S i n a i

Makna

We Arabs, especially the educated among us, look with deepest sympathy on the Zionist movement ... We will wish the Jews a hearty welcome home ... We are working together for a reformed and revised Near East, and our two movements complement one another ... The movement is national and not imperialistic. There is room in Syria for us both. Indeed, I think that neither can be succesful without the other. THE EMIR FEISAL TO FELIX FRANKFURTER 3 MARCH 1919

Red Sea

© Martin Gilbert

If, as may well happen, there should be created in our own lifetime by the banks of the Jordan a Jewish State under the protection of the British Crown which might comprise three or four millions of Jews, an event will have occurred in the history of the world which would from every point of view be beneficial, and would be especially in harmony with the truest interests of the British Empire WINSTON CHURCHILL ILLUSTRATED SUNDAY HERALD 8 FEB 1920

Map 3

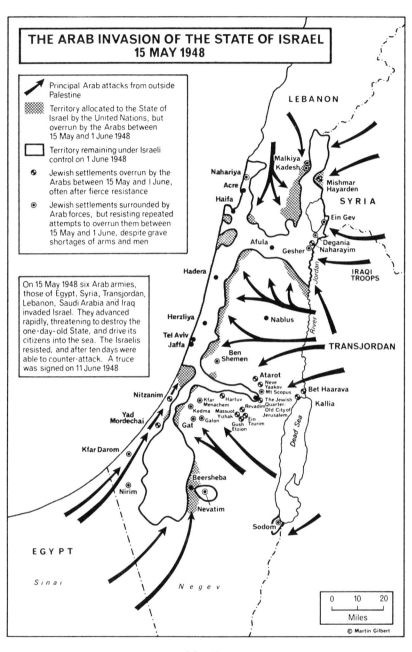

THE ARAB INVASION OF THE STATE OF ISRAEL
15 MAY 1948

Principal Arab attacks from outside Palestine

Territory allocated to the State of Israel by the United Nations, but overrun by the Arabs between 15 May and 1 June 1948

Territory remaining under Israeli control on 1 June 1948

⊘ Jewish settlements overrun by the Arabs between 15 May and 1 June, often after fierce resistance

◉ Jewish settlements surrounded by Arab forces, but resisting repeated attempts to overrun them between 15 May and 1 June, despite grave shortages of arms and men

On 15 May 1948 six Arab armies, those of Egypt, Syria, Transjordan, Lebanon, Saudi Arabia and Iraq invaded Israel. They advanced rapidly, threatening to destroy the one-day-old State, and drive its citizens into the sea. The Israelis resisted, and after ten days were able to counter-attack. A truce was signed on 11 June 1948

LEBANON

SYRIA

TRANSJORDAN

EGYPT

Sinai

Negev

Nahariya
Acre
Haifa
Malkiya
Kadesh
Mishmar Hayarden
Ein Gev
Afula
Gesher
Degania
Naharayim
IRAQI TROOPS
Hadera
Herzliya
Tel Aviv
Jaffa
Nablus
Ben Shemen
Atarot
Neve Yaakov
Mt Scopus
Bet Haarava
Nitzanim
Kfar Menachem
Hartuv
Revadim
The Jewish Quarter:
Old City of Jerusalem
Kallia
Kedma
Massuot
Yizhak
Galon
Ein Tzurim
Gush Etzion
Yad Mordechai
Gat
Kfar Darom
Beersheba
Nirim
Nevatim
Sodom

Jordan River

Dead Sea

0   10   20
Miles

© Martin Gilbert

Map 4

139

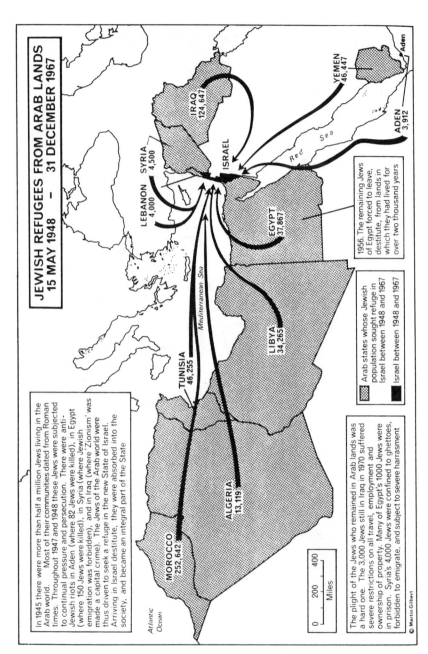

Map 5

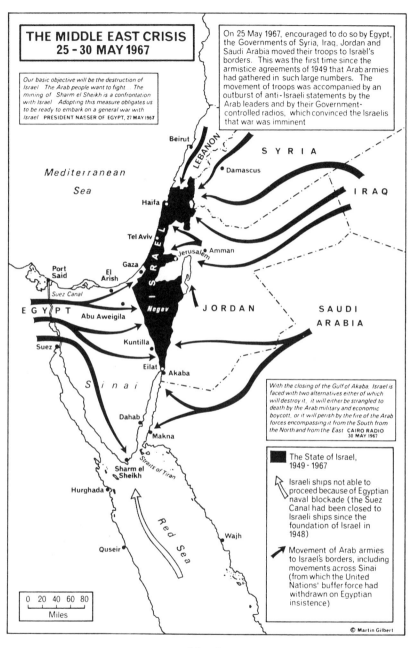

THE MIDDLE EAST CRISIS
25 - 30 MAY 1967

Our basic objective will be the destruction of Israel The Arab people want to fight ... The mining of Sharm el Sheikh is a confrontation with Israel Adopting this measure obligates us to be ready to embark on a general war with Israel PRESIDENT NASSER OF EGYPT, 27 MAY 1967

On 25 May 1967, encouraged to do so by Egypt, the Governments of Syria, Iraq, Jordan and Saudi Arabia moved their troops to Israël's borders. This was the first time since the armistice agreements of 1949 that Arab armies had gathered in such large numbers. The movement of troops was accompanied by an outburst of anti-Israeli statements by the Arab leaders and by their Government-controlled radios, which convinced the Israelis that war was imminent

Beirut

Mediterranean

Sea

Haifa

LEBANON

S Y R I A

Damascus

I R A Q

Tel Aviv

Jerusalem Amman

Port Said

Gaza

El Arish

Suez Canal

E G Y P T

Abu Aweigila

Negev

J O R D A N

S A U D I

A R A B I A

Suez

Kuntilla

Eilat Akaba

S i n a i

Dahab

Makna

With the closing of the Gulf of Akaba, Israel is faced with two alternatives either of which will destroy it, it will either be strangled to death by the Arab military and economic boycott, or it will perish by the fire of the Arab forces encompassing it from the South from the North and from the East CAIRO RADIO 30 MAY 1967

Sharm el Sheikh

Straits of Tiran

Hurghada

Red Sea

Wajh

Quseir

0 20 40 60 80
Miles

The State of Israel, 1949 - 1967

Israeli ships not able to proceed because of Egyptian naval blockade (the Suez Canal had been closed to Israeli ships since the foundation of Israel in 1948)

Movement of Arab armies to Israel's borders, including movements across Sinai (from which the United Nations' buffer force had withdrawn on Egyptian insistence)

© Martin Gilbert

Map 6

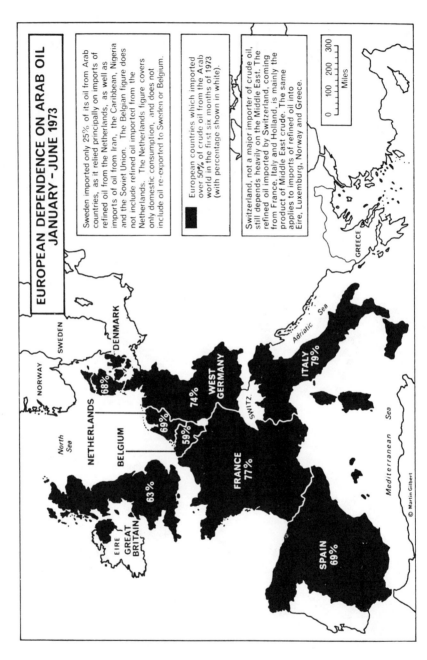

EUROPEAN DEPENDENCE ON ARAB OIL
JANUARY – JUNE 1973

Sweden imported only 25% of its oil from Arab countries, as it relied principally on imports of refined oil from the Netherlands, as well as imports of oil from Iran, the Caribbean, Nigeria and the Soviet Union. The Belgian figure does not include refined oil imported from the Netherlands. The Netherlands figure covers only domestic consumption, and does not include oil re-exported to Sweden or Belgium.

■ European countries which imported over 50% of crude oil from the Arab world in the first six months of 1973 (with percentage shown in white).

Switzerland, not a major importer of crude oil, still depends heavily on the Middle East. The refined oil imported by Switzerland, coming from France, Italy and Holland, is mainly the product of Middle East crude. The same applies to imports of refined oil into Eire, Luxemburg, Norway and Greece.

0 100 200 300
Miles

NORWAY

SWEDEN

DENMARK

North
Sea

NETHERLANDS
68%

BELGIUM
69%

59%

WEST
GERMANY
74%

SWITZ.

EIRE

GREAT
BRITAIN
63%

FRANCE
77%

SPAIN
69%

ITALY
79%

Adriatic Sea

GREECE

Mediterranean Sea

© Martin Gilbert

Map 7

142

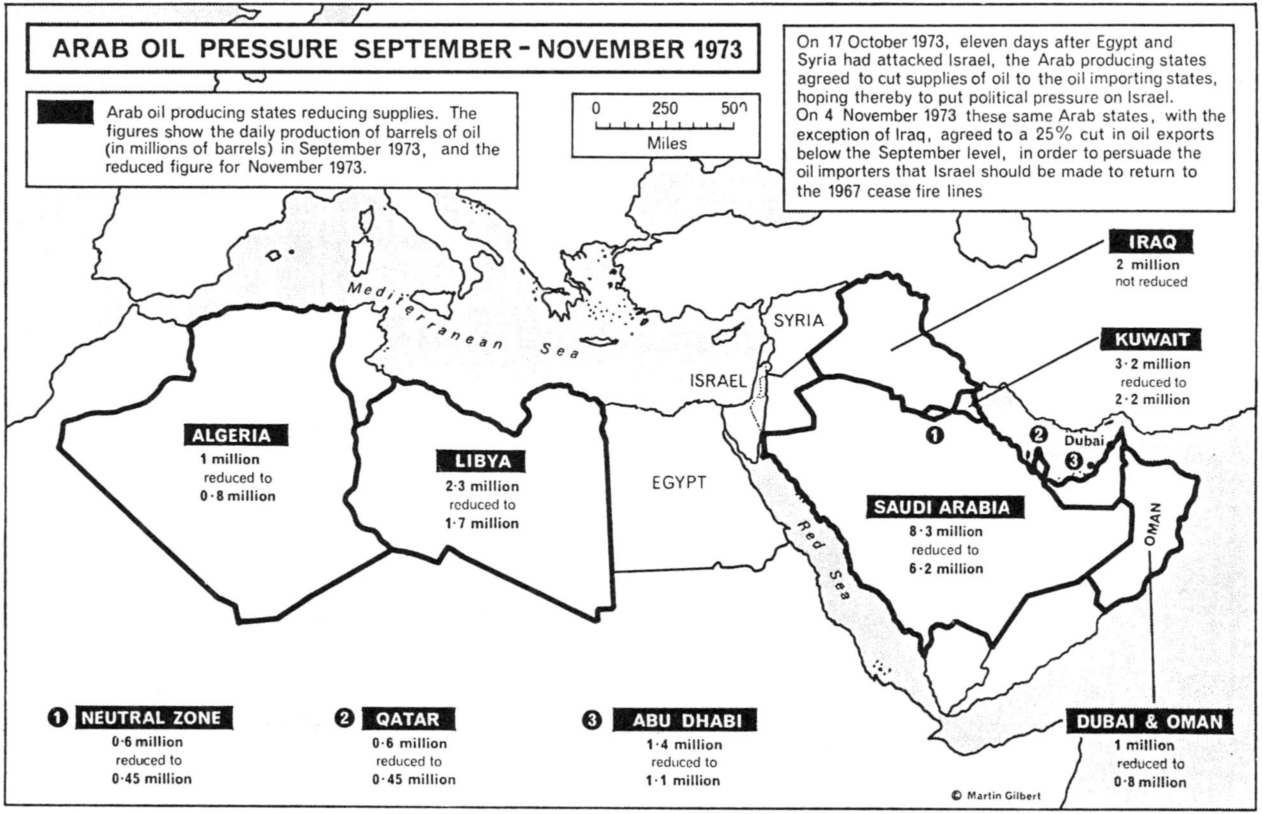

ARAB OIL PRESSURE SEPTEMBER - NOVEMBER 1973

Arab oil producing states reducing supplies. The figures show the daily production of barrels of oil (in millions of barrels) in September 1973, and the reduced figure for November 1973.

0 ___ 250 ___ 500
Miles

On 17 October 1973, eleven days after Egypt and Syria had attacked Israel, the Arab producing states agreed to cut supplies of oil to the oil importing states, hoping thereby to put political pressure on Israel. On 4 November 1973 these same Arab states, with the exception of Iraq, agreed to a 25% cut in oil exports below the September level, in order to persuade the oil importers that Israel should be made to return to the 1967 cease fire lines

IRAQ
2 million
not reduced

KUWAIT
3·2 million
reduced to
2·2 million

DUBAI & OMAN
1 million
reduced to
0·8 million

SAUDI ARABIA
8·3 million
reduced to
6·2 million

OMAN

Dubai

Red Sea

SYRIA

ISRAEL

EGYPT

Mediterranean Sea

LIBYA
2·3 million
reduced to
1·7 million

ALGERIA
1 million
reduced to
0·8 million

❶ NEUTRAL ZONE
0·6 million
reduced to
0·45 million

❷ QATAR
0·6 million
reduced to
0·45 million

❸ ABU DHABI
1·4 million
reduced to
1·1 million

© Martin Gilbert

Map 8

143

Documents

· · · · ·

1. "The Basle Programme" for Jewish Self-Determination, August, 1897.   146
2. The Balfour Declaration, November 2, 1917.   146
3. Letter from A. Henry McMahon to the *Times,* July 23, 1937.   146
4. The Feisal-Weizmann Agreement, January 3, 1919.   147
5. The Mandate for Palestine Confirmed by the League Council on July 24, 1922, and the British Memorandum Relating to Transjordan Approved by the Council on September 16, 1922 (Excerpts).   148
6. Congressional Resolution Favoring the Establishment in Palestine of a National Home for the Jewish People, September 21, 1922.   151
7. Treaty of Lausanne, July 24, 1923 (Excerpts).   152
8. Declaration of Independence of the State of Israel, May 14, 1948.   152
9. Security Council Resolution 49 (1948) of May 22, 1948, Calling for a Cease-Fire in Palestine.   154
10. Security Council Resolution 54 (1948) of July 15, 1948, Determining a Threat to the Peace and Ordering a Cease-Fire in Palestine.   155
11. Security Council Resolution 73 (1949) of August 11, 1949, Reaffirming the Order to Observe an Unconditional Cease-Fire.   155
12. General Assembly Resolution 273(III), Admitting Israel to Membership in the United Nations, May 11, 1949.   156
13. Security Council Resolution 95 (1951) of September 1, 1951, Concerning the Passage of Israeli Shipping through the Suez Canal.   157
14. Charter of the United Nations (Excerpts).   158
15. Definition of Aggression, General Assembly Resolution 3314(XXIX), of December 14, 1974.   161
16. The Palestinian National Charter, 1966, as Amended in 1968 (Excerpts).   163
17. Security Council Resolution 242 (1967) on the Principles for a Just and Lasting Peace in the Middle East, of November 22, 1967.   165

1. THE BASLE PROGRAMME, AUGUST 1897 (FROM ISRAEL
COHEN, THE ZIONIST MOVEMENT [1946], P. 77)

"The aim of Zionism is to create for the Jewish people a home in Palestine secured by public law.

"In order to attain this object the Congress adopts the following means:

"1. The systematic promotion of the settlement of Palestine with Jewish agriculturists, artisans, and craftsmen.

"2. The organisation and federation of all Jewry by means of local and general institutions in conformity with the local laws.

"3. The strengthening of Jewish sentiment and national consciousness.

"4. Preparatory steps for the procuring of such Government assents as are necessary for achieving the object of Zionism."

2. THE BALFOUR DECLARATION, NOVEMBER 2, 1917 (REPRINTED IN
3 NORTON MOORE 32)

Foreign Office,
November 2nd, 1917.

Dear Lord Rothschild,

I have much pleasure in conveying to you, on behalf of His Majesty's Government, the following declaration of sympathy with Jewish Zionist aspirations which has been submitted to, and approved by, the Cabinet.

"His Majesty's Government view with favour the establishment in Palestine of a national home for the Jewish people, and will use their best endeavours to facilitate the achievement of this object, it being clearly understood that nothing shall be done which may prejudice the civil and religious rights of the existing non-Jewish communities in Palestine, or the rights and political status enjoyed by Jews in any other country".

I should be grateful if you would bring this declaration to the knowledge of the Zionist Federation.

[Yours sincerely]
[Signed] Arthur James Balfour

3. LETTER FROM A. HENRY McMAHON TO THE *TIMES*, JULY 23, 1937
(REPRINTED FROM THE *TIMES*, FRIDAY, JULY 23, 1937)

Independence of the Arabs: "The McMahon Pledge"
A DEFINITE STATEMENT TO THE EDITOR OF THE TIMES

Sir.—Many references have been made in the Palestine Royal Commission Report and in the course of the recent debates in both Houses of Parliament to the "McMahon Pledge," especially to that portion of the pledge which concerns Palestine and of which one interpretation has been claimed by the Jews and another by the Arabs.

It has been suggested to me that continued silence on the part of the giver of that pledge may itself be misunderstood.

I feel, therefore, called upon to make some statement on the subject, but I will confine myself in doing so to the point now at issue—i.e., whether that portion of Syria now known as Palestine was or was not intended to be included in the territories in which the independence of the Arabs was guaranteed in my pledge.

I feel it my duty to state, and I do so definitely and emphatically, that it was not intended by me in giving this pledge to King Hussein to include Palestine in the area in which Arab independence was promised.

I also had every reason to believe at the time that the fact that Palestine was not included in my pledge was well understood by King Hussein.

Yours faithfully,
A. HENRY MCMAHON,
5, Wilton Place, S.W.1, July 22.

4. THE FEISAL-WEIZMANN AGREEMENT, JANUARY 3, 1919

(3 DAVID HUNTER MILLER, *MY DIARY AT THE*

PEACE CONFERENCE OF PARIS, WITH DOCUMENTS [1928], PP. 188-89)

His Royal Highness the Emir FEISAL, representing and acting on behalf of the Arab Kingdom of Hedjaz, and DR. CHAIM WEIZMANN, representing and acting on behalf of the Zionist Organization,
mindful of the racial kinship and ancient bonds existing between the Arabs and the Jewish people, and realizing that the surest means of working out the consummation of their national aspirations, is through the closest possible collaboration in the development of the Arab State and Palestine, and being desirous further of confirming the good understanding which exists between them,
have agreed upon the following articles:

ARTICLE I.

The Arab State and Palestine in all their relations and undertakings shall be controlled by the most cordial goodwill and understanding and to this end Arab and Jewish duly accredited agents shall be established and maintained in the respective territories.

ARTICLE II.

Immediately following the completion of the deliberations of the Peace Conference, the definite boundaries between the Arab State and Palestine shall be determined by a Commission to be agreed upon by the parties hereto.

ARTICLE III.

In the establishment of the Constitution and Administration of Palestine all such measures shall be adopted as will afford the fullest guarantees for carrying into effect the British Government's Declaration of the 2nd of November, 1917.

ARTICLE IV.

All necessary measures shall be taken to encourage and stimulate immigration of Jews into Palestine on a large scale, and as quickly as possible to settle Jewish immigrants upon the land through closer settlement and intensive cultivation of the soil. In taking such measures the Arab peasant and tenant farmers shall be protected in their rights, and shall be assisted in forwarding their economic development.

ARTICLE V.

No regulation nor law shall be made prohibiting or interfering in any way with the free exercise of religion; and further the free exercise and enjoyment of religious profession and worship without discrimination or preference shall forever be allowed. No religious test shall ever be required for the exercise of civil or political rights.

ARTICLE VI.

The Mohammedan Holy Places shall be under Mohammedan control.

ARTICLE VII.

The Zionist Organisation proposes to send to Palestine a Commission of experts to make a survey of the economic possibilities of the country, and to report upon the best means for its development. The Zionist Organisation will place the afore-mentioned Commission at the disposal of the Arab State for the purpose of a survey of the economic possibilities of the Arab State and to report upon the best means for its development. The Zionist Organisation will use its best efforts to assist the Arab State in providing the means for developing the natural resources and economic possibilities thereof.

ARTICLE VIII.

The parties hereto agree to act in complete accord and harmony on all matters embraced herein before the Peace Congress.

ARTICLE IX.

Any matters of dispute which may arise between the contracting parties shall be referred to the British Government for arbitration.

EMIR FEISAL.
CHAIM WEIZMANN.

5. THE MANDATE FOR PALESTINE CONFIRMED BY THE LEAGUE COUNCIL ON JULY 24, 1922, AND THE BRITISH MEMORANDUM RELATING TO TRANSJORDAN APPROVED BY THE COUNCIL ON SEPTEMBER 16, 1922 (EXCERPTS, AS REPRINTED IN REPORT TO THE GENERAL ASSEMBLY OF THE UNITED NATIONS SPECIAL COMMITTEE ON PALESTINE, VOL. 2, ANNEXES, APPENDIX, AND MAPS 18-22, U.N.DOC.A/364 ADD.1 [SEPT. 9, 1947])

The Council of the League of Nations:

Whereas the Principal Allied Powers have agreed, for the purpose of giving effect to the provisions of Article 22 of the Covenant of the League of Nations, to entrust to a Mandatory selected by the said Powers the administration of the territory of Palestine, which formerly belonged to the Turkish Empire, within such boundaries as may be fixed by them; and

Whereas the Principal Allied Powers have also agreed that the Mandatory should be responsible for putting into effect the declaration originally made on November 2nd, 1917, by the Government of His Britannic Majesty, and adopted by the said Powers, in favour of the establishment in Palestine of a national home for the Jewish people, it being clearly understood that nothing should be done which might prejudice the civil and religious rights of existing non-Jewish communities in Palestine, or the rights and political status enjoyed by Jews in any other country; and

Whereas recognition has thereby been given to the historical connection of the Jewish people with Palestine and to the grounds for reconstituting their national home in that country; and

Whereas the Principal Allied Powers have selected His Britannic Majesty as the Mandatory for Palestine; and

Whereas the mandate in respect of Palestine has been formulated in the following terms and submitted to the Council of the League for approval; and

Whereas His Britannic Majesty has accepted the mandate in respect of Palestine and undertaken to exercise it on behalf of the League of Nations in conformity with the following provisions; and

Whereas by the aforementioned Article 22 (paragraph 8) it is provided that the degree of authority, control or administration to be exercised by the Mandatory, not having been previously agreed upon by the Members of the League, shall be explicitly defined by the Council of the League of Nations;

Confirming the said mandate, defines its terms as follows:

ARTICLE 1

The Mandatory shall have full powers of legislation and of administration, save as they may be limited by the terms of this mandate.

ARTICLE 2

The Mandatory shall be responsible for placing the country under such political, administrative and economic conditions as will secure the establishment of the Jewish national home, as laid down in the preamble, and the development of self-governing institutions, and also for safeguarding the civil and religious rights of all the inhabitants of Palestine, irrespective of race and religion.

ARTICLE 3

The Mandatory shall, so far as circumstances permit, encourage local autonomy.

ARTICLE 4

An appropriate Jewish agency shall be recognized as a public body for the purpose of advising and co-operating with the Administration of Palestine in such economic, social and other matters as may affect the establishment of the Jewish national home and the interests of the Jewish population in Palestine, and, subject always to the control of the Administration, to assist and take part in the development of the country.

The Zionist organization, so long as its organization and constitution are in the opinion of the Mandatory appropriate, shall be recognized as such agency. It shall take steps in consultation with His Britannic Majesty's Government to secure the co-operation of all Jews who are willing to assist in the establishment of the Jewish national home.

ARTICLE 5

The Mandatory shall be responsible for seeing that no Palestine territory shall be ceded or leased to, or in any way placed under the control of the Government of any foreign Power.

ARTICLE 6

The Administration of Palestine, while ensuring that the rights and position of other sections of the population are not prejudiced, shall facilitate Jewish immigration under suitable conditions and shall encourage, in co-operation with the Jewish agency referred to in Article 4, close settlement by Jews on the lands, including State lands and waste lands not required for public purposes.

.   .   .

ARTICLE 23

The Administration of Palestine shall recognize the holy days of the respective communities in Palestine as legal days of rest for the members of such communities.

ARTICLE 24

The Mandatory shall make to the Council of the League of Nations an annual report to the satisfaction of the Council as to the measures taken during the year to carry out the provisions of the mandate. Copies of all laws and regulations promulgated or issued during the year shall be communicated with the report.

ARTICLE 25

In the territories lying between the Jordan and the eastern boundary of Palestine as ultimately determined, the Mandatory shall be entitled, with the consent of the Council of the League of Nations, to postpone or withhold application of such provisions of this mandate as he may consider inapplicable to the existing local conditions, and to make such provisions for the administration of the territories as he may consider suitable to those conditions, provided that no action shall be taken which is inconsistent with the provisions of Articles 15, 16 and 18.*

ARTICLE 26

The Mandatory agrees that, if any dispute whatever should arise between the Mandatory and another Member of the League of Nations relating to the interpretation or the application of the provisions of the mandate, such dispute, if it cannot be settled by negotiation, shall be submitted to the Permanent Court of International Justice provided for by Article 14 of the Covenant of the League of Nations.

ARTICLE 27

The consent of the Council of the League of Nations is required for any modification of the terms of this mandate.

ARTICLE 28

In the event of the termination of the mandate hereby conferred upon the Mandatory, the Council of the League of Nations shall make such arrangements as may be deemed necessary for safeguarding in perpetuity, under guarantee of the

---

*Article 15 deals with freedom of conscience, religious discrimination and education, Article 16 with religious or eleemosynary bodies, and Article 18 with discrimination against nationals or trade of other States than the Mandatory.

League, the rights secured by Articles 13 and 14,** and shall use its influence for securing, under the guarantee of the League, that the Government of Palestine will fully honour the financial obligations legitimately incurred by the Administration of Palestine during the period of the mandate, including the rights of public servants to pensions or gratuities.

The present instrument shall be deposited in original in the archives of the League of Nations and certified copies shall be forwarded by the Secretary-General of the League of Nations to all Members of the League.

Done at London the twenty-fourth day of July, one thousand nine hundred and twenty-two.

Article 25 of the Palestine Mandate
Memorandum by the British Representative

Approved by the Council on September 16th, 1922
1. Article 25 of the Mandate for Palestine provides as follows:
"In the territories lying between the Jordan and the eastern boundary of Palestine as ultimately determined, the Mandatory shall be entitled, with the consent of the Council of the League of Nations, to postpone or withhold application of such provisions of this Mandate as he may consider inapplicable to the existing local conditions, and to make such provisions for the administration of the territories as he may consider suitable to those conditions, provided that no action shall be taken which is inconsistent with the provisions of Articles 15, 16 and 18."
2. In pursuance of the provisions of this article, His Majesty's Government invite the Council to pass the following resolution:
"The following provisions of the Mandate for Palestine are not applicable to the territory known as Transjordan, which comprises all territory lying to the east of a line drawn from a point two miles west of the town of Akaba on the Gulf of that name up the centre of the Wady Araba, Dead Sea and River Jordan to its junction with the River Yarmuk: thence up the centre of that river to the Syrian frontier.
"*Preamble.* Recitals 2 and 3.
"*Article 2.*
"The words 'placing the country under such political administration and economic conditions as will secure the establishment of the Jewish national home, as laid down in the Preamble, and . . .'
"*Article 4.*
"*Article 6.*

6. CONGRESSIONAL RESOLUTION FAVORING THE ESTABLISHMENT IN PALESTINE OF A NATIONAL HOME FOR THE JEWISH PEOPLE, SEPTEMBER 21, 1922 (42 STAT. 1012 [PART 1, 1922])

Resolved by the Senate and House of Representatives of the United States of America in Congress assembled, That the United States of America favors the establishment in Palestine of a national home for the Jewish people, it being clearly

**These deal with free access to the Holy Places and freedom of worship therein.

understood that nothing shall be done which may prejudice the civil and religious rights of Christian and all other non-Jewish communities in Palestine, and that the holy places and religious buildings and sites in Palestine shall be adequately protected.

Approved, September 21, 1922.

7. TREATY OF LAUSANNE, JULY 24, 1923 (EXCERPTS, 28 LEAGUE OF NATIONS TREATY SERIES NO. 701, 13-113, AT 15, 23 [1924])

ARTICLE 1

From the coming into force of the present Treaty, the state of peace will be definitely re-established between the British Empire, France, Italy, Japan, Greece, Roumania and the Serb-Croat-Slovene State of the one part, and Turkey of the other part, as well as between their respective nationals.

Official relations will be resumed on both sides and, in the respective territories, diplomatic and consular representatives will receive, without prejudice to such agreements as may be concluded in the future, treatment in accordance with the general principles of international law.

.   .   .

ARTICLE 16

Turkey hereby renounces all rights and title whatsoever over or respecting the territories situated outside the frontiers laid down in the present Treaty and the islands other than those over which her sovereignty is recognised by the said Treaty, the future of these territories and islands being settled or to be settled by the parties concerned.

The provisions of the present Article do not prejudice any special arrangements arising from neighbourly relations which have been or may be concluded between Turkey and any limitrophe countries.

8. DECLARATION OF INDEPENDENCE OF THE STATE OF ISRAEL, MAY 14, 1948 (*LAWS OF THE STATE OF ISRAEL,* VOL. 1 [1948], PP. 3-5)

ERETZ-ISRAEL[1] was the birthplace of the Jewish people. Here their spiritual, religious and political identity was shaped. Here they first attained to statehood, created cultural values of national and universal significance and gave to the world the eternal Book of Books.

After being forcibly exiled from their land, the people kept faith with it throughout their Dispersion and never ceased to pray and hope for their return to it and for the restoration in it of their political freedom.

Impelled by this historic and traditional attachment, Jews strove in every successive generation to re-establish themselves in their ancient homeland. In recent decades they returned in their masses. Pioneers, *ma'pilim*[2] and defenders, they made deserts bloom, revived the Hebrew language, built villages and towns, and created a thriving community, controlling its own economy and culture, loving

[1] I.e. Land of Israel, Palestine.
[2] I.e. immigrants from oppressive discrimination.

peace but knowing how to defend itself, bringing the blessings of progress to all the country's inhabitants, and aspiring towards independent nationhood.

In the year 5657 (1897), at the summons of the spiritual father of the Jewish State, Theodore Herzl, the First Zionist Congress convened and proclaimed the right of the Jewish people to national rebirth in its own country.

This right was recognised in the Balfour Declaration of the 2nd November, 1917, and re-affirmed in the Mandate of the League of Nations which, in particular, gave international sanction to the historic connection between the Jewish people and Eretz-Israel and to the right of the Jewish people to rebuild its National Home.

The catastrophe which recently befell the Jewish people—the massacre of millions of Jews in Europe—was another clear demonstration of the urgency of solving the problem of its homelessness by re-establishing in Eretz-Israel the Jewish State, which would open the gates of the homeland wide to every Jew and confer upon the Jewish people the status of a fully-privileged member of the comity of nations.

Survivors of the Nazi holocaust in Europe, as well as Jews from other parts of the world, continued to migrate to Eretz-Israel, undaunted by difficulties, restrictions and dangers, and never ceased to assert their right to a life of dignity, freedom and honest toil in their national homeland.

In the Second World War, the Jewish community of this country contributed its full share to the struggle of the freedom and peace-loving nations against the forces of Nazi wickedness and, by the blood of its soldiers and its war effort, gained the right to be reckoned among the peoples who founded the United Nations.

On the 29th November, 1947, the United Nations General Assembly passed a resolution calling for the establishment of a Jewish State in Eretz-Israel; the General Assembly required the inhabitants of Eretz-Israel to take such steps as were necessary on their part for the implementation of that resolution. This recognition by the United Nations of the right of the Jewish people to establish their State is irrevocable.

This right is the natural right of the Jewish people to be masters of their own fate, like all other nations, in their own sovereign State.

ACCORDINGLY WE, MEMBERS OF THE PEOPLE'S COUNCIL, REPRESENTATIVE OF THE JEWISH COMMUNITY OF ERETZ-ISRAEL AND OF THE ZIONIST MOVEMENT, ARE HERE ASSEMBLED ON THE DAY OF THE TERMINATION OF THE BRITISH MANDATE OVER ERETZ-ISRAEL AND, BY VIRTUE OF OUR NATURAL AND HISTORIC RIGHT AND ON THE STRENGTH OF THE RESOLUTION OF THE UNITED NATIONS GENERAL ASSEMBLY, HEREBY DECLARE THE ESTABLISHMENT OF A JEWISH STATE IN ERETZ-ISRAEL, TO BE KNOWN AS THE STATE OF ISRAEL.

WE DECLARE that, with effect from the moment of the termination of the Mandate, being tonight, the eve of Sabbath, the 6th Iyar, 5708 (15th May, 1948), until the establishment of the elected, regular authorities of the State in accordance with the Constitution which shall be adopted by the Elected Constituent Assembly not later than the 1st October 1948, the People's Council shall act as a Provisional Council of State, and its executive organ, the People's Administration, shall be the Provisional Government of the Jewish State, to be called "Israel."

THE STATE OF ISRAEL will be open for Jewish immigration and for the Ingathering of the Exiles; it will foster the development of the country for the benefit of all its inhabitants; it will be based on freedom, justice and peace as envisaged by the prophets of Israel; it will ensure complete equality of social and political rights to all its inhabitants irrespective of religion, race or sex; it will guarantee freedom of religion, conscience, language, education and culture; it will safeguard the Holy Places of all religions; and it will be faithful to the principles of the Charter of the United Nations.

THE STATE OF ISRAEL is prepared to cooperate with the agencies and representatives of the United Nations in implementing the resolution of the General Assembly of the 29th November, 1947, and will take steps to bring about the economic union of the whole of Eretz-Israel.

WE APPEAL to the United Nations to assist the Jewish people in the building-up of its State and to receive the State of Israel into the comity of nations.

WE APPEAL—in the very midst of the onslaught launched against us now for months—to the Arab inhabitants of the State of Israel to preserve peace and participate in the upbuilding of the State on the basis of full and equal citizenship and due representation in all its provisional and permanent institutions.

WE EXTEND our hand to all neighbouring states and their peoples in an offer of peace and good neighbourliness, and appeal to them to establish bonds of cooperation and mutual help with the sovereign Jewish people settled in its own land. The State of Israel is prepared to do its share in a common effort for the advancement of the entire Middle East.

WE APPEAL to the Jewish people throughout the Diaspora to rally round the Jews of Eretz-Israel in the tasks of immigration and upbuilding and to stand by them in the great struggle for the realization of the age-old dream—the redemption of Israel.

PLACING OUR TRUST IN THE ALMIGHTY, WE AFFIX OUR SIGNATURES TO THIS PROCLA-MATION AT THIS SESSION OF THE PROVISIONAL COUNCIL OF STATE, ON THE SOIL OF THE HOMELAND, IN THE CITY OF TEL-AVIV, ON THIS SABBATH EVE, THE 5TH DAY OF IYAR, 5708 (14TH MAY, 1948).

David Ben-Gurion
[signatures of other members follow]

9. SECURITY COUNCIL RESOLUTION 49 (1948) OF MAY 22, 1948,

CALLING FOR A CEASE-FIRE IN PALESTINE (3 U.N. S.C.O.R., SUPP.

FOR MAY 1948, AT 97, U.N.DOC.S/773 [MAY 22, 1948])

The Security Council,

Taking into consideration that previous resolutions of the Security Council in respect to Palestine have not been complied with and that military operations are taking place in Palestine;

Calls upon all Governments and authorities, without prejudice to the rights, claims or position of the parties concerned, to abstain from any hostile military action in Palestine and to that end to issue a cease-fire order to their military and para-military forces to become effective within thirty-six hours after midnight New York Standard Time, 22 May 1948;

Calls upon the Truce Commission and upon all parties concerned to give the highest priority to the negotiation and maintenance of a truce in the City of Jerusalem;

Directs the Truce Commission established by the Security Council by its resolution of 23 April 1948 to report to the Security Council on the compliance with the two preceding paragraphs of this resolution;

Calls upon all parties concerned to facilitate by all means in their power the task of the United Nations Mediator appointed in execution of the resolution of the General Assembly of 14 May 1948.

10. SECURITY COUNCIL RESOLUTION 54 (1948) OF JULY 15, 1948, DETERMINING A THREAT TO THE PEACE AND ORDERING A CEASE-FIRE IN PALESTINE (3 U.N. S.C.O.R., SUPP. FOR JULY 1948, AT 76-77, U.N.DOC.S/902 [1948])

The Security Council,
Taking into consideration that the Provisional Government of Israel has indicated its acceptance in principle of a prolongation of the truce in Palestine; that the States members of the Arab League have rejected successive appeals of the United Nations Mediator, and of the Security Council in its resolution of 7 July 1948, for the prolongation of the truce in Palestine; and that there has consequently developed a renewal of hostilities in Palestine;
Determines that the situation in Palestine constitutes a threat to the peace within the meaning of Article 39 of the Charter;
Orders the Governments and authorities concerned, pursuant to Article 40 of the Charter of the United Nations, to desist from further military action and to this end to issue cease-fire orders to their military and para-military forces, to take effect at a time to be determined by the Mediator, but in any event not later than three days from the date of the adoption of this resolution;
Declares that failure by any of the Governments or authorities concerned to comply with the preceding paragraph of this resolution would demonstrate the existence of a breach of the peace within the meaning of Article 39 of the Charter requiring immediate consideration by the Security Council with a view to such further action under Chapter VII of the Charter as may be decided upon by the Council;
Calls upon all Governments and authorities concerned to continue to co-operate with the Mediator with a view to the maintenance of peace in Palestine in conformity with the resolution adopted by the Security Council on 29 May 1948.

11. SECURITY COUNCIL RESOLUTION 73 (1949) OF AUGUST 11, 1949, REAFFIRMING THE ORDER TO OBSERVE AN UNCONDITIONAL CEASE-FIRE PENDING A FINAL PEACE. (4 U.N. S.C.O.R., RESOLUTIONS AND DECISIONS OF THE SECURITY COUNCIL 1949, AT 8, U.N.DOC.S/1376,II[1949])

The Security Council,
Having noted with satisfaction the several Armistice Agreements[1] concluded by means of negotiations between the parties involved in the conflict in Palestine in pursuance of its resolution 62 (1948) of 16 November 1948,

[1] See S.C.O.R. *Fourth Year, Special Supplements Nos. 1, 2, 3 and 4.*

1. *Expresses the hope* that the Governments and authorities concerned, having undertaken, by means of the negotiations now being conducted by the Conciliation Commission for Palestine, to fulfil the request of the General Assembly in its resolution 194 (III) of 11 December 1948 to extend the scope of the armistice negotiations and to seek agreement by negotiations conducted either with the Conciliation Commission or directly, will at an early date achieve agreement on the final settlement of all questions outstanding between them;

2. *Finds* that the Armistice Agreements constitute an important step toward the establishment of permanent peace in Palestine and considers that these agreements supersede the truce provided for in Security Council resolutions 50 (1948) of 29 May and 54 (1948) of 15 July 1948;

3. *Reaffirms,* pending the final peace settlement, the order contained in its resolution 54 (1948) to the Governments and authorities concerned, pursuant to Article 40 of the Charter of the United Nations, to observe an unconditional cease-fire and, bearing in mind that the several Armistice Agreements include firm pledges against any further acts of hostility between the parties and also provide for their supervision by the parties themselves, relies upon the parties to ensure the continued application and observance of these Agreements;

4. *Decides* that all functions assigned to the United Nations Mediator in Palestine having been discharged, the Acting Mediator is relieved of any further responsibility under Security Council resolutions;

5. *Notes* that the Armistice Agreements provide that the execution of those Agreements shall be supervised by mixed armistice commissions whose chairman in each case shall be the Chief of Staff of the United Nations Truce Supervision Organization in Palestine or a senior officer from the observer personnel of that organization designated by him following consultation with the parties to the Agreements;

6. *Requests* the Secretary-General to arrange for the continued service of such of the personnel of the present Truce Supervision Organization as may be required in observing and maintaining the cease-fire, and as may be necessary in assisting the parties to the Armistice Agreements in the supervision of the application and observance of the terms of those Agreements, with particular regard to the desires of the parties as expressed in the relevant articles of the Agreements;

7. *Requests* the Chief of Staff mentioned above to report to the Security Council on the observance of the cease-fire in Palestine in accordance with the terms of this resolution, and to keep the Conciliation Commission for Palestine informed of matters affecting the Commission's work under General Assembly resolution 194 (III) of 11 December 1948.

12. GENERAL ASSEMBLY RESOLUTION 273(III) ADMITTING ISRAEL
TO MEMBERSHIP IN THE UNITED NATIONS, MAY 11, 1949 (G.A. RES.
273(III), 3 U.N. G.A.O.R., PT. II, RESOLUTIONS APRIL 5-MAY 18, 1949,
AT 18, U.N.DOC.A/900 [MAY 31, 1949])

Having received the report of the Security Council on the application of Israel for membership in the United Nations,[1]

[1]Document A/818.

Noting that, in the judgment of the Security Council, Israel is a peace-loving State and is able and willing to carry out the obligations contained in the Charter,

Noting that the Security Council has recommended to the General Assembly that it admit Israel to membership in the United Nations,

Noting furthermore the declaration by the State of Israel that it "unreservedly accepts the obligations of the United Nations Charter and undertakes to honour them from the day when it becomes a Member of the United Nations,"[2]

Recalling its resolutions of 29 November 1947[3] and 11 December 1948[4] and taking note of the declarations and explanations made by the representative of the Government of Israel[5] before the *ad hoc* Political Committee in respect of the implementation of the said resolutions,

THE GENERAL ASSEMBLY,

Acting in discharge of its functions under Article 4 of the Charter and rule 125 of its rules of procedure,

1. *Decides* that Israel is a peace-loving State which accepts the obligations contained in the Charter and is able and willing to carry out those obligations;

2. *Decides* to admit Israel to membership in the United Nations.

Two hundred and seventh plenary meeting,
11 May 1949.

13. SECURITY COUNCIL RESOLUTION 95 (1951) OF SEPTEMBER 1, 1951, CONCERNING THE PASSAGE OF ISRAELI SHIPPING THROUGH THE SUEZ CANAL (6 U.N. S.C.O.R., 558TH MEETING, AT 2-3, U.N.DOC. S/2322 [1951]).

The Security Council,

1. *Recalling* that in its resolution of 11 August 1949 (S/1376) relating to the conclusion of Armistice Agreements between Israel and the neighbouring Arab States it drew attention to the pledges in these Agreements 'against any further acts of hostility between the Parties,'

2. *Recalling* further that in its resolution of 17 November 1950 (S/1907 and Corr. 1), it reminded the States concerned that the Armistice Agreements to which they are parties contemplate 'the return of permanent peace in Palestine', and therefore urged them and other States in the area to take all such steps as will lead to the settlement of the issues between them,

3. *Noting* the report of the Chief of Staff of the Truce Supervision Organization to the Security Council of 12 June 1951 (S/2194),

4. *Further noting* that the Chief of Staff of the Truce Supervision Organization recalled the statement of the senior Egyptian delegate in Rhodes on 13 January 1949, to the effect that his delegation was 'inspired with every spirit of co-operation, conciliation and a sincere desire to restore peace in Palestine', and that the Egyptian

---

[2]Document A/1093.
[3]G. A. *Resolutions,* Second Session, pp. 131-32.
[4]G.A. *Resolutions* Third Session, Part I 21-25.
[5]Documents A/AC.24/SR.45-48, 50 and 51.

Government has not complied with the earnest plea of the Chief of Staff made to the Egyptian delegate on 12 June 1951, that it desist from the present practice of interfering with the passage through the Suez Canal of goods destined for Israel,

5. *Considering* that since the armistice regime, which has been in existence for nearly two and a half years, is of a permanent character, neither party can reasonably assert that it is actively a belligerent or requires to exercise the right of visit, search, and seizure for any legitimate purpose of self-defence,

6. *Finds* that the maintenance of the practice mentioned in paragraph 4 above is inconsistent with the objectives of a peaceful settlement between the parties and the establishment of a permanent peace in Palestine set forth in the Armistice Agreement;

7. *Finds further* that such practice is an abuse of the exercise of the right of visit, search and seizure;

8. *Further finds* that the practice cannot in the prevailing circumstances be justified on the ground that it is necessary for self-defence;

9. *And further noting* that the restrictions on the passage of goods through the Suez Canal to Israel ports are denying to nations at no time connected with the conflict in Palestine valuable supplies required for their economic reconstruction, and that these restrictions together with sanctions applied by Egypt to certain ships which have visited Israel ports represent unjustified interference with the rights of nations to navigate the seas and to trade freely with one another, including the Arab States and Israel,

10. *Calls upon* Egypt to terminate the restrictions on the passage of international commercial shipping and goods through the Suez Canal wherever bound and to cease all interference with such shipping beyond that essential to the safety of shipping in the Canal itself and to the observance of the international conventions in force.

14. CHARTER OF THE UNITED NATIONS (EXCERPTS)

Chapter 1
Purposes and Principles
Article 1

The Purposes of the United Nations are:

1. To maintain international peace and security, and to that end: to take effective collective measures for the prevention and removal of threats to the peace, and for the suppression of acts of aggression or other breaches of the peace, and to bring about by peaceful means, and in conformity with the principles of justice and international law, adjustment or settlement of international disputes or situations which might lead to a breach of the peace;

2. To develop friendly relations among nations based on respect for the principle of equal rights and self-determination of peoples, and to take other appropriate measures to strengthen universal peace;

3. To achieve international cooperation in solving international problems of an economic, social, cultural, or humanitarian character, and in promoting and encouraging respect for human rights and for fundamental freedoms for all without distinction as to race, sex, language, or religion; and

4. To be a center for harmonizing the actions of nations in the attainment of these common ends.

Article 2

The Organization and its Members, in pursuit of the Purposes stated in Article 1, shall act in accordance with the following Principles.

1. The Organization is based on the principle of the sovereign equality of all its Members.

2. All Members, in order to ensure to all of them the rights and benefits resulting from membership, shall fulfill in good faith the obligations assumed by them in accordance with the present Charter.

3. All Members shall settle their international disputes by peaceful means in such a manner that international peace and security, and justice, are not endangered.

4. All Members shall refrain in their international relations from the threat or use of force against the territorial integrity or political independence of any state, or in any other manner, inconsistent with the Purposes of the United Nations.

5. All Members shall give the United Nations every assistance in any action it takes in accordance with the present Charter, and shall refrain from giving assistance to any state against which the United Nations is taking preventive or enforcement action.

6. The Organization shall ensure that states which are not Members of the United Nations act in accordance with these Principles so far as may be necessary for the maintenance of international peace and security.

7. Nothing contained in the present Charter shall authorize the United Nations to intervene in matters which are essentially within the domestic jurisdiction of any state or shall require the Members to submit such matters to settlement under the present Charter; but this principle shall not prejudice the application of enforcement measures under Chapter VII.

. . . . . .

Chapter VII

Action with Respect to Threats to the Peace, Breaches of the Peace, and Acts of Aggression

Article 39

The Security Council shall determine the existence of any threat to the peace, breach of the peace, or act of aggression and shall make recommendations, or decide what measures shall be taken in accordance with *Articles 41* and *42,* to maintain or restore international peace and security.

Article 40

In order to prevent an aggravation of the situation, the Security Council may, before making the recommendations or deciding upon the measures provided for in Article 39, call upon the parties concerned to comply with such provisional measures as it deems necessary or desirable. Such provisional measures shall be without prejudice to the rights, claims, or position of the parties concerned. The Security Council shall duly take account of failure to comply with such provisional measures.

Article 41

The Security Council may decide what measures not involving the use of armed force are to be employed to give effect to its decisions, and it may call upon the Members of the United Nations to apply such measures. These may include complete or partial interruption of economic relations and of rail, sea, air, postal, telegraphic, radio, and other means of communications, and the severance of diplomatic relations.

Article 42

Should the Security Council consider that measures provided for in *Article 41* would be inadequate or have proved to be inadequate, it may take such action by air, sea, or land forces as may be necessary to maintain or restore international peace and security. Such action may include demonstrations, blockade, and other operations by air, sea, or land forces of Members of the United Nations.

Article 43

1. All Members of the United Nations, in order to contribute to the maintenance of international peace and security, undertake to make available to the Security Council, on its call and in accordance with a special agreement or agreements, armed forces, assistance, and facilities, including rights of passage, necessary for the purpose of maintaining international peace and security.

2. Such agreement or agreements shall govern the numbers and types of forces, their degrees of readiness and general location, and the nature of the facilities and assistance to be provided.

3. The agreement or agreements shall be negotiated as soon as possible on the initiative of the Security Council. They shall be concluded between the Security Council and Members or between the Security Council and groups of Members and shall be subject to ratification by the signatory states in accordance with their respective constitutional processes.

Article 44

When the Security Council has decided to use force it shall, before calling upon a Member not represented on it to provide armed forces in fulfilment of the obligations assumed under Article 43, invite that Member, if the Member so desires, to participate in the decisions of the Security Council concerning the employment of contingents of that Member's armed forces.

. . .

Article 46

Plans for the application of armed force shall be made by the Security Council with the assistance of the Military Staff Committee.

. . .

Article 48

1. The action required to carry out the decisions of the Security Council for the maintenance of international peace and security shall be taken by all the Members of the United Nations or by some of them, as the Security Council may determine.

2. Such decisions shall be carried out by the members of the United Nations directly and through their action in the appropriate international agencies of which they are members.

Article 49

The Members of the United Nations shall join in affording mutual assistance in carrying out the measures decided upon by the Security Council.

Article 50

If preventive or enforcement measures against any state are taken by the Security Council, any other state, whether a Member of the United Nations or not, which finds itself confronted with special economic problems arising from the carrying out of those measures shall have the right to consult the Security Council with regard to a solution of those problems.

Article 51

Nothing in the present Charter shall impair the inherent right of individual or collective self-defense if an armed attack occurs against a Member of the United Nations, until the Security Council has taken measures necessary to maintain international peace and security. Measures taken by Members in the exercise of this right of self-defense shall be immediately reported to the Security Council and shall not in any way affect the authority and responsibility of the Security Council under the present Charter to take at any time such action as it deems necessary in order to maintain or restore international peace and security.

15. DEFINITION OF AGGRESSION (RESOLUTION ADOPTED BY THE GENERAL ASSEMBLY ON THE REPORT OF THE SIXTH COMMITTEE [A/9890] A/RES/3314[XXIX], 14 DECEMBER 1974)

· · ·

Definition of Aggression

The General Assembly,

Basing itself on the fact that one of the fundamental purposes of the United Nations is to maintain international peace and security and to take effective collective measures for the prevention and removal of threats to the peace, and for the suppression of acts of aggression or other breaches of the peace,

Recalling that the Security Council, in accordance with Article 39 of the Charter of the United Nations, shall determine the existence of any threat to the peace, breach of the peace or act of aggression and shall make recommendations, or decide what measures shall be taken in accordance with Articles 41 and 42, to maintain or restore international peace and security,

Recalling also the duty of States under the Charter to settle their international disputes by peaceful means in order not to endanger international peace, security and justice,

Bearing in mind that nothing in this Definition shall be interpreted as in any way affecting the scope of the provisions of the Charter with respect to the functions and powers of the organs of the United Nations,

Considering also that, since aggression is the most serious and dangerous form of the illegal use of force, being fraught, in the conditions created by the existence of all types of weapons of mass destruction, with the possible threat of a world conflict and all its catastrophic consequences, aggression should be defined at the present stage,

Reaffirming the duty of States not to use armed force to deprive peoples of their right to self-determination, freedom and independence, or to disrupt territorial integrity,

Reaffirming also that the territory of a State shall not be violated by being the object, even temporarily, of military occupation or of other measures of force taken by another State in contravention of the Charter, and that it shall not be the object of acquisition by another State resulting from such measures or the threat thereof,

Reaffirming also the provisions of the Declaration on Principles of International Law concerning Friendly Relations and Co-operation among States in accordance with the Charter of the United Nations,

Convinced that the adoption of a definition of aggression ought to have the effect of deterring a potential aggressor, would simplify the determination of acts of aggression and the implementation of measures to suppress them and would also facilitate the protection of the rights and lawful interest of, and the rendering of assistance to, the victim,

Believing that, although the question whether an act of aggression has been committed must be considered in the light of all the circumstances of each particular case, it is nevertheless desirable to formulate basic principles as guidance for such determination,

Adopts the following Definition of Aggression:*

*Explanatory notes on articles 3 and 5 are to be found in paragraph 20 of the report of the Special Committee on the Question of Defining Aggression (*Official Records of the General Assembly, Twenty-ninth Session, Supplement No. 19* [A/9619 and Corr. 1]). Statements on the Definition are contained in paragraphs 9 and 10 of the report of the Sixth Committee (A/9890).

Article 1

Aggression is the use of armed force by a State against the sovereignty, territorial integrity or political independence of another State, or in any other manner inconsistent with the Charter of the United Nations, as set out in this Definition.

Explanatory note: In this Definition the term "State":

(a) Is used without prejudice to questions of recognition or to whether a State is a Member of the United Nations;

(b) Includes the concept of a "group of States" where appropriate.

Article 2

The first use of armed force by a State in contravention of the Charter shall constitute *prima facie* evidence of an act of aggression although the Security Council may, in conformity with the Charter, conclude that a determination that an act of aggression has been committed would not be justified in the light of other relevant circumstances, including the fact that the acts concerned or their consequences are not of sufficient gravity.

Article 3

Any of the following acts, regardless of a declaration of war, shall, subject to and in accordance with the provisions of article 2, qualify as an act of aggression:

(a) The invasion or attack by the armed forces of a State of the territory of another State, or any military occupation, however temporary, resulting from such invasion or attack, or any annexation by the use of force of the territory of another State or part thereof;

(b) Bombardment by the armed forces of a State against the territory of another State or the use of any weapons by a State against the territory of another State;

(c) The blockade of the ports or coasts of a State by the armed forces of another State;

(d) An attack by the armed forces of a State on the land, sea or air forces, or marine and air fleets of another State;

(e) The use of armed forces of one State which are within the territory of another State with the agreement of the receiving State, in contravention of the conditions provided for in the agreement or any extension of their presence in such territory beyond the termination of the agreement;

(f) The action of a State in allowing its territory, which it has placed at the disposal of another State, to be used by that other State for perpetrating an act of aggression against a third State;

(g) The sending by or on behalf of a State of armed bands, groups, irregulars or mercenaries, which carry out acts of armed force against another State of such gravity as to amount to the acts listed above, or its substantial involvement therein.

Article 4

The acts enumerated above are not exhaustive and the Security Council may determine that other acts constitute aggression under the provisions of the Charter.

Article 5

1. No consideration of whatever nature, whether political, economic, military or otherwise, may serve as a justification for aggression.

2. A war of aggression is a crime against international peace. Aggression gives rise to international responsibility.

3. No territorial acquisition or special advantage resulting from aggression is or shall be recognized as lawful.

Article 6

Nothing in this Definition shall be construed as in any way enlarging or diminishing the scope of the Charter, including its provisions concerning cases in which the use of force is lawful.

Article 7

Nothing in this Definition, and in particular article 3, could in any way prejudice the right to self-determination, freedom and independence, as derived from the Charter, of peoples forcibly deprived of that right and referred to in the Declaration on Principles of International Law concerning Friendly Relations and Co-operation among States in accordance with the Charter of the United Nations, particularly peoples under colonial and racist régimes or other forms of alien domination; nor the right of these peoples to struggle to that end and to seek and receive support, in accordance with the principles of the Charter and in conformity with the above-mentioned Declaration.

Article 8

In their interpretation and application the above provisions are interrelated and each provision should be construed in the context of the other provisions.

16. THE PALESTINIAN NATIONAL CHARTER, 1966, AS
AMENDED IN 1968 (DECISIONS OF THE NATIONAL CONGRESS OF
THE PALESTINE LIBERATION ORGANIZATION HELD IN CAIRO
FROM 1-17 JULY 1968, EXCERPTS)

Article 1: Palestine is the homeland of the Arab Palestinian people; it is an indivisible part of the Arab homeland, and the Palestinian people are an integral part of the Arab nation.

Article 2: Palestine, with the boundaries it had during the British mandate, is an indivisible territorial unit.

Article 3: The Palestinian Arab people possess the legal right to their homeland and have the right to determine their destiny after achieving the liberation of their country in accordance with their wishes and entirely of their own accord and will.

Article 4: The Palestinian identity is a genuine, essential and inherent characteristic; it is transmitted from parents to children. The Zionist occupation and the dispersal of the Palestinian Arab people, through the disasters which befell them, do not make them lose their Palestinian identity and their membership of the Palestinian community, nor do they negate them.

Article 5: The Palestinians are those Arab nationals who, until 1947, normally resided in Palestine regardless of whether they were evicted from it or have stayed there. Anyone born, after that date, of a Palestinian father—whether inside Palestine or outside it—is also a Palestinian.

Article 6: The Jews who had normally resided in Palestine until the beginning of the Zionist invasion will be considered Palestinians. . . .

Article 9: Armed struggle is the only way to liberate Palestine. Thus it is the overall strategy, not merely a tactical phase. The Palestinian Arab people assert their absolute determination and firm resolution to continue their armed struggle and to work for an armed popular revolution for the liberation of their country and their return to it. They also assert their right to normal life in Palestine and to exercise their right to self-determination and sovereignty over it. . . .

Article 14: The destiny of the Arab nation, and indeed Arab existence itself, depends upon the destiny of the Palestine cause. From this interdependence springs the Arab nation's pursuit of, and striving for, the liberation of Palestine. The people of Palestine play the role of the vanguard in the realization of this sacred national goal.

Article 15: The liberation of Palestine, from an Arab viewpoint, is a national duty and it attempts to repel the Zionist and imperialist aggression against the Arab homeland, and aims at the elimination of Zionism in Palestine. Absolute responsibility for this falls upon the Arab nation—peoples and governments—with the Arab people of Palestine in the vanguard.

. . .

Article 19: The partition of Palestine in 1947 and the establishment of the state of Israel are entirely illegal, regardless of the passage of time, because they were contrary to the will of the Palestinian people and to their natural right in their homeland, and inconsistent with the principles embodied in the Charter of the United Nations, particularly the right to self-determination.

Article 20: The Balfour Declaration, the mandate for Palestine and everything that has been based upon them, are deemed null and void. Claims of historical and religious ties of Jews with Palestine are incompatible with the facts of history and the true conception of what constitutes statehood. Judaism, being a religion, is not an independent nationality. Nor do Jews constitute a single nation with an identity of its own; they are citizens of the states to which they belong.

Article 21: The Arab Palestinian people, expressing themselves by the armed Palestinian revolution, reject all solutions which are substitutes for the total liberation of Palestine and reject all proposals aiming at the liquidation of the Palestinian problem, or its internationalization.

. . .

Article 23: The demands of security and peace, as well as the demands of right and justice, require all states to consider Zionism an illegitimate movement, to outlaw its existence, and to ban its operations, in order that friendly relations among peoples may be preserved, and the loyalty of citizens to their respective homelands safeguarded.

Article 24: The Palestinian people believe in the principles of justice, freedom, sovereignty, self-determination, human dignity, and in the right of all peoples to exercise them.

. . .

Article 27: The Palestine Liberation Organization shall cooperate with all Arab states, each according to its potentialities; and will adopt a neutral policy among them in the light of the requirements of the war of liberation; and on this basis it shall not interfere in the internal affairs of any Arab state.

. . .

Article 33: This Charter shall not be amended save by (vote of) a majority of two-thirds of the total membership of the National Congress of the Palestine Liberation Organization (taken) at a special session convened for that purpose.

17. SECURITY COUNCIL RESOLUTION 242 (1967) ON THE PRINCIPLES FOR A JUST AND LASTING PEACE IN THE MIDDLE EAST, NOVEMBER 22, 1967 (22 U.N. S.C.O.R., 1382d MEETING, AT 8-9 [1967])

The Security Council,

Expressing its continuing concern with the grave situation in the Middle East,

Emphasizing the inadmissibility of the acquisition of territory by war and the need to work for a just and lasting peace in which every state in the area can live in security,

Emphasizing further that all Member States in their acceptance of the Charter of the United Nations have undertaken a commitment to act in accordance with Article 2 of the Charter,

1. *Affirms* that the fulfilment of Charter principles requires the establishment of a just and lasting peace in the Middle East which should include the application of both the following principles:

(i) Withdrawal of Israel armed forces from territories occupied in the recent conflict;

(ii) Termination of all claims or states of belligerency and respect for and acknowledgement of the sovereignty, territorial integrity and political independence of every State in the area and their right to live in peace within secure and recognized boundaries free from threats or acts of force;

2. *Affirms further* the necessity

(*a*) For guaranteeing freedom of navigation through international waterways in the area;

(*b*) For achieving a just settlement of the refugee problem;

(*c*) For guaranteeing the territorial inviolability and political independence of every State in the area, through measures including the establishment of demilitarized zones;

3. *Requests* the Secretary-General to designate a Special Representative to proceed to the Middle East to establish and maintain contacts with the States concerned in order to promote agreement and assist efforts to achieve a peaceful and accepted settlement in accordance with the provisions and principles in this resolution;

4. *Requests* the Secretary-General to report to the Security Council on the progress of the efforts of the Special Representative as soon as possible.

Adopted unanimously at the
1382d meeting.

Discourse 1

·····

Limited Bearing on International Law Issues of the *Elon Moreh* Case (*Dweikat & Others* v. *Government of Israel & Others*)

Considerable attention has been focused on the decision of the Supreme Court of Israel in the *Elon Moreh* case (High Court of Justice [H.C.J.] Judgment of Oct. 22, 1979,[1] in the context of charges of "illegality" of Jewish settlements in Judea and Samaria. When emanating from rejectionist Arab quarters, such allegations base themselves on the assertion that those territories are "Arab lands" in which not only new settlements of Jews, but the very presence of Israel authorities, including the Israel Defence Forces (I.D.F.), violates international law, and even constitutes continuing "aggression." But, of course, these critics also join in any case in the charge that such new settlements violate the restraints on belligerent occupying powers imposed by international law, and in particular by the Fourth Geneva Convention, Relative to the Protection of Civilian Persons in Time of War, 1949, Article 49(6). The United States' position, so far as it has been spelled out, rests on the assertion that while the Israel presence as a belligerent occupant is consistent with international law, the particular activity of authorizing or even permitting Jewish settlements to be established is ultra vires of the authority of an occupying power under international law, and in particular, under the above Geneva Convention. The narrower question of occupation law will be examined in Discourse 2.

In a wider political context, the Israel Supreme Court decision in the *Elon Moreh* case has been interpreted in some quarters as confirming such constrictions placed by international law upon Israel's territorial standing in Judea and Samaria (the West Bank) and Gaza. It is the more important to point out, therefore, as this discourse will do, that that decision of the Supreme Court of Israel, while it held that the customary law of belligerent occupation did not permit the requisition of land for a Jewish settlement at Elon Moreh in Judea, has on a correct reading no bearing on the validity of the other international law bases of Israel's standing in these territories. More than one such base, as submitted in Chapters 3 and 7, may suffice to establish its sovereign title in these areas, as against (for example) the state of Jordan. At the least, as there shown, they also certainly support the right of Jews to settle in these territories.

The present analysis will show that the Supreme Court in the *Elon Moreh* case (as well as in the *Beit-El* case, H.C.J. 606/78, Judgment of March 15, 1979, which preceded it)[2] limited itself to the question whether the requisitioning of the petitioners' private property in certain land was lawful under Israel municipal law, as it stood for the time being under Israel legislation, the applicable common law, and the military commander's requisition order, as invoked in the pleading and argument of the respondent authorities in those cases. Israel courts, following in this matter the Anglo-American common law principle they share with British and United States courts, regard the municipal law as including any rules of customary international law relevant to the issue before them. The court's decision that the present state of Israel municipal law, the form of the military requisition order, and the respondent authorities' pleading and argument directed it to the international law concerning belligerent occupation, as the *only* appropriate test for the legality of the action of the Israel authorities, led the court to an important ruling on the law of belligerent occupation. By that ruling, however, the Court in no way passed upon the question whether, on a full view of the operation of international law as between the states concerned, Israel was entitled to rights of territorial sovereignty in the area concerned, or other rights over and beyond the rights of a belligerent occupant.

This commentary will show that, not only in the *Beit-El* case but also in the *Elon Moreh* case, the court applied the customary law of belligerent occupation as a frame because the respondent authorities of the state of Israel, by their procedures of requisition and *in lite,* required the court to judge their official acts by this limited body of law.[3] The court decided these cases *as if* the lawfulness of settlement-related requisitions depended wholly on the customary law of belligerent occupation, deemed on common law principles to be incorporated into Israel municipal law. Whether, like *Beit-El,* the cases upheld the requisition, or like *Elon Moreh,* they struck it down, these cases in no way finally determine either Israel's territorial rights, or the rights of Jews to settle in Judea and Samaria (the West Bank) and Gaza. The determination of such rights involves the application of other rules of international law than those concerning belligerent occupation. But recourse by the Supreme Court to any of these other bodies of law was, as a technical matter, excluded by the nature and terms of the requisition order, and of the pleading and argument before the court, and the prevailing state of Israel law—in short, by the issue before them.

The other bases of Israel's territorial entitlement, and the principles of international law involved, were examined in Chapter 7. They include: (1) The rule that would attribute sovereign title in Judea and Samaria (the West Bank) and Gaza to Israel, by virtue of the fact that Israel is the state in lawful possession of territory affected by a "sovereignty vacuum" (view of E. Lauterpacht); (2) The rule that in a situation of disputed sovereignty that state is entitled that can establish the best title thereto, a rule well recognized by the International Court of Justice; (3) The rule that a state in lawful possession of territory to which no other sovereign has a supportable claim of sovereignty is entitled to take the step of formal annexation; (4) The rule laid down by the International Court of Justice, that territories subject to a League of Nations mandate whose disposition has not been otherwise determined remain subject to the obligations of the mandate, here the mandate for Palestine of which the primary obligation was the establishment of a Jewish national home. Far from dismissing such formidable bases of title, this analysis will show that the judgments of the Supreme Court of Israel carefully reserved the effects of such other rules, the court regarding itself as debarred from addressing them by the manner in which the case was presented.

This restricted import of the judgments is quite explicit in them. On pp. 16-17 of the translation of the *Elon Moreh* opinions, for example, Justice Landau (deputy president as he then was) referred to the arguments based on the fact that at the time of the I.D.F.'s entry into Judea and Samaria, the territory "was not occupied by a sovereign power whose occupation thereafter enjoyed international recognition." (This, in effect, refers to the first two bases of title discussed in the last paragraph of Chapter 7 above.) The court, he said in *Beit-El*, would not deal with this question, which, he said, "joins the bundle of reservations mentioned by me in H.C.J. 302/72 (p. 177, D) (*Hilu* case) which remain undisposed of by this Court" (p. 20). The judge in this connection observed that Major-General Orly's affidavit began with the words, "Without going into the legal question of the applicability of the rules of international law in the area occupied since 1967 . . ." (*Elon Moreh* transl., p. 20). This is obviously wide enough to embrace the other several grounds recalled in the last section for attribution of territorial rights to Israel.[4]

Witkon J., also, in the *Elon Moreh* case was very emphatic that the court must entirely reserve all international law issues other than those as to the law of belligerent occupation raised by the government's pleadings. He there stated, after referring to the hypothetical case of the right of Jewish settlers to enter land as to which no requisition order has'been issued by the military authorities, "This answer is basic in the law. Furthermore had some serious doubt been raised here as regards the status of the land in question, we would be obliged to refer to the Ministry of Foreign Affairs and ask them for an official certificate defining the status of the land. This question is not justiciable and thus the Court will act according to the decision of the Government" (*Elon Moreh* transl., p. 42). It should be clear that the reason why the question of the consistency of the requisition with the customary international law of belligerent occupation was dealt with, but not the other questions, is precisely that the government had by its requisition procedure, pleading, and argument directed the court's attention exclusively to the question of validity of the requisition on the assumption that this was governed by the international law of belligerent occupation.[5]

The judges were clear in *Elon Moreh* as to their reasons for reserving these wider questions as to Israel's territorial entitlements. The Deputy President Justice Landau (as he then was) wrote the opinion in that case in which the other judges concurred. He there observed (transl., pp. 15-17) that "the framework of the hearing . . . is delimited first and foremost by the requisition order issued by the Commander of the region, and all agree that the direct source for this order lies in the powers that international law accords to the Military Commander in the area occupied by his forces in a war."[6] The framework is also delimited, said the learned judge, by "the legal principles" followed by the regional military commander that were "also based on the laws of war in international law" (transl., p. 15). These principles the court found in the military commander's proclamations no. 1 of July 6, 1967, and no. 2, paragraph 2, of the same date, so far as consistent with this or other proclamations, and "with the changes stemming from the establishment of rule by the Israel Defence Forces (I.D.F.) in the region"; and paragraph 4 of Proclamation no. 2, which tranferred all movable and immovable property belonging to the state or government of Jordan to the military commander.

These 1967 proclamations were still in force at the date of the *Elon Moreh* case. It is true that section 1 of the Area of Jurisdiction and Powers Ordinance, 5708/1948, issued by the Provincial Council of State, applied any law of the state of Israel also to "any part of Palestine which the Minister of Defence has defined by proclamation as being held by the I.D.F." Counsel for the Gush Emunim respondents (not, be it noted, counsel for the military commander or the government) argued that even though the minister of defense had not issued any proclamation defining Judea and Samaria as being so held by the I.D.F., that Ordinance was "an exercise of legislative sovereignty by the Council which evidenced the sovereignty of Israel over areas including Judea and Samaria" (*Elon Moreh* transl., p. 16).

Justice Landau's observation on this effort of the nonofficial respondents to raise issues going beyond the law of belligerent occupation reinforces the conclusions of the present analysis as to the severely restricted import of the *Elon Moreh* decision. He noted that neither the minister of defense under section 1 above, nor the government of Israel in any other manner had yet exercized the above power to extend by proclamation the area in which Israel law applied, though it had applied Israel law to East Jerusalem under the Law and Administration Ordinance 5708/1948, section 11B (transl., p. 16). It was the duty of the court to apply Israel municipal law as it stood at the present time, and this duty could not be affected by the fact that the legal outcome in the *Elon Moreh* case might have been different if the power given by section 1 of the above Area of Jurisdiction and Powers Ordinance had been exercised in respect of Judea and Samaria. In his summation of the matter, "when we come to consider the legal basis of Israeli rule in Judea and Samaria, our interest is in the legal norms which actually exist and not just those which exist potentially."[7] Justice Landau, indeed, did go so far as to observe that there was "great force" to the argument that since there is no state that is sovereign reversioner of Judea and Samaria, the factual situation before the court was not one for which the customary law of belligerent occupation was appropriate. Consistently with the present analysis of the judgments, however, he reserved this question as going beyond the matrix of occupation law within which the court's decision was held.[8] He relegated the question of the effect of these other rules, therefore, to "the international arena." (transl., pp. 15-16.) Once again, in short, it was made clear that the *Elon Moreh* case did not determine the question of Israel's final territorial entitlements under international law.[9]

Recognition that the matrix fixed by the Israel authorities for the court's decision in the *Elon Moreh* case prevented that decision passing on any standing of Israel in the territories concerned other than that of military occupant, raises questions in turn concerning this attitude of the authorities vis-à-vis its courts. While this is strictly beyond the scope of the present legal analysis, certain observations proximate to the legal issues may be helpful.

Governmental attitudes in Israel have obviously reflected that state's assessment of the need to avoid action provocative to the Arab states, such as formal acts of annexation, whether by legislative or executive action, or even (as this discourse has shown) by permitting the sovereignty issue to be passed on by its courts. Even through the years when the Arab states all insisted on the triple nay, of no recognition, no negotiation, no peace, of the Khartoum formula, successive governments of Israel have striven to keep the way open for peace negotiations.

In a real sense, indeed, it may be said that this very restraint in asserting the full potentialities of its territorial entitlements under international law, and preventing their being passed on by its courts, has obscured the strength of these entitlements. On the one hand, the government has insisted, in the present view correctly, that by virtue of Israel's lawful entry in the course of self-defense onto territory to which Jordan, by virtue of her unlawful entry and the principle of *ex iniuria non oritur ius* had no title, and by the operation thereafter of the principle *uti possidetis,* Israel was entitled to expect that the peace negotiations would provide such territorial adjustments as her security required.

Israel rejected from the earliest debates after the cease-fire of 1967 charges that she had annexed the territories, and even that she had annexed Jerusalem. She has still not formally annexed even East Jerusalem.[10] Her representative did not sufficiently articulate that she could in international law lawfully annex them, in case solution by negotiation proved impossible. Yet this has certainly been implicit in her position. Her adversaries have undoubtedly had this in mind in the repetitively premature charges, beginning as early as June 1967, that she had annexed Jerusalem, and was proceeding to annex other territories. Of course, such charges, though incorrect as statements of international law, were part of an understandable and even skillful strategy of political warfare. As such they tended to limit the options short of annexation open to Israel, and to obfuscate and even subvert the undoubted rules of international law that entitled Israel in the final resort to territorial rights well beyond those of a mere belligerent occupant.

Israel governments have (wisely or unwisely) refused to be forced into either annexation or withdrawal (except to boundaries duly negotiated in treaties of peace). Annexation would arguably have increased the dangers of renewed war; unilateral withdrawal would have been a renunciation of legal rights vital to her future security. But this very self-denying ordinance, which kept her from the act of annexation, turned the clear position under international law into obscuring paradox. As long as Israel refrained from an unequivocal claim of sovereignty, the only alternative status that existing international law seemed to offer was that of belligerent occupant. Yet, as frequently observed in the preceding chapters, that limited status, with its severe restraints on the occupant's action, was inappropriate to, and indeed quite incongruous with, her full legal position in Judea and Samaria (the West Bank) and Gaza. And this for at least two main reasons.

First, as spelled out in Chapter 7, under "Bases of Sovereignty under International Law," the customary law of belligerent occupation seems, by its very terms, applicable only where reversionary sovereign rights over the territory are vested in the ousted state. Here the ousted state, Jordan, had no territorial title whatsoever in Judea and Samaria. Even as a former belligerent occupant, her standing was vitiated by illegality. Once she was ousted by Israel's self-defensive action—*ex iniuria non oritur ius.* And similarly with Egypt in Gaza. Second, the persistent refusal of Jordan and Egypt to negotiate produced, after the lapse of so many years, a situation that had as little relation to the usual assumptions of belligerent occupation as does (for example) the present status of West Berlin. West Berlin still remains, technically speaking, under the belligerent occupation of the former principal allies in World War II. It would be strange, however, to try to describe the governmental regime of West Berlin solely or even mainly in terms of the law of belligerent occupation. The point of this comparison is merely the obvious inadequacy in both cases of belligerent occupation law as a matrix for territorial arrangements of long and indefinite regimes. The contrast is no less significant, that while the Great Powers in West Berlin have no other legal basis for their presence than occupation law, Israel has wider claims, including claims to sovereignty, resting on other independent grounds.

The official Israel position has for these reasons often seemed ambivalent. While not accepting that its territorial standing was that merely of belligerent occupant, legally hemmed in by the customary rules on that matter, the authorities have as occasion arose, especially before the courts, insisted that (as it were, de facto) they do observe and are ready to be judged by the customary law of belligerent occupation, *as if* this were the basis of their presence. Beyond matters of military security the government of Israel has, for example, recognized the continued tenure in office of Jordanian officials in Judea and Samaria, allowing them to receive Jordanian stipends and continue their relations with Amman. Within similar limits, and indeed partly beyond them, the Jordanian laws in force in Judea and Samaria in 1967 have been continued in force.[11] Among the rare exceptions is the instruction to Israel military courts never to inflict capital punishment in respect of some of the offenses so punishable by Jordanian law. Moreover, on the central matter that here concerns us, namely, cases of property rights before the civil courts of Israel, the governmental authorities have by their modes of requisition, pleading, and argument required the courts to adjudicate as if Israel's status in the territories were that merely of a belligerent occupant—so that the powers of the authorities, including military authorities, and the rights of the inhabitants, were to be determined, hypothetically and provisionally, for the limited purposes of the particular litigation, on the basis of the customary international law of belligerent occupation.

It was on this basis that, as this analysis has shown, the Supreme Court of Israel decided in the *Beit-El* case in 1979, that the requisition of certain Arab-owned land for settlements was lawful, since the requisition was for the purposes of the security of the occupying forces and the occupied area. For such civilian settlements played a security role, for instance, in preempting terrorist activity in an area where this was endemic. It was on a similar basis that the same court held, in the *Elon Moreh* case, that the requisition was not lawful, since certain evidence that emerged in the prceedings, both in the military authorities' replies to the court's questionnaire, and the evidence led by some of the "Gush Emunim" Israel settlers who intervened in the case (transl., esp. pp. 25 ff.) showed that the objectives with which the settlements were established arose primarily from initiatives not directed to military security in the above sense, so that the dominant motive among the mixture of motives operating was not that of military security.[12] This evidence, the court concluded, showed that both the initiative towards the requisition, and a predominant purpose of carrying it through, went beyond measures of military security authorized by belligerent occupation law to which it was required to limit itself. So that here again the court's language indicates that it did not regard itself as passing on the territorial rights that the state of Israel might have in the broader arena of international law other than rules governing belligerent occupation. As in earlier cases, wider questions were "reserved" by the court.[13]

The constrictions thus imposed on the law applied by a municipal court, whose task is limited to applying the municipal law to the precise issue before it, have long been recognized, sometimes with a certain frustration, by the Supreme Court of Israel. In the *Hilu* case in 1972, for example, Justice Landau observed that certain questions concerning the international law position must "be added to the bundle of problems as to which we are not, in this litigation, required to express a binding opinion, and I wish to reemphasize that they are all problems which remain open in this Court" (transl., p. 5).[14] Justice Witkon went further (transl., p. 8), observing that the "concession made . . . so generously" by the authorities "has resulted in a confusion of topics and a distortion of the rules of law in this area." Such agreements, further observed Justice Witkon, "given from time to time, and relating to certain restricted subjects and without any commitment that it will be given in all repetitions yet to come, turn our hearings into a kind of arbitration which depends on the consent of the defendant. This court was not created for that purpose" (transl., p. 11-12).

It will already have become clear that one main clue to understanding the strictly limited bearing of the *Elon Moreh* and similar cases on Israel's rights under international law, is to recognize that these are municipal court decisions applying municipal law. This being so, the legal principles to be applied were limited by the issue that the facts (including the type of requisition), the mode of pleading, and argument of the parties presented for the decision and the law municipally applicable thereto. The court found that these required it to decide the case *as if* Israel were a belligerent occupant. This it did, reserving all other questions of international law affecting the territorial title of Israel.

Insofar as the court thus did not consider other international law bases of Israel's entitlement, the outcome was to decide the case against the Israel authorities by reference to a limited part of customary international law incorporated as such into municipal law. Insofar as Israel might have additional entitlements under the other, unconsidered, parts of international law, the decision on the municipal level seemed to disfavor, but in reality simply "reserved" Israel's rights on the full level of international law. Other parts of the judgment in the *Elon Moreh* case illustrate the fact that "favor" or "disfavor" of the rights and powers of the state of Israel are merely by-products of rules concerning the degree of incorporation of international law into the municipal law, which, as a municipal court, the Supreme Court of Israel was required to apply.

Thus, the Supreme Court was concerned in the *Elon Moreh* case to reject arguments by the petitioners against the respondent authorities based on the 1949 Fourth Geneva Convention, Relative to the Protection of Civilian Persons in Time of War, Article 49(6) of which, it was claimed, expressly forbad the belligerent occupant to settle its metropolitan population in occupied territories. The present discussion is not concerned with the question of interpretation of Article 49(6) involved.[15] Nor was the court willing to enter into the question at all. Instead the judgments "reserved" the question whether that treaty provision did prohibit the settlements under question. This, too, was a "reservation" of questions of international law from the scope of the decision, but for a reason different from those that led the court to focus only on Israel's authority as a belligerent occupant under international law. This reason was one shared generally, if not universally, by common law countries. While the rules of customary international law are deemed by such courts to be incorporated into the municipal law, and therefore to be applicable by such courts, rules of mere treaty law, even if the treaty has been signed and ratified—and is thus binding on the state on the international level—do not by that fact become part of the municipal law applicable by the court.[16] In order to become so applicable, treaties must be incorporated in municipal statutes duly enacted, and (if they are not in self-executing terms) must be accompanied by the necessary legislation for implementation. This is so even for the common law of the United States, except insofar as the constitutional provision that self-implementing treaties approved by two-thirds of the Senate and duly proclaimed by the president, become automatically "the supreme law of the land." Thus, international engagements, such as executive agreements that do not meet these requirements or treaties that are not "self-implementing," still require legislative incorporation before the courts will apply them.

As to the Fourth Geneva Convention, therefore, merely because the Supreme Court of Israel did not apply its provisions to the facts before it, the court did not deny that these might give rise to obligations of Israel under international law. Since treaty law as such was not part of the municipal law, the convention as such was not part of the law on which the court was free to pass either way. On this point the constrictions on the law applicable in that municipal court favored the respondent authorities. On the point, on the other hand, of Israel's territorial entitlements, the restriction of the law applicable by the court to belligerent occupation law, for the different reasons above set out, favored the petitioners as against the respondent authorities. The failure of the court to apply the provisions of the Geneva Convention against the Israel authorities left open the questions whether Israel had obligations under that convention, and what these might be. So, too, questions were also left open by the court's abstention from considering, besides the law of belligerent occupation forced on it by the requisitional and pleading procedure, what might be Israel's territorial rights under other relevant parts of customary international law. As shown at length in Chapters 3, 7, and 8 of the text, such relevant parts include the rules of *uti possidetis,* of the lawfulness of a state's self-defensive action, and of the principle *ex iniuria non oritur ius.* Here also the decision left open what these rights of Israel might be under those other rules of international law.

The complexity of the analysis thus necessary to delimit the precise bearing of the *Elon Moreh* case on the questions of international law at issue between Israel and Jordan and Egypt, will no doubt in the future attract the admirable industry of candidates for advanced degrees. More immediately, they have already afforded opportunities for hostile assertions by adversaries of Israel that her claims in Judea and Samaria (the West Bank) and Gaza violate international law. It is, after all, an irresistible temptation for political warfare to present the *Elon Moreh* case as one in which the most learned justices of Israel's own Supreme Court unanimously held that Israel's only territorial standing in Judea and Samaria (the West Bank) and Gaza under international law is that of a belligerent occupant; and that settlement of Jews in these territories or even tolerance of this by the authorities of the state, and any other activities of Israel there, are legally limited to those sanctioned by the astringent law of belligerent occupation.

The present analysis has shown that such a presentation is legally incorrect in important respects. To correct it has required a careful spelling out of the decision in a series of statements that may now be summarized. What the judges held was not what is asserted in the preceding paragraph. It was rather that, in view of the mode in which the power to requisition was purported to be exercized through the military authorities, and of the mode of pleading and argument consequentially pursued *in lite* by the respondent authorities, the only matter placed in issue before the court concerned the conformity of the requisition with that part of customary international law governing belligerent occupation, and that under common law principles this customary law was deemed to be incorporated into the municipal law of Israel, which the court was required to apply. It is true that under other parts of customary international law, deemed under the same common law principles to be also incorporated into Israel law, the decision might have been different. But in view of the issues placed before the court by the positions of the respondent authorities manifest in their above modes of requisition, pleading, and argument, the Court was debarred from considering such other parts of customary law. Once these other bases of possible territorial entitlements of Israel were thus excluded from consideration, the court felt compelled to hold that the action of the Israel authorities exceeded the limited powers granted by international law to the role of belligerent occupant. In short, it was required, by the legal matrix into which the case was cast, to leave out of consideration the cardinal principles of international law that base the full territorial entitlements of Israel.

This statement of the *Elon Moreh* case is complex. The complexity is inherent in the interactions of municipal and international law involved in cases of this kind. It is correct in law despite its complexity. And insofar as this is so, it is clear beyond doubt that, important as the case may be for interpreting the powers of belligerent occupants, it has no bearing, either one way or the other, on the more general and important questions, central to the body of the present work, as to what title and powers the state of Israel may have over the territories in question when all the rules of international law that bear on those matters are taken into consideration.[17]

The *Elon Moreh* holding may, indeed, be regarded as a landmark in the law concerning belligerent occupation in several respects. First, it presents an unusual setting of the denial of the belligerent occupant's authority by that state's own courts, to which the state authorities yielded. Second, by denying, for the *Elon Moreh* requisitions, the legality that the court had accorded to requisitions in the *Beit-El* and earlier cases, the Supreme Court asserted that the test of "military requirements" of the occupying army, was not to be regarded as a merely formal test, and was to be seriously applied to the facts of each requisition. Third, the court felt able to enter into a full analysis of the respective roles of the political authorities (the defence minister, the prime minister, the Ministerial Defence Committee, and the cabinet plenum) as well as the military authorities, and to determine on this basis that even though the settlement would serve military purposes, the purposes dominant in its establishment were political and not military.

The judges of the Supreme Court of Israel have indeed, on these accounts, received high praise. Professor Werner Kagi in the *Neue Züricher Zeitung* of February 16-17, 1980, hails their courage in enforcing the rules concerning belligerent occupation, even as against the defense concerns of their own small state surrounded by implacably hostile neighbors; and in countering the claims of the Gush Emunim settler-respondents to divine authority. The counsel for the settler-respondents invoked Numbers 33:53—"And you shall take possession of the land and settle in it, for I have given the land to you to possess it." Justice Landau replied with Leviticus 19:33-34[18]—"And if a stranger sojourn with you in your land you shall not do him wrong. The stranger that sojourneth with you shall be as the home-born among you, and thou shalt love him as thyself" (transl., p. 13). They are praised no less as exemplars of faithfulness to the principles of "the constitutional State" even in the face of emergency conditions. And they are praised finally for their courage in not shirking the duty of judges to apply the law, despite the risk of seeming to "descend into the arena of public debate" (Justice Landau, in *Elon Moreh,* transl. at 1-2), nor seeking refuge in doctrines of nonjusticiability.

The present writer shares the admiration that underlies such praises. It may conceivably be that, in the respects mentioned, the *Elon Moreh* case will prove to be, as Professor Kagi thinks, "one of the most significant legal decisions ever in the history of the modern constitutional State." But all this makes it the more crucial that its substantive holding be correctly delimited. The judges did not decide, but on the contrary carefully reserved, all questions of the territorial entitlements of Israel in these areas under other parts of international law than the rules of belligerent occupation.

This insistence on the correct interpretation of the *Elon Moreh* holding will not, of course, in itself prevent the use of incorrect versions of it as a weapon of political warfare against Israel. It may to some degree neutralize such meretricious use. More important, however, the correct understanding of the case is deeply related to the main themes of the present work. For this has shown at length that, quite apart from the status of belligerent occupant, there are no less than four bases of Israel's territorial entitlements in Judea and Samaria (the West Bank) and Gaza, all of them solidly resting on international law principles. In a context where a Peace Treaty with Egypt has for the first time opened the way somewhat to the negotiation of peace between Israel and the other Arab states, these principles are an essential part of the dialogue through which final accommodation and pacification must be sought. One may be permitted to believe that the judges concerned would not wish to be interpreted in any other sense.

Discourse 2

· · · · ·

Jewish Settlements in Judea and Samaria (the West Bank) and Geneva Convention, IV, Article 49(6) Relative to the Protection of Civilian Persons in Time of War

Perhaps the central current criticism against the government of Israel in relation to its administration of the territories occupied after the 1967 War concerns its alleged infractions of the final paragraph (6) of Article 49, of the Fourth Geneva Convention, Relative to the Protection of Civilian Persons in Time of War, of August 12, 1949. The preceding paragraphs deal with deportation or transfer of a population out of the occupied territory. The final paragraph (6) reads as follows: "The Occupying Power shall not deport or transfer parts of its own civilian population into the territory it occupies." The Supreme Court of Israel in the *Beit-El* and *Elon Moreh* cases regarded this issue as not within its purview on the ground that that convention had not been enacted into the municipal law of Israel, and that, according to common law principles, it is only the rules of customary international law that are deemed to be so incorporated without enactment, and are thus applicable in that municipal court.[1] In view of its importance the writer ventures some observations as to the correctness of the above current assertions that settlement of Jews in the "occupied" territories is "illegal," presumably for violating the above provision.[2]

It has been shown in Chapters 3 and 7 that there are solid grounds in international law for denying any sovereign title to Jordan in the West Bank, and therefore any rights as reversioner state under the law of belligerent occupation. The grounds on which Israel might now or in the future claim to have such title have also there been canvassed. The initial point that arises under Article 49(6) of Geneva Convention IV of 1949 is more specific. Not only does Jordan lack any legal title to the territories concerned, but the Convention itself does not by its terms apply to these territories. For, under Article 2, that Convention applies "to cases of . . . occupation of the territory of a High Contracting Party," by another such Party. Insofar as the West Bank at present held by Israel does not belong to any other State, the Convention would not seem to apply to it at all. This is a technical, though rather decisive, legal point.

It is also important to observe, however, that even if that point is set aside, the claim that Article 49 of the Convention forbids the settlement of Jews in the West Bank is difficult to sustain.

It is clear that in its drafting history, Article 49 as a whole was directed against the heinous practice of the Nazi regime during the Nazi occupation of Europe in World War II, of forcibly transporting populations of which it wished to rid itself, into or out of occupied territories for the purpose of "liquidating" them with minimum disturbance of its metropolitan territory, or to provide slave labor or for other inhumane purposes. The genocidal objectives, of which Article 49 was concerned to prevent future repetitions against other peoples, were in part conceived by the Nazi authorities as a means of ridding the Nazi occupant's metropolitan territory of Jews—of making it, in Nazi terms, *judenrein*. Such practices were, of course, prominent among the offenses tried by war crimes tribunals after World War II.[3] They were covered by counts in the charter of the International Military Tribunal of 1945 for the trial of major war criminals, including "deportation to slave labour or for any other purpose, of civilian population of or in occupied territory,"[4] and also (under Article 6[c]) as crimes against humanity, defined to include "murder, extermination, enslavement, deportation and other inhuman acts committed against any civilian population" or "persecution on political, social and religious grounds," committed before or during the war in connection with another crime within the Tribunal's jurisdiction.

In the words of Dr. Jean Pictet's commentary on the convention:

It will suffice to mention that millions of human beings were torn from their homes, separated from their families and deported from their country, usually under inhumane conditions. These mass transfers took place for the greatest possible variety of reasons, mainly as a consequence of the formation of a forced labour service. The thought of the physical and mental suffering endured by these "displaced persons," among whom there were a great many women, children, old people and sick, can only lead to thankfulness for the prohibition embodied in this paragraph, which is intended to forbid such hateful practices for all time.[5]

These remarks were directed primarily to paragraph 1 of Article 49 prohibiting "regardless of their motive" all "individual or mass forcible transfers, as well as deportations of protected persons from occupied territory to the territory of the Occupying Power or to that of any other country."

Article 49, paragraph 6, uses similar language, though with significant differences, forbidding the occupying power to "deport or transfer parts of its own civilian population into the territory it occupies." Notably, paragraph 6 does not include the peremptory clause "regardless of motive," so that the spirit of its provision, as well as the letter, requires attention. Dr. Pictet's commentary acknowledges "some hesitation" and some doubts in the drafting as to its relation to the above main preoccupation of Article 49. He observes, "It is intended to prevent a practice adopted during the Second World War by certain Powers, which transferred portions of their own population to occupied territory for political and racial reasons or in order, as they claimed, to colonize those territories. Such transfers worsened the economic situation of the native population and endangered their separate existence as a race."[6] He feels it to be particularly difficult that the terms "deportation" and "transfer" are used in paragraph 1 to refer to "protected persons" (which under Article 4 excludes nationals of the occupying power); and in paragraph 6, where they clearly refer to the occupant's own civilian population (which obviously includes the occupant's own nationals).

It is clear that historically the victims of the terrible abuses that Dr. Pictet, as well as this writer, regards as a key to interpreting paragraph 1, included many thousands who were nationals of the Nazi occupying power in Nazi metropolitan territory, and who were deported (e.g., to Poland). Many of these, for example the Jews, had shortly before the relevant time been deprived of German nationality, presumably in order to expose them more easily to arbitrary action. Dr. Pictet, somewhat ambiguously, refers to this when he describes the transfers of the occupant's own population forbidden by paragraph 6 as "transfers for political and racial reasons."[7] He tends, however, in the end (still with some ambiguity) to think that the gist of paragraph 6 is to protect the "native population" of the occupied territory against impairment of their "economic situation" or "their separate existence."

In the present view, the ambit of the text of Article 49(6) is wide enough to forbid conduct of the occupying power that involves either of the above evils. As there indicated, the historical background would make it quite incongruous for a legislator to ignore in relation to the occupant's own population, those same heinous and inhuman acts against civilians that (as Dr. Pictet freely acknowledges) were the immediate background for the provisions of Article 49. If and insofar, therefore, as Israel's position in Judea and Samaria (the West Bank) is merely that of an occupying power, Article 49 would forbid "deportation" or "transfer" of its own population onto the West Bank whenever this action has the consequence of serving as a means of either (1) impairment of the economic situation or racial integrity of the native population of the occupied territory; or (2) inhuman treatment of its own population. These were the two aspects of the application of Article 49(6) detected by the present writer as long ago as 1954.[8] It is necessary to consider separately each of these possible taints.

Impairment of Racial Integrity of the Native Population of the Occupied Territory. The prominence of the question of legality of Jewish settlements on the West Bank reflects the tensions of the peace process, rather than the magnitude of any demographic movement. There appear to be in the whole of Judea and Samaria (the West Bank) about 20,000 (excluding 2,500 in military postings in the Jordan valley) Jews amid a native population approaching 700,000 (excluding 111,000 Arabs of East Jerusalem). Despite vociferous political warfare pronouncements on both sides, it seems clear, therefore, that no serious dilution (much less extinction) of the "separate racial existence" of the native population has either taken place or is in prospect. Nor do well-known facts of dramatic improvement in the "economic situation" of the inhabitants since 1967 permit any suggestion that that situation has been worsened or impaired.

Insofar, moreover, as these or future settlements are merely directed to the requirements of military security in the occupied territory they do not violate either the spirit or the letter of this aspect of Article 49. And they also conform, as the preceding discourse has shown, to the general requirements of customary international law, embracing the relevant provisions of the Fourth Hague Convention of 1907, and its annexed regulations.

Inhuman Treatment of the Occupant State's Own Population. The second aim of the prohibition in Article 49(6) was, as has been seen, to protect the inhabitants of the occupant's own metropolitan territory from genocidal and other inhuman acts of the occupant's government. That this was part of, if not the main intention of Article 49(6) seems clear from the use of the term "deport," which clearly refers to a coerced movement of its population. The addition of the term "or transfer" does not alter this import. The word "deport" is usually associated with the involuntary removal by a government of aliens from its territory, and the addition of "transfer" as a synonym seems only directed to indicate that the prohibition was intended to protect the occupant state's own nationals as well as other elements in its population. In the case of the genocidal transfer of German Jews to Poland for destruction, as observed above, the Nazi government had indeed first deprived most of the victims of German nationality. So that it is understandable that the draftsmen might wish to make it clear that the prohibition of forced transfer of elements of its own population is in no way dependent on technicalities of nationality. And the word "transfer" in itself implies that the movement is not voluntary on the part of the persons concerned, but a magisterial act of the state concerned.

As contrasted with this main evil at which Article 49 was aimed, the diversion of the meaning of paragraph 6 to justify prohibition of the voluntary settlement of Jews in Judea and Samaria (the West Bank) carries an irony bordering on the absurd. Ignoring the overall purpose of Article 49, which would *inter alia* protect the population of the state of Israel from being removed against their will into the occupied territory, it is now sought to be interpreted so as to impose on the Israel government a duty to prevent any Jewish individual from voluntarily taking up residence in that area. For not even the most blinkered adversary of Israel could suggest that the individual Jews who (for example) are members of the small Gush Emunim groups, are being in some way forced to settle in Judea and Samaria (the West Bank)! The issue is rather whether the government of Israel has any obligation under international law to use force to prevent the voluntary (often the fanatically voluntary) movement of these individuals.

On that issue, the terms of Article 49(6), however they are interpreted, are submitted to be totally irrelevant. To render them relevant, we would have to say that the effect of Article 49(6) is to impose an obligation on the state of Israel to ensure (by force if necessary) that these areas, despite their millennial association with Jewish life, shall be forever *judenrein*. Irony would thus be pushed to the absurdity of claiming that Article 49(6), designed to prevent repetition of Nazi-type genocidal policies of rendering Nazi metropolitan territories *judenrein,* has now come to mean that Judea and Samaria (the West Bank) must be made *judenrein* and must be so maintained, if necessary by the use of force by the government of Israel against its own inhabitants.

Common sense as well as correct historical and functional context exclude so tyrannical a reading of Article 49(6). So does the consideration, discussed at the end of Chapter 7, that Judea and Samaria (the West Bank) are residual areas of the original Palestine mandate. As such, in Eugene Rostow's cogent view there examined, they have to be regarded as still subject to the substantive obligations of that mandate.[9] Among these the establishment of a Jewish national home, if not "the soul of the Mandate" (as stated in the Permanent Mandates Commission in 1935), was at least its "primary purpose." A demand that this territory be kept *judenrein* would be a gross travesty of this legal position, turning international law on its head.

This is, of course, quite a separate issue from that of the limits of the government of Israel's power to requisition land owned by Arabs, and of its general powers to see to its own security and the security of its forces. It is, however, a very fundamental issue. Insofar as we must reject the interpretation of Article 49(6) that would require the areas concerned to be kept *judenrein,* the issue of the extent and conditions for entry and residence by Jews, now and in the future, is a matter to be negotiated as a part of the peace process.

It is true that during its period of unlawful possession from 1948 to 1967, Jordan did apply a Nazi-type law of exclusion of Jews from Jerusalem and Judea and Samaria. If the unlawfulness of these Jordanian positions there were overlooked, it could conceivably be argued that when Jordan was ousted by Israel's lawful entry in 1967, Israel's occupation was nevertheless subject to the limits of Article 43 of the Hague Rules, under which it must respect the laws in force unless "absolutely prevented." Therefore, it might be said, Israel as a belligerent occupant was bound to maintain the Jordanian law excluding Jews—of *Judenreinlichkeit.* Even on such assumptions, however, it would have to be said, most emphatically, that such a demand that international law sanctify the obnoxious policy of *Judenreinlichkeit* for Judea and Samaria (the West Bank) would fly in the face of principles of belligerent occupation law established after World War II. The Allies in Germany in 1944 provided immediately for the abolition of the basic Nazi discriminatory legislation. And the authorities seem to hold that this was justified squarely on the ground that the occupants were "absolutely prevented," within the terms of Article 43, from continuing laws so repugnant to elementary conceptions of justice.[10] The removal therefore by Israel, even in the role of belligerent occupant, of the Jordanian discriminatory laws against Jews, was equally lawful on precisely the same ground.

Notes

· · · · ·

Introduction

1. J. Stone, *International Guarantees of Minority Rights* (Oxford: Oxford Univ. Press, 1932); J. Stone, *Regional Guarantees of Minority Rights* (Cambridge: Harvard Univ. Press, 1933).

2. The author's term, from J. Stone, *Legal Controls of International Conflict* (1954; repr., Sydney, 1959), pp. 242-84.

3. J. Stone, *Aggression and World Order* (1958; repr., 1976), pp. 161 ff.

4. These studies and the abbreviations hereafter used for them are listed in this footnote for later cross-reference: *The Origins and Evolution of the Palestine Problem* (New York, 1978), 2 pts. (ST/SG/Ser F/1) (hereafter referred to as *Origins*); *The Right of Return of the Palestinian People* (ST/SG Ser F/2), New York, 1979) (hereafter referred to as *Return*); *The Right to Self-Determination of the Palestinian People* (ST/SG/Ser F/3, New York, 1979) (hereafter referred to as *Self-Determination*); *An International Law Analysis of the Major United Nations Resolutions Concerning the Palestine Question* (ST/SG/Ser F/4, New York, 1979) (hereafter referred to as *Resolutions*).

5. See, e.g., *No Peace-No War in the Middle East* (Sydney, 1969); "The 'November Resolution' and Middle East Peace—Pitfall or Guidepost?" *Univ. of Toledo L. Rev.* (1971), pp. 43-69; "Peace and the Palestinians" *N. Y. Univ. J. of Int. L. and Politics* 3 (1970): 247-62; "Behind the Cease-Fire Lines: Israel's Administration in Gaza and the West Bank," in S. Shoham, ed., *Of Law and Man: Essays in Honor of Haim H. Cohn* (New York, 1971); "Between Cease Fires in the Middle East," *Israel L. Rev.* 6 (1971): 165-87; "Palestinian Resolution: Zenith or Nadir of the General Assembly," *N. Y. Univ. J. of Int. L. and Politics* 1 (1975): 1-18. A number of these are reprinted (in whole or in part) in J. Norton Moore, *The Arab-Israel Conflict,* 3 vols. (Princeton, 1974), hereafter cited as "Norton Moore."

Chapter 1

1. Paragraphs 1 and 2 of Resolution 3236(XXIX), adopted Nov. 22, 1974, at the 2296th Plenary Meeting, also sought retrospectively to interpret references in earlier resolutions to "inalienable rights" of the Palestinian people as if they included the "rights of self-determination and national independence and sovereignty." See below Chapter 5 for discussion of these attempts to rewrite history.

For the full titles and citations of this series from the Committee on the Exercise of the Inalienable Rights of the Palestinian People, see *supra* Introduction, n. 4, where the abbreviations here in use are also listed.

2. *The Right to Self-Determination of the Palestinian People* (ST/SG/Ser F/2, 1979), p. 37. (Hereafter referred to as *Self-Determination.*)

3. J. C. Hurewitz, ed., *The Middle East, North Africa, and World Politics: A Documentary Record,* vol. 2, *British-French Supremacy, 1914-1945* (1956; rev. ed., New Haven,

1979), pp. 180-81. Thus, also, the second Palestine Conference held at Jericho on Dec. 1, 1948, in its first resolution, saw Palestine as historically "a part of natural Syria." See text in M. M. Whiteman, *Digest of International Law* 2 (Washington, D.C., 1963): 1163.

4. Quoted in James Dorsey, *Trouw,* Mar. 31, 1977.

5. See U.S. *Congressional Record,* vol. 53 (1916): 8854.

6. See *Foreign Relations of the United States,* Paris Peace Conference, 1919, vol. 12, pp. 781, 787 (Report of the King-Crane Commission of Aug. 28, 1919), repr. J. Norton Moore, ed., *The Arab-Israel Conflict* (1974), vol. 3, *Documents,* pp. 5 ff. (hereafter cited with volume number as Norton Moore). It is significant that this report did not ground its advocacy of a restrictive application of the Balfour Declaration on Palestinian-Arab nationalism, but, on the contrary, on the Syrian nature of the whole area and the shared hostility to Zionism of Arabs "throughout Syria." Much of the King-Crane report manifests the simplism of its recommendation that the United States become the single mandatory for all Syria, including Palestine. See 3 Norton Moore, pp. 56-59.

7. For texts cf. 3 Norton Moore 618 (original text of 1964) and 705 (revised text of 1968).

8. For convenient texts of the Covenant of 1966 and of the same as amended at Cairo in July 1968, see 3 Norton Moore 700-705, 706-11 respectively. The deadly Article 6, introduced in 1968 and maintained since, provided that only "the Jews who normally resided in Palestine until the beginning of the Zionist invasion will be considered Palestinians." It made quite explicit the threat already present in the 1966 version: "Jews *of Palestinian origin* shall be considered Palestinian if they desire to undertake to live in loyalty and peace in Palestine." (Emphasis supplied.) Loyalty to whom?

9. For the texts of the Feisal-Frankfurter exchange see 3 Norton Moore 43-44, and of the preceding Feisal-Weizmann Agreement of Jan. 3, 1919, 3 Norton Moore 40-42. Texts or extracts of the latter, of the Palestinian National Charter, its Mandate, and other key documents hereafter referred to will be found in the Documents section of the Appendixes.

10. See this exchange reprinted in 3 Norton Moore 6-21, passim.

11. See W. T. Mallison, "The Zionist-Israel Juridical Claims . . ." *Geo. Wash. Univ. L. Rev.* (1964), 983, at 1011. A main question-begging theme of that paper is that since Jews can be characterized only by religion (*sic*) Israel cannot be a Jewish state. Insofar as it is (on this view) not a Jewish state, it has no legitimate relation to the Jewish people. He is concerned, obviously, to support the campaign of the small but fanatically anti-Israel "American Council for Judaism," of which he was a former consultant.

12. Text in 3 Norton Moore 32, with surrounding documents at 4-49. The declaration went on to promise that the U.K.: "will use its best endeavours to facilitate the achievement of this object, it being clearly understood that nothing shall be done which may prejudice the civil and religious rights of the existing non-Jewish communities in Palestine, or the rights and political status enjoyed by Jews in any other country."

It was the understanding of the Jewish and Arab leaders not merely that there should be *a* Jewish home in Palestine, but that Palestine should be the Jewish homeland. This was also the intention of the British government. In the Frankfurter-Brandeis-Balfour Interview of June 24, 1919 (repr. 3 Norton Moore 46-49 from *Documents on British Foreign Policy, 1919-1939,* 1st ser. London: 1952, pp. 1276-78), Mr. Justice Brandeis put to Lord Balfour: "First, that Palestine should be the Jewish homeland and not merely that there be a Jewish Homeland in Palestine. That, he assumed, is the commitment of the Balfour Declaration . . ." (46). Balfour expressed entire agreement (47).

The suggestion sometimes made that Lord Balfour believed that the Jewish national home would conflict with the self-determination principle is a misleading wrenching of his words out of context. Balfour was merely explaining in the above interview why President Wilson's notion of sending a commission to each location in the Middle East "to find out *what the people really wanted*" was inappropriate and impractical. (Emphasis supplied.) The commitment was to "reconstitute the Jewish community," so that the test was not a "numerical majority" of Jews in Palestine now. Balfour was criticizing Wilson's naively simple proposal. With him, as with Emir Feisal, the two peoples to be endowed were the Jewish people and the Arab people (including the Palestinians, whose identity as a separate nation was still unconceived).

Nowhere in this discussion is there any evidence that Palestinian Arabs—as a national group—either existed or played any role. The target was Wilson's simplification. The use made in *Self-Detemination,* pp. 17-18, of certain quotations from Lord Balfour is misleading insofar as it ignores their true context, namely, the Anglo-French-American altercations about how to implement self-determination. Balfour was concerned emphatically to deny that the Arabs of Palestine (as distinct from Arabs of the Middle East generally) were even "on the way" to becoming a distinct nation; while (he said) the Jewish claims were "rooted in age-old traditions, in present needs, and in future hopes." (See 3 Norton Moore 46 ff.)

13. See the King-Crane Commission Report, Aug. 28, 1919 (U.S. Foreign Relations, Paris Peace Conference 1919, 787, repr. 3 Norton Moore 51, 55-56).

14. See *Origins,* pt. 1 p. 82, n. 7. The Feisal-Weizmann text is in 3 Norton Moore 40 and the Documents section of the Appendixes. See also ibid. for the Balfour Declaration.

15. It has been cogently argued, indeed, precisely on this basis, that under the principle of self-determination *"l'Etat d'Israël a été créé essentiellement par des Juifs arrivés en Palestine avant le Mandat."* So that on this ground as well as others, Israel as a state rests solidly on the principle of self-determination. See J. le Morzellec, *La Question de Jerusalem devant le O.N.U.* Thèse, Univ. de Jean-Moulin, Lyon III, 1976, vol. 1, p. 285, now published under the same title (Emile Bruylant: Brussels, 1979).

See Map 2 in the Appendixes (The Jews of Palestine before the Arab Conquest, 1000 BC-636 AD).

16. D. Hunter Miller, *My Diary at the Peace Conference at Paris,* vol. 4 (New York, 1924), p. 264.

17. Permanent Mandates Commission, Minutes of the 32d (Extraordinary) Session, 1837, *Report,* p. 229.

18. *Report of the Royal Commission, June 22, 1937.* Great Britain, Parliamentary Paper, C.M.D. 5479, pp. 8-9, here referred to as "Peel Commission Report."

19. The statement in para. 176 of the *U.N. Special Committee on Palestine, Report,* Sept. 3, 1947, United Nations General Assembly Official Records (U.N.G.A.O.R.) Supp. 11 (1947), 3 Norton Moore 259-312, that the principle of self-determination after World War I was not applied to Palestine "obviously because of the intention to make possible the creation of a Jewish National Home" proceeds on these compounded errors.

20. A main purpose of the excision was to create a throne for Emir Abdullah of Hedjaz—later King Abdullah—in the context of a conflict involving Abdullah and his brother Feisal (later King Feisal of Iraq), on one side, and the French government on the other. Another was to accommodate Palestinian Arabs, Transjordan being the major part of Mandated Palestine. Cf. the deprecation of this excision in the Peel Commission Report, Ch. 20, para. 20.

See Map 1 in the Appendixes (The Arab World, 1945-1962) and Map 3 (Britain and the Jewish National Home: Pledges and Border Changes, 1917-1923). For the Palestine Mandate of July 24, 1922, and the British Memorandum excising Transjordan therefrom, see the Documents section of the Appendixes.

21. International Court of Justice (I.C.J.) Reports, 1971, p. 4, at 31 ff. Cf. the Advisory Opinion on the International Status of S.W. Africa, I.C.J. Reports, 1950, p. 137; and the Opinion on Western Sahara, I.C.J. Reports, 1975, pp. 31 ff.

22. Cf. also the heavy labors involved in ascertaining the relation of "compromise" in the General Assembly, to the discovery of the "consistency" of that body's various relevant resolutions *inter se* (e.g., I.C.J. Reports, 1975, pp. 35 ff.)

23. Stephen M. Schwebel, "Wars of Liberation—as Fought in U.N. Organs," in J. N. Moore, ed., *Law and Civil War in the Modern World* (Baltimore, 1974), pp. 446-57, at

456-57. Cf. the formidable analysis of similar tenor by Professor G. Arangio-Ruiz, *The Normative Role of the General Assembly of the United Nations and the Declaration of Principles of Friendly Relations,* Hague Academy of International Law, *Recueil des Cours,* 1972-iii (Leyden, 1974), pp. 431-628, esp. 561-71. See the literature there cited at 561-63. And see infra the further examination of the writer's position in Ch. 2, sects. 2-4.

24. In "Wars of Liberation—as Fought in U.N. Organs," 455.

25. It may be that other parts also of the Friendly Relations resolution reinforce Professor Schwebel's conclusion. The preamble, for example, recited the "convictions" as: (1) the obligation of states not to intervene in the affairs of any other state and that "the practice of any form of intervention" violates and threatens international peace; (2) the obligation *of states* to refrain in their relations from "military, political, economic or other form of coercion aimed against the political independence or territorial integrity of *any State*"(emphasis supplied); (3) the obligation of states to refrain from threat or use of force in terms of Article 2(4) of the charter; (4) the principle of the sovereign equality of states; (5) the importance for friendly relations of states based on sovereign equality of the principle of equal rights and self-determination of peoples as a "significant contribution to contemporary international laws"; and (6) the conviction "that any attempt aimed at the partial or total disruption of the national unity and territorial integrity or political independence of a State" is "incompatible with the Charter" (unnumbered paras. 8, 9, 10, 12, 14-15). The preamble (in its penultimate paragraph) recited also a range of "considerations" similar to the convictions (1-5) above as a preliminary to the provisions as to the principle of equal rights and self-determination, freedom, and independence quoted, followed by those in paras. 7-8 of the section on threat or use of force as to prohibitions of the use of armed bands for incursions into another state, and (in the last two paragraphs of the section on self-determination) of action to "dismember or impair . . . the territorial integrity or political unity of sovereign and independent States" conforming to that principle, quoted in the text above.

26. See supra, n. 19. As of 1920, concludes the most comprehensive study yet made of the use of the name "Palestine," that term "included both banks of the Jordan." See B. Lewis, "Palestine: On the History and Geography of a Name," *International History Review,* 11, no. 1, pp. 1-12, at 11. This distinguished historian also points out that the River Jordan did not figure as a division either under the Romans (p. 3), or under Arab administration after the seventh-century Arab conquest (p. 4), or after the Arab defeat of the Crusaders (p. 5), nor even in nineteenth-century Christian usage (pp. 6-7).

27. According to L. W. Holborn, in *World Refugees* (Washington, D.C., American Association of University Women, Committee on International relations, 1960), truncated West Germany, after World War II, absorbed and rehabilitated no less than 5,978,000 displaced persons from Poland and 1,891,000 from Czechoslovakia. Austria received 178,000 Hungarian refugees in the aftermath of the Hungarian revolution of 1956 (Elfan Rees, *Century of the Homeless Man,* International Conciliation no. 515, New York, 1957). Italy received 585,000 Italians displaced from territory ceded to Yugoslavia, and from various parts of Africa. France received 1,372,000 refugees (including Algerian Moslems) displaced by emergent new states in North Africa and Indo-China (*New York Times,* Dec., 1961, Nov., 1962). The tiny Netherlands settled 230,000 refugees from Indonesia; Turkey resettled 150,000 Turks expelled from Communist Bulgaria. India and Pakistan, despite conditions of terrible passion and violence, resettled between them nearly fifteen million human beings. Israel itself, of course, even apart from refugees from Europe, received within her small area 700,000 Jews driven from their Arab "homelands."

It may be noted as a sample of the ratios of resettlement in new countries to repatriation after World War II, that of 1,208,586 persons assisted by the International Refugee Organization as of 1951, no less that 1,038,750 were resettled in new countries, and only 72,834 were repatriated to their country of origin or former domicile. In short, 86 percent were settled in new countries, and only 14 percent were repatriated. (Cf. L. W. Holborn, *The International Refugee Organisation* (London, 1956) 200-201.)

Ms. Holborn estimates (ibid., p. 15) that the dimensions of the displaced persons problem after World War II were of the order of eighty-one and one-half million, including at least twenty-one million Germans, eight and one-half million non-Germans in forced labor in Germany, twenty million non-German Europeans elsewhere, twenty million Chinese, and twelve million such persons in Japan.

The failure to solve by comparable methods the problem of half a million Arab refugees, mostly displaced during the same historical epoch as the displacements just cited, suggests deliberation rather than neglect.

28. For the purported bases of Jordan's claim to the right to amalgamate the West Bank with Jordan see: the resolutions of the Second Palestine Arab Conference held at Jericho, Dec. 1, 1948; the policy statement of the Jordanian Council of Ministers of Dec. 9, 1948, favoring the general election of Apr. 11, 1950, for a Jordanian parliament equally representing both Banks (in which 70 percent of the West Bank Arabs are claimed to have voted), and the resolution of unity of the newly elected National Assembly of Apr. 24, 1950. All of these are in M. M. Whiteman, *Digest of International Law* 2, 1163-67.

29. This position was reflected in Jordanian nationality policies. Palestinians other than Jews resident in Transjordan before Dec. 1949 became Jordanian citizens. Such Palestinians fleeing to Jordan after 1948 or to the West Bank after 1954 were also eligible for citizenship. During the Jordanian occupation of the West Bank there was considerable migration from the West Bank to the East, so that the West Bank sank from 62 percent to 38 percent of the whole Jordanian population; 400,000 Palestinian Arabs voluntarily migrated from the West to the East bank. Since 1967 Jordanian passports are also grantable to stateless Palestinians of Gaza.

30. See also the further discussion of this matter, infra Chap. 5, opening section, "Right of Return." And see Map 5 in the Appendixes (Jewish Refugees from Arab Lands, 15 May 1948-31 December 1967).

Chapter 2

1. Pp. 39-44.

2. Count Folke Bernadotte, Progress Report of Sept. 16, 1948, 3 United Nations General Assembly Official Records (U.N.G.A.O.R.), Supp. 11, 1-19, at 18, U.N.Doc.A/648, 21 Sept.-12 Dec. 1948.

3. *An International Law Analysis of the Major United Nations Resolutions Concerning the Palestine Question* (ST/SG/Ser F/4, N.Y.: 1979), (hereafter referred to as *Resolutions*).

4. Ibid.

5. See the voting figures in *Resolutions,* pp. 57 ff.

6. International Court of Justice (I.C.J.) Reports, 1955, pp. 115 ff. His further explanation that repeated flouting of such recommendations may overstep the "line between impropriety and illegality" (p. 120), has reference to the special case of exercise of standing supervisory competence over the trusteeship system under the charter. It is not of general application.

7. See *Institut de Droit International, Livre du Centenaire* (Basel, 1978) 268-70.

8. *The Development of International Law through the Political Organs of the United Nations* (London, Oxford University Press, 1963) 2.

9. Second phase, I.C.J., 1966, 6, at 248.

10. P. 5.

11. *Resolutions,* p. 8.

12. Ibid., pp. 3-4.

13. See generally for a recent and most valuable survey of the literature manifesting these doubts and disputes, Christoph Schreuer, "Recommendations and the Traditional Sources of International Law," *German Yearbook of International Law* 20 (1977): 103-18.

14. C. Schreuer, "Recommendations," p. 117.

15. See on the history and scope of this article, Stone, *Of Law and Nations* (1974) Ch. 8, pp. 231-51.

16. U.N.Doc.A/AC77/14, repr. Report of Special Committee on the Definition of Aggression, 1956, G.A.O.R. XII, Supp. no. 16 (A/3574 A/AC77, 1.13). Cf. the Soviet 1933 proposal in the League of Nations context, repr. in the Secretary-General's Report, G.A.O.R. VII, Ann. Agenda Item 54, pp. 34 ff. See Stone, *Aggression and World Order* (Berkeley, 1958), pp. 34-35, 201-2 (texts); 58-60, 66 ff. (discussion).

17. A/C.SR 1472, pp. 5-6. And see Stone, *Conflict Through Consensus* (Baltimore, 1977), pp. 87-104, and documentation there cited.

18. See the discussion in Stone, ibid., esp. pp. 96-104.

19. See ibid., pp. 101-5. See Map 7 in the Appendixes (European Dependence on Arab Oil, January-June, 1973) and Map 8 (Arab Oil Pressure, September-November, 1973).

20. See the discussion in Stone, ibid., pp. 103-4.

21. See, e.g., Mr. Jazic (Yugoslavia) U.N.Doc.A/C6SR 1442, pp. 13, 15 and related positions cited in Stone, *Conflict Through Consensus,* pp. 103-4.

22. Hague Academy of International Law, *Recueil des Cours,* vol. 1972-iii (Leyden, 1974), p. 419.

23. Ibid., p. 476, n. 26.

24. Security Council Resol. 338, 28 U.N. Security Council Official Records, Resol. and Dec. 1973, at 10, U.N.Doc.S/INF/29 provides:

The Security Council

1. *Calls upon* all parties to the present fighting to cease all firing and terminate all military activity immediately, no later than 12 hours after the moment of the adoption of this decision, in the positions they now occupy;

2. *Calls upon* the parties concerned to start immediately after the cease-fire the implementation of Security Council resolution 242 (1967) in all of its parts;

3. *Decides* that, immediately and concurrently with the cease-fire, negotiations start between the parties concerned under appropriate auspices aimed at establishing a just and durable peace in the Middle East.

For the text of Resolution 242 see the Documents section in the Appendixes.

25. See Stone, "The Palestinian Resolution, Zenith or Nadir of the General Assembly" *Journal of International Law and Politics* 1 (1975): 1-18.

26. The record shows no fewer than 181 P.L.O. attacks on civilians in Israel from June 12, 1967, to July 30, 1979, and no fewer than 201 P.L.O. attacks on aircraft, their passengers and crews, and on other civilians outside Israel from July 23, 1968, to July 30, 1979. The terrorist acts outside Israel attacked the sovereign rights, property, and nationals of at least forty states.

27. For Resolution 242 see appendix.

28. Resolution Adopted on the Report on the Ad Hoc Committee on the Palestine Question, G.A. Resol. 181(II), 2 U.N.G.A.O.R. Resol., at 131, U.N.Doc.A/519 (1947). Only the sense of Resol. 181(II) is here involved; as to the failure of this resolution to come into effect, see infra Ch. 4.

29. It is incorrect to assume that the names "Judea" and "Samaria" are archaic revivals by Israel authorities. Thus Sir John Glubb's *A Soldier with the Arabs* (London, 1957), p. 107, stated that "the three areas of Palestine which the Legion was charged to defend formed the three distinct districts of Samaria, Judea and Hebron." Sir John, of course, served the state of Jordan, not the state of Israel. So also, as of Dec. 30, 1939, the Palestine *Gazette* extraordinary no. 974 refers to the "Samaria District"; and the topographical map

of the Palestine Government's Department of Survey, 1937, even earlier, devotes a map to "Central Judea."

30. West of the river the areas are Israel (within the "Green Lines") 8461; West Bank, 2270; and Gaza, 140 square miles.

31. *Shuiun Falastiniyya* (Beirut, 1974)

32. Resolution 3236(XXIX), of Nov. 22, 1974, para. 5.

33. Ibid., at para. 6. The succeeding words in para. 6—"in accordance with the Purposes and Principles of the Charter"—are quite ambivalent as to whether any limits are to be read into that extraordinary appeal.

34. Press Release U.S.-U.N.-191(74), Dec. 6, 1974.

Chapter 3

1. The draft resolution (U.N.Doc.A/L521, June 26, 1967) was defeated on July 4, 1967, by seventy-one votes against twenty-two, with twenty-seven absentions (repr. 3 Norton Moore 782-84, 6 *International Legal Materials* [Washington D.C., 1962], 840).
See Map 4 in the Appendixes (The Arab Invasion of the State of Israel, May 15, 1948) and Map 6 (The Middle East Crisis, May 25-30, 1967).

2. L. Oppenheim, *International Law,* vol. 1, para. 130 (6th ed. by H. Lauterpacht, London, 1944), p. 266. This book is cited hereafter as "Oppenheim-Lauterpacht, *International Law.*"

3. See the Soviet note of Dec. 5 (3) 1929 [sic], *U.S. Foreign Relations,* Washington D.C., 1929, vol. 2, p. 405.

4. For the exchanges in the *Caroline Case* see Moore, *Digest of International Law* 2 (Washington, D.C., 1906): 409-14, and for discussion see Ch. 3 under "Aggression by Attacks by Armed Bands."

5. Soviet texts on the contrary continue to stigmatize as aggression hostilities that breach cease-fire and armistice agreements. See Academy of Sciences of the Soviet Union, *Course of International Law,* vol. 5 (1969), p. 405, as translated in N. Feinberg, "Sovereignty over Palestine," repr. in 1 Norton Moore 225, pp. 247-48. See for the cease-fire resolutions of 1948: Apr. 16, 1948, Security Council Official Records (S.C.O.R.), 3d year, Supp. for Apr., 1948, at 7-8, repr. 3 Norton Moore 341-42; May 22, 1948, S.C.O.R., 3d year Supp. for May, 1948, at 97, repr. 3 Norton Moore 359; May 29, 1948, S.C.O.R., 3d year, Supp. for May, 1948, at 3-4, repr. 3 Norton Moore 361; ditto Resol. of July 15, 1948, "Determining that the Situation in Palestine Constitutes a Threat to the Peace and Ordering a Cease-Fire," S.C.O.R., 3d year, Supp. for July, 1948, at 76-77, repr. in 3 Norton Moore 363-64.

6. These are too numerous and notorious to require listing here.

7. Cf. Q. Wright, "The Middle East Situation," *Law and Contemporary Problems* 33 (1968): 5, 17. See extracts repr. in 2 Norton Moore 107-32, esp. 114-16.

8. M. R. García-Mora, *International Responsibility for Hostile Acts of Private Persons against Foreign States* (The Hague, 1962), pp. 30-66 (hereafter cited as "García-Mora, *Responsibility* ").

9. Cf. Q. Wright, "The Prevention of Aggression," *Am. J. Int. L.* 50 (1956): 514, 527, there cited.

10. Agreeing with V. F. García-Amador, "State Responsibility in the Light of New Trends, . . ." *Am. J. Int. L.* 49 (1955): 339, at 345.

11. García-Mora, *Responsibility,* pp. 39-46.

12. E. de Vattel, *Le Droit des Gens,* trans. C. G. Fenwick, Bk. 2, Ch. 6, sect. 78, cited in García-Mora, *Responsibility,* p. 110.

13. García-Mora, *Responsibility,* pp. 112-13.

14. Ibid., pp. 113-14. Cf. J. Stone, *Aggression and World Order* (Berkeley, 1958), pp. 35, 115, 135, 201-8, 216, where the texts are also collected.

15. J. L. Kunz, "Sanctions in International Law" *Am. J. Int. L.* 54 (1960): 324, 331-32, citing U.S. Instructions, Law of Naval Warfare.

16. For which, see J. B. Moore, *Digest of International Law* 2 (Washington, D.C., 1906): 409-14.

17. García-Mora, *Responsibility*, pp. 115-30. He cites in support only Q. Wright, "U.S. Intervention in the Lebanon" *Am. J. Int. L.* 53 (1959): 112, 115. He also gives little or no attention to contrary positions, e.g., in J. Stone, *Legal Controls of International Conflict* (New York, 1954), pp. 243-81; idem, *Aggression and World Order,* pp. 92-103; idem, *Of Law and Nations* (Buffalo, 1974), Ch. 1, though he frequently cites the first of the above works.

18. See Stone, *Legal Controls,* esp. pp. 192-200, 207-16, 224-27, 243-81; idem, *Quest for Survival* (Cambridge, Mass., 1961), passim; idem, *Of Law and Nations,* Ch. 1, pp. 1-38.

19. García-Mora, *Responsibility,* pp. 119-20.

20. See the exchanges in J. B. Moore, *Digest of International Law* 2 (Washington, D.C., 1906): 409-14, and Professor García-Mora's observations, ibid., pp. 115 ff.

21. Professor García-Mora is gracious enough to cite my own view that self-defense cannot be thought of as part of what he terms "orderly world community processes." However, I did not mean this observation to deny that self-defense still enjoys a range of legal license by international law even after the charter's limitations on this range are delimited. What I meant, and what I spelled out on the very next page of the cited book, was rather somewhat to the contrary: we must recognize that international law, even as it is after the charter, does not actually embody such "orderly world community processes," even as to the major dimension of force associated with war. Consequently, to assume that there is a blanket prohibition of lesser coercions, while uses of major violence associated with war remain "licit or at least tolerated," might even be a disservice to peace as well as to international law. García-Mora, *Responsibility,* pp. 116-17, citing Stone, *Legal Controls of International Conflict* (1954), p. 287. And see ibid., p. 288.

22. Arab Summit, Khartoum, Sept. 1, 1967, summary of resolution repr. in 3 Norton Moore 787-88. Secretary of State Vance therefore was correct on the law when he observed in 1979 that it is "an open question as to who has the legal right to the West Bank." (Quoted by William Safire, *New York Times,* May 24, 1979.) It is regrettable in these circumstances that other U.S. spokesmen have asserted with less circumspection that Israel's entry onto the West Bank gave her only the status of a belligerent occupant under international law, and that therefore any settlement of Jews there is "illegal" as violating Article 49 of the Fourth Geneva Convention on the protection of civilian population. (Herbert Hansell, Apr. 21, 1978, reported ibid.) Cf. Ambassador Yost's Statement of July 1, 1969, in the Security Council, repr. 3 Norton Moore 993-94, which added that the occupied area was to be maintained "as intact and unaltered as possible" subject to "the immediate needs of the occupation."

This ignores the fact that because of the *ex iniuria* principle, Jordan never had nor now has any legal title in the West Bank, nor does any other state even claim such title. Article 49 seems thus simply not applicable. (Even if it were, it may be added that the facts of recent voluntary settlements seem not to be caught by the intent of Article 49 which is rather directed at the forced transfer of the belligerent's inhabitants to the occupied territory, or the displacement of the local inhabitants, for other than security reasons.) The Fourth Geneva Convention applies only, according to Article 2, to occupation of territory belonging to "another High Contracting Party"; and Jordan (as already explained) cannot show any such title to the West Bank, nor Egypt to Gaza.

At most the secretary of state's view of the law noted above can lead only to demands for some regime on the.West Bank that avoids attribution of sovereignty altogether. And this should provide common ground with Prime Minister Begin's position that "full autonomy" of the West Bank inhabitants is an autonomy of people that does not necessarily entail any attribution of ultimate sovereignty in territory. (See Chapter 8, final section, and Appendixes: Discourse 2.)

23. In response to the purported annexation, the Political Committee of the Arab League voted that this violated the League's antiannexation resolution of April 12, 1950, referring presumably to the League Council resolution of April 13, 1950, for text of which see H. A. Hassouna, *The League of Arab States and Regional Disputes* . . . (Dobbs Ferry, 1975), pp. 34-35. All other League members voted that the annexation violated the League resolution of April 13. Egypt, Saudi Arabia, Syria, and Lebanon voted on May 16, 1950, to expel Jordan from the League. After Iraqi mediation, Jordan, on May 31, 1950, informed the League that annexation was without prejudice to the final settlement of the Palestinian issue. See Arab League Note of Dec. 14, 1948, to Transjordan and subsequent proceedings in M. M. Whiteman, *Digest of International Law* 2 (Washington, D.C., 1963): 1164-67, and H. A. Hassouna, *The League of Arab States,* pp. 33-43.

For the U.K. recognition, see Whiteman, *Digest of International Law* 2 (Washington, 1963): 1167 (statement of Minister of State Younger in the House of Commons). It reserved two matters. One is the frontier between the annexed territory and Israel, left to the relevant Armistice Agreement or final settlement replacing it. The other was as to Jerusalem, where recognition of Jordan's sovereignty was expressly withheld, though Jordanian de facto authority in the area occupied by her was recognized. Subject to similar reservation the statement accorded *"de jure* recognition" to the State of Israel.

While there has been no formal U.S. recognition statement, Secretary of State Acheson told a press conference on April 26, 1950, after the West Bank and East Bank election, and before the new parliament "ratified" the amalgamation—"Now, our American attitude is that normally we have no objection whatever to the union of peoples mutually desirous of this new relationship." (Circular Telegram to certain diplomatic and consular offices, April 26, 1950. Ms. file 784.0214-2650, Whiteman, *Digest of International Law* 2 [Washington, D.C., 1963]: 1167.)

24. See, e.g., J. Stone, *No Peace—No War in the Middle East* (Sydney, 1967), pp. 34-35, repr. 2 Norton Moore 141-58; A. Lall, *The U.N. and the Middle East Crisis 1967* (New York, 1968), pp. 260-63 (as to the omission of the words "all the" before "territories"). And see J. Stone, "The 'November Resolution' and Middle East Peace," *Univ. of Toledo L. Rev.* (1971): 43-69 (repr. 2 Norton Moore 801-27).

For the official Security Council (S.C.) account, see Report of S.C., 16 July 1967-15 July 1968, 23 G.A.O.R. Supp. 2, 13-23, U.N.Doc.A/7202 (1968), 3 Norton Moore 1008-42. The relevant meetings were the 1373d (Nov. 9, 1967), 1379th (Nov. 16, 1967), 1381st (Nov. 20, 1967), and 1382d (Nov. 22, 1967). See esp. para. 90 (the unsuccessful draft of India, Mali, and Nigeria, S/8227, Nov. 7, 1967); para. 133 (the unsuccessful Soviet draft, S/8253 of similar import); para. 127 (the accepted Caradon [U.K.] draft, S/8247); paras. 128, 138, and 155-56 (Arab state rejection of the Caradon formula, as not requiring complete withdrawal); para. 141 (Indian attempted stipulation that Caradon draft required complete withdrawal); para. 143 (Caradon nonacceptance of Indian stipulation); para. 148 (Israel nonacceptance of Indian stipulation); paras. 146, 161 (various other members nonacceptance of Indian stipulation).

Syntactically, the Russian text is unambiguous, matching the English main negotiating text, and the Spanish text was finally corrected accordingly. The French text, for syntactic reasons, was ambiguous. See the elegant study in S. Rosenne, "On Multi-Lingual Interpretation," *Israel L. Rev.* 6 (1971): 360-66.

25. S.C.O.R. 22d year, 1360th meeting, June 14, 1967, p. 18. The majorities rejecting (including abstentions in each case) were of the order of 88 against 32, 98 against 22, 81 against 36, and 80 against 36. G.A.O.R. (E.S. V) 1548th Plenary Meeting, July 4, 1967,

p. 1416. See J. Stone, *The Middle East under Cease-Fire* (Sydney, 1967), sections II-IX, pp. 2-10.

26. See J. W. Halderman, ". . . Constitutional Aspects of the Palestine Case" in Symposium, "The Middle East Crisis and International Law," *Law & Contemporary Problems* 33 (1968): 1-193, at 79, 89-90.

27. Cf. A. Lall, *The U.N. and the Middle East Crisis 1967* (1968), p. 247, quoting Abba Eban in the Security Council, S.C.O.R., 22d year 1375th meeting, 13 Nov. 1967, para. 49, Nov. 13, 1967, S/PV.1375, p. 28.

The Security Council's two 1980 resolutions on Jerusalem (Resol. 476 and Resol. 478) "reaffirm" this recital from Resolution 242 (1967). They are still subject, in this aspect, to the comments and conclusions in the text and cannot bear the meaning that Arab States target on Israel while rejecting it for themselves.

28. See the analysis of the drafting in J. Stone, *Conflict through Consensus* (Baltimore, 1977) 56-66. The Thirteen-Power Draft ("Third World" Draft) (A/AC.134/L.16 and Add. 1 & 2) para. 8, had proposed a text harmonious with the Arab state desire. See infra under "Arab States' Resistance to *ex iniuria non oritur ius*" and later sections. on other aspects of this definition important for understanding the matters here discussed.

29. After this failure of their main efforts, the Arab states then sought the inclusion in para. 20 of the Special Committee's Report (G.A.O.R., 29th session, Supp. no. 19 (A/9619 and Corr. 1)) of an enigmatic Note 4: "4. With reference to the third paragraph of Art. 5. . . . this paragraph should not be construed so as to prejudice the established principles of international law relating to the inadmissibility of territorial acquisition resulting from the threat or use of force." Since, as indicated in the text, international law is precisely what Article 5 (as distinct from Arab counterproposals) affirmed, the purport of the note seems to be to keep alive the precise words of the relevant recital in Resol. 242, in the hope presumably that its first sight ambiguity could continue to be exploited by the Arab side in the Middle East conflict. (See Stone, *Conflict through Consensus* [Baltimore, 1977], pp. 63-64.)

30. See above, Ch. 2, esp. the first sections.

31. P. v.

32. A curiosity within a curiosity. It presumably refers to *travaux préparatoires* available other than in official U.N. records. *Sed quaere?* And it is positively startling thereafter to find the authors on p. 26 deliberately invoking the negotiating history of the Palestine mandate to make a point that the authors, at any rate, believe favorable to Arab claims.

33. See Stone, *No Peace—No War in the Middle East*, pp. 33-35, and the decisive details of the *travaux préparatoires* cited supra n. 24.

34. *Resolutions*, p. 41. Cf. the description of the distinguished Professor Nathan Feinberg as a "Zionist lawyer," ibid., p. 26.

35. The only real use the authors seek to make of this supposedly "basic juridical distinction" is for ventilating some criticisms of the early Jewish liberation movement, or of Israel by rather isolated Jewish individuals and a few extreme Jewish religious sects. See ibid., pp. 9-14, passim. And whatever else is to be said about this use, it is in no sense "juridically basic" to the Mallisons' terms of reference.

36. Ibid., pp. 9-17.

37. *The Origins and Evolution of the Palestine Problem* (New York, 1978), 2 pts. (ST/SG/Ser F/1); pt. 1, pp. 35-37. (Hereafter referred to as *Origins*.)

38. Another credential claimed by Professor Mallison in his principal other publication in this area is that he was at one time a consultant of the American Council for Judaism, a group formed to oppose the establishment of the state of Israel. See W. T. Mallison, "The Zionist-Israel Juridical Claims . . ." *Geo. Wash. Univ. L. Rev.* 32 (1964): 983-1074, on the "defamatory" and "question-begging" and "amateurish" allegations against which see Ben Halpern, "The Anti-Zionist Phobia—Legal Style" *Midstream* 2 (1965): 74-85. These writings

are reprinted respectively in 1 Norton Moore 88-177, and 179-90. See especially 1 Norton Moore 181-82, 185-86, and 187-88.

Chapter 4

1. General Assembly Official Records (G.A.O.R.) Resolutions Sept. 16-Nov. 29, 1947, pp. 131 ff., repr. 3 Norton Moore 314-39. (These resolutions are not to be confused with the study here referred to as *Resolutions,* concerning which see supra, "Introduction," at n. 4.)

2. *Resolutions,* p. v.

3. *Resolutions,* pp. 22-23.

4. See, e.g., H. Cattan, *Palestine and International Law* (2d ed., London, 1976), on which the authors heavily rely.

5. Pp. 24-25.

6. See G.A.O.R. 1st Special Session, Plenary, Gen. series, U.N.Doc.A/286.

7. The *locus classicus* is Sir Hersch Lauterpacht's concurring opinion in the S.W. Africa Voting Procedure Advisory Opinion, International Court of Justice (I.C.J.) Reports, 1955, pp. 67, 115 ff. And see D.H.N. Johnson, "The Effect of Resolutions of the General Assembly, . . ." *B.Y.B. Int. L.* 32 (1955-56): 97. See supra under "Standing of Resolutions: Simplistic Assumptions."

8. E. Lauterpacht, *Jerusalem and the Holy Places* (London, 1968), p. 39, repr. in 2 Norton Moore, 929-1009, at 960.

9. Ibid.

10. Ibid. And see supra, Ch. 3.

11. Certainly, insofar as all the parties concerned allowed it to become operative, it would become binding on them and on all concerned. And it was on this assumption, that it might still become operative, that Moshe Shertok, speaking for the Jewish Agency, distinguished at the time between this partition resolution and other resolutions of the General Assembly, and stated on April 27, 1948, that the partition resolution would (that is, if it became operative) have a binding force. U.N.Doc.A/C/SR 127, p. 7. The context was a particular and ephemeral one of 1948, namely, whether the General Assembly would be able to revoke the 1947 resolutions and impose a U.N. trusteeship on Palestine. This statement is quoted in *Resolutions* 25-26, in disregard of context, and of the assumption that the resolution was to become operative.

12. Official translation in *Laws of the State of Israel,* Vol. 1, *Ordinances, 5708-1948* (Jerusalem, 1948), pp. 3-5, repr. in 3 Norton Moore, pp. 349-51, and in the Documents section of the Appendixes.

13. *Resolutions,* p. 26.

14. As already noted, the Arab states were on this account subject, under para. C of the Partition Resolution, to Security Council action against them as aggressors. The Mallisons themselves, as already observed, blow hot and cold as to whether, at its moment of proposed implementation, the Partition Resolution was or was not "valid," let alone binding on the states concerned (see above, Ch. 4, and *Resolutions,* pp. 23-25). But one is finally told (p. 27) that, viewed from 1979, thirty-one years after the Arab states launched the aggression that prevented its ever coming into force, "it is not possible to conclude as a matter of law that it was invalid per se."

15. Security Council Official Records (S.C.O.R.), 3d year, No. 72, 302d Meeting, p. 43.

See Map 4 in the Appendixes (The Arab Invasion of the State of Israel, May 15, 1948).

16. S.C.O.R., 3rd year, No. 71, 299th Meeting, p. 7. For pertinent resolutions of the Security Council on the hostilities resulting from the Arab invasion, 1948-49, see the Documents section of the Appendixes.

17. *Resolutions,* pp. 25-27.

18. Ibid., pp. 26-27.

19. This is the nearest reference the Mallisons permit themselves to the war of aggression by which the Arab states prevented the resolution ever coming into effect.

20. Presumably the authors mean to refer by this "violation of the self-determination principle" to the recognition of Israel's right of self-determination.

21. Except perhaps those which affect the duties and authorities of the Secretariat and other U.N. officers.

22. *Resolutions,* pp. 25-27, at 27.

23. They draw a distinction, on p. 27, between this question of validity and what they call "subsequent effectuation," and urge that lack of the latter does not affect the former. But the question whether the plan came into legal operation is different from both of these. Obviously the question whether the resolution ever came into legal effect is also different from whether, after they did so, the parties concerned observed it.

24. For these quite explicit objectives of the attack see the statements collected in (1946-48) Keesing's *Contemporary Archives,* 9244; e.g., on the intent to seize the whole of Palestine, King Abdullah's statement of April 22, 1948, and the decision of the Arab League Premiers and Foreign Ministers of December 8 and 17, 1947, declaring the intent to enter battle against the U.N. decision to partition Palestine. See G.A.O.R., Second Session, Plenary, vol. 2, p. 1425 (Saudi Arabia); ibid., p. 1427 (Iraq, Syria, Yemen), S.C.O.R. (third year) no. 25, p. 299 (Egypt); S.C.O.R. (third year), Supp. for May 1948, p. 90, and U.N.Doc.S/748 (1948) (Jordan).

Cf. the surprised regret of Mr. Gromyko (U.S.S.R.) that Arab states were "carrying out military operations aimed at the suppression of the national liberation movement in Palestine" (i.e., of the new state of Israel). (S.C.O.R. [Third Year], no. 71, p. 7.) For the formal Security Council determination that the Arab states' actions constituted "a threat to the peace" under Article 39 of the charter, see Security Council Resol. 54 (1948) of July 15, 1948.

25. Reported by William Safire, *New York Times,* May 24, 1979.

26. P. 27.

Chapter 5

1. *Resolutions,* pp. 31-37.

2. Ibid., pp. 31-32. Certainly they were so treated by the commission. See, e.g., as to refugees, the negotiations reported in the U.N. Conciliation Commission Report of June 21, 1949, 4 G.A.O.R. [General Assembly Official Records] Ad Hoc Political Committee, Annex to Summary Records, vol. ii at 5-9 (1949), repr. 3 Norton Moore 485 ff. The commission there concluded that the immediate problem facing the commission consisted in linking together the negotiations on the refugee problem and those on "territorial questions" (ibid. at 9). In its next report (Dec. 11, 1949-Oct. 23, 1950, 5 G.A.O.R. Supp. 18, 1-21, 30-31, repr. 3 Norton Moore 496-537) the commission observed in Ch. 1, paras. 3-5, that as between the Arab states' position that Israel's acceptance of the right to return was a preliminary *sine qua non* to all negotiation, and Israel's willingness to discuss this in the framework of peace negotiations, the commission "did not consider it possible to separate any one problem from the rest of the peace negotiations or from the final peace settlement." This was in reply to the Arab states' reliance on para. 11 of Resol. 194(III) on refugees. And in its Supplementary Report of Oct. 23, 1950, paras. 8-9 (3 Norton Moore 538, 540-41) the commission called for attention to possible resettlement with compensation "in the Arab countries" of refugees, as also called for by Resol. 194(III). Cf. also the conclusions in paras. 83-85 of the commission's Report of Jan. 23 to Nov. 19, 1951, 6 G.A.O.R. Supp. 18 at 1-10, repr. 3 Norton Moore 544-67 at 566-67.

3. This is made even clearer since the immediately preceding recital refers to Israel "unreservedly accepting" the obligations of the charter. See M. van Dusen, "Jerusalem, the Occupied Territories, and the Refugees," in M. Khadduri, ed., *Major Middle Eastern Problems in International Law* (1972), pp. 37, 55-56, for contrary Arab positions. However, as N. Feinberg ("Arab-Israel Conflict in International Law" (1970), repr. in 1 Norton Moore 386-93) has pointed out, the Arab representatives at the General Assembly meeting of May 11, 1949, admitting Israel, complained precisely that she was admitted without having given the assurances that they had demanded.

4. See Elihu Lauterpacht, *Jerusalem and the Holy Places* (London, 1968), pp. 27 ff.

5. *Resolutions,* pp. 34 ff.

6. *Resolutions,* pp. 28-30.

7. *Self-Determination,* ST/SG/Ser.F/3 (1979). For the full title and citation of this study see supra "Introduction" at n. 4.

8. *Self-Determination,* p. 1.

9. Ibid.

10. See R. Rao, "The Right of Self-Determination: Its Status and Role in International Law," *Internationales Recht und Diplomatie* (1968), pp. 24-28. And see infra at n. 27.

11. See below under "Is Self-Determination Prescribed by International Law" and "Inter-Temporal Law and Self-Determination."

12. *Self-Determination,* p. 5, and see generally, pp. 1-13.

13. See, e.g., on pp. 5, 19-20, the invocations of W. E. Hocking, *The Spirit of World Politics* (New York, 1932), pp. 196, 354, 372-74.

14. P. 12.

15. P. 12.

16. At pp. 12-13. Their main authority on *ius cogens* is a statement of Mr. Gros Espiel, Implementation of United Nations Resolutions, E/C.N.4/Sub.2/405, esp. at 33-35. They also cite Professor Georg Schwarzenberger, *International Law and Order* (New York, 1971) as if in support of their positions. This is startling, to say the least. That book contains a long and penetrating chapter (pp. 27-56) on *ius cogens,* but not a word that supports such a status of the self-determination principle, and much that implies a denial of it. For example, the most pertinent principle that that distinguished author believes to approach *ius cogens* status, is the principle forbidding premature recognition of insurgent movements against established states—a view obviously not sanctifying "wars of liberation" (32-33). Conversely, he denies *ius cogens* status to any rule imposing affirmative obligations to recognize even entities meeting the full qualifications of statehood (p. 33). How much more, therefore, would he deny this status to the supposed duty to recognize (and indeed assist) self-determination movements, which usually involve disruption or destruction of established states.

Nor in this misleading presentation of Professor Schwarzenberger as elevating the self-determination principle to *ius cogens* status on the basis of resolutions of the General Assembly do these anonymous authors trouble to mention his trenchant view (with which I agree) on this very matter. This is that where the General Assembly's authority is to "recommend," "no repetition, however insistent, can transform the right of individual Member States not to take any action on any such recommendation into . . . a legal duty to accept such a recommendation" (p. 44). Nor do they care to notice that author's deep scepticism as to the *ius cogens* doctrine embodied in Article 53 itself, as to which he makes a sharp distinction between its "legal ambit" and its abuse in "ideological warfare." (See ibid., pp. 53-54.) All this was to be expected from an author who, in his work *Frontiers of International Law* (London, 1962), pp. 308 ff., did not even include the right of self-determination in his discussion of "fundamental rights and freedoms."

These matters suggest disquieting departures from standards of scholarship and collegiality in the Secretariat unit on Palestinian rights.

17. This was in a report of Mr. Aureliu Cristescu as Special Rapporteur for the Commission on Human Rights, Sub-Commission on Prevention of Discrimination and Protection of Minorities. See E/CN.4/Sub.2/404 (vol. 1) July 3, 1978. "The Historical and Current Development of the Right of Self-Determination on the Basis of the Charter of the U.N. and other Instruments Adopted by U.N. Organs, with Particular Reference to the Promotion and Protection of Human Rights and Fundamental Freedoms." The statement quoted is in para. 152. Mr. Cristescu's study is no less clear in para. 153 where it states that "No United Nations instrument places equal rights and self-determination of peoples among the general principles of law," and that "equal rights and self-determination of peoples cannot be regarded as general principles of law."

The authors of *Self-Determination* do not refer to Mr. Cristescu's report on these points.

18. *Self-Determination*, pp. 14-21. On the liberation drive of the so-called "Basle Program" drawn up by this Congress, see 3 Norton Moore 4. And see supra Ch. 1, n. 12.

19. At pp. 22-28.

20. At p. 32.

21. See supra passim, esp. Ch. 1-2.

22. Pp. 33-37.

23. *Resolutions*, sec. IV, pp. 39-48.

24. It was in fact shortly preceded by an oblique reference in Resol. 2649 of November 30, 1970.

25. P. 33.

26. Ser.F/3, p. 37.

27. See R. Rao, "The Right of Self-Determination: Its Status and Role in International Law" *Internationales Recht und Diplomatie* (1968), 24-28.

Chapter 6

1. *Resolutions*, pp. 39-48.

2. Ibid., p. 8.

3. Ibid. See Ch. 2, text accompanying notes 11-12.

4. Ibid., pp. 22-27.

5. Ibid., p. 27.

6. Ibid., pp. 44-46. They deal first with the Partition Resolution of 1947 as the first recognition of "the Palestinian National Right of Self-Determination" (p. 44). In view of the emphatic conclusion in the *Self-Determination* pamphlet dating General Assembly recognition from about 1970, this must have been a recognition by anticipation, or even perhaps, self-fulfilling prophecy. See supra, Ch. 1, under "Parallel Liberations: 'Arab Asia' and Jewish Palestine," and Ch. 2, under "Pronouncements on Palestinian Self-Determination."

7. *Resolutions*, pp. 46 ff.

8. Ibid., p. 47.

9. Doc.A/31/35, para. 33.

10. *The International Status of the Palestinian People* (1979), pp. 22-29, at 27. Published by the United Nations, New York, with the description—"Prepared for, and under the guidance of the Committee on the Exercise of the Inalienable Rights of the Palestinian People." No author is disclosed.

11. *Resolutions*, p. 47.

12. See, e.g., General Assembly (G.A.) Resol. 3236(XXIX) of Nov. 22, 1974, paras. 5, 6 (89 for, 8 against, 37 abstentions); G.A. Resol. 32/14 of Nov. 7, 1977 (113 for, 3 against, 18 abstentions).

13. U.N.Doc.A/5746, p. 42.

14. See Stephen M. Schwebel, "Wars of Liberation—as Fought in U.N. Organs," in J. N. Moore, *Law and Civil War* (Baltimore, 1974), pp. 446, 446-48. Cf. on the lack of international legal basis for the Indian action, Q. Wright, "The Goa Incident," *Am. J. Int. L.* 56 (1962): 617.

15. For the text of the Consensus Definition see appended documents.

16. G.A. Res. 2625(XXV). For a commentary on the Declaration see R. Rosenstock, "The Declaration of Principles of International Law Concerning Friendly Relations: A Survey," *Am. J. Int. L.* 65 (1971): 713-35.

17. G.A. Resol. 2734(XXV), para. 18.

18. A/C.6/SR.1477, pp. 9-10. This, in substance, was also the position of M. Bessou (France). Article 7 was "alien to the text" since not concerned with "aggression as defined in Article 1, i.e. between sovereign States." The text did not guarantee that States supporting self-determination struggles could not be guilty of aggression. See General Assembly Official Records (G.A.O.R.) (XXIX) Supp. No. 19 (A/9619), p. 22, repr. B. B. Ferencz, *Defining International Aggression* (Dobbs Ferry, Oceana, 1975), p. 73. So also U.S. Delegate Rosenstock, A/CS.R.1480, p. 24 (also in G.A.O.R.(XXIX) Supp. No. 19 (A/9619), p. 24).

19. A/C.6/SR.1478, pp. 13-14.

20. Soviet bloc spokesmen would no doubt justify the continued suppression of Baltic, Ukrainian, and Jewish nationalist aspirations as "ordinary police action" in M. Ustor's term. The bland assumption that they can have it both ways is not surprising if we recall that as to the ten States with which the Soviet Union made treaties containing a definition of aggression, she sooner or later committed acts against most of them clearly falling within the agreed definition. See S. Schwebel, *Aggression, Intervention and Self-Defence, Hague Recueil* (1972) vol. 2, 419, at 443. These lectures were of course delivered in the author's personal capacity.

21. A/C.6/SR.1478, p. 3.

22. A/C.6/SR.1472, p. 15.

23. Cf. B. B. Ferencz, "Defining Aggression: Where It Stands and Where It's Going," *Am. J. Int. L.* 66 (1972): 491, 498.

Three main proposals by states were before the Special Committee, namely, from (1) U.S.S.R. (A/AC.134/L.12); (2) Columbia, Cyprus, Ecuador, Ghana, Guyana, Haiti, Iran, Madagascar, Mexico, Spain, Uganda, Uruguay, and Yugoslavia ("Thirteen-Power Draft," A/AC.134/L.16 and Add. 1 and 2); and (3) Australia, Canada, Italy, Japan, U.K., U.S.A. ("Six-Power Draft (A/AC.134/L.17 and Add. 1 and 2). (These appear in Annex. 1 to the Special Committee's 1970 Report, G.A.O.R. (XXV) Supp. no. 19 (A/5019) pp. 55-60, repr. in G.A.O.R. (XXVIII) Supp. No. 19 (A/9619), pp. 7-12. In addition a Consolidated Text, with notes and table of state proposals, was prepared in 1973 ("Consolidated Text," Appendix A to the Special Committee's 1973 Report, G.A.O.R. (XXVIII) Supp. no. 19 (A/9019), pp. 15-21).

24. A/C.6/SR.1475, pp. 10-11.

25. A/AC.134/SR.111, pp. 10-11.

26. Originally in Doc. A/C.6/L264, G.A.O.R., Seventh Session, Annexes, Agenda Item 54, and repeated verbatim in subsequent draft definitions submitted by the U.S.S.R. delegation. Drafts of the armed bands clause in various U.N. committee proceedings are collected in J. Stone, *Aggression and World Order* (Berkeley, 1958), pp. 201 ff., including notably by Paraguay (202), Iran and Panama (203), Mexico (203), Dominican Republic et al. (204-5), Bolivia (205), U.N. Secretariat (from G.A.O.R. [IX] Supp. No. 9 [a/2693] ciii, p. 2), M. Yepes (207), M. Hsu (207), M. Cordova (207), China (208), Mr. Robert H. Jackson (216).

27. Op. cit. supra n. 23. Mr. Ferencz (*Defining International Aggression,* vol. 2 [Dobbs Ferry, 1975], pp. 48-49) in his sharpest censure of the 1974 Definition, observes that the

opposing parties might interpret it to their own advantage should the need arise. And cf. ibid., pp. 22-23, on the "vexing dilemma" of "how to reaffirm the right to self-determination and still restrain the use of force."

28. S. Schwebel, "Aggression, Intervention, and Self-Defense in Modern International Law," in Hague Academie de Droit International, *Recueil des Cours* 1972-ii (Leyden, 1974), pp. 411-97, at 419.

29. On the various drafts see supra n. 23.

30. Presumably "to that end" refers to "the right of self-determination, etc."; but not clearly so.

31. Article 3(e) stigmatizing the use of one state's armed forces, which are by agreement of a host state within the territory of that state, contrary to agreed conditions, or beyond the agreed term, may raise related questions. This provision was proposed in the Six-Power Draft (para. IV.B.[2]). See A/AC.134/L.7 and Add. 1 and 2, repr. A/9019 (1973), pp. 11-12. It has other problems of its own. Since, unlike the original Six-Power Proposal (A/8019, Doc. 18 at 58, 60), Article 3(e) states the offense without any qualifications as to the purpose or intent, the fault stigmatized might be quite trivial. Cf. Ferencz, *Defining International Aggression,* vol. 1, p. 38. Presumably the Security Council could exculpate such trivia under Article 2 of the definition. On the other hand, Article 3(e) situations that are not trivial might be thought to be caught in any case by Article 3(a), as a kind of constructive "invasion."

32. A/C.6/SR.1477, p. 6.

33. The Italian representative, A/C.6/SR.1472, p. 10. Cf. the Kenyan representative, A/C.6/SR.1474, p. 9.

34. As to the impotence of the host state in face of such unlawful use of its hospitality see the Politis Report of 1933 (Conf. D/CG./108; Conf. D./C.P./C.RS19).

35. See generally D. W. Bowett, "Reprisals Involving Recourse to Armed Force," *Am. J. Int. L.* 66 (1972): 1, and esp. 20. The analysis in R. A. Falk, "The Beirut Raid and the International Law of Retaliation" *Am. J. Int. L.* 63 (1969): 415, esp. 434-38, is centrally affected by uncertainty as to whether the incident in question was to be judged as a peacetime reprisal, as Y. Z. Blum ("The Beirut Raid and the International Double Standard" *Am. J. Int. L.* 64 [1970]: 73) points out (at 78). Other issues included the relevance of international law authorities (including Lauterpacht-Oppenheim, Kelsen, and the International Law Commission) asserting the international law responsibility of the host state in respect of operations of armed bands from its territory (see citations in Blum, ibid., pp. 79-87), and the adequacy of notices given to Lebanon (see ibid., pp. 87-89). (Citations ibid., pp. 87-89.)

36. See G.A.O.R. (XXV), Supp. no. 19, A/8019, Doc. 18, pp. 47-48, paras. 131-34. And see on the Soviet position, A/AC.6/SR.63, p. 5 (Mr. Schwebel) and A/AC.6/SR.74, p. 8 (Mr. Steel), and Ferencz, *Defining International Aggression,* vol. 2 (Dobbs Ferry, 1975), p. 46. And see U.N.Doc.A/AC.134/SR./97, p. 4 for the Soviet reasoning on burden of proof.

For further detailed discussion of the varied attitudes of states on these matters in the 1967 Special Committee, see J. Stone, *Conflict Through Consensus* (Baltimore, 1977), pp. 74-76, 80-86. The text of the 1974 Definitions will be found in the Documents section of the Appendixes.

37. A/9019 (1973), p. 19.

38. The Consolidated Text stated in para. 6 of the preamble of the duty of states not to use armed force to deprive peoples of their right to "self-determination, freedom and independence." In the final draft of the Consensus Definition there was added, "or to disrupt territorial integrity." This might be read to imply that any license to support self-determination ceases at the point when such support would disrupt the territorial integrity of a state. This would support the Western view of the final articles 6 and 7.

39. See, e.g., among studies denying or severely constricting any such existing legal right, Muhammed Aziz Shakri, *The Concept of Self-Determination in the United Nations*

(1965); Calogeropoulos-Shatis, *Le Droit des Peuples à Disposer d'Eux-Mêmes* (1973). And cf. R. Rao, "The Right of Self-Determination," *Internationales Recht und Diplomatie* (1968), pp. 24-28.

40. See U.N. press release NB/464/30 Sept. 1975. Also U.K. Parliamentary Papers, Cmd. 6198 (1975); Dept. of State Bulletin, vol. 76, no. 1888, p. 323.

41. See the record of debate in the U.N. *Monthly Chronicle,* vol. 13, no. 3 (March 1976): 5-14, and the historical discussion in J. Binet, "Les Comores au seuil de l'independence," *Afrique Contemporaine* 84 (Mar.-Apr., 1976): 16-20, esp. 19-20.

42. See Stone, *Conflict Through Consensus* (Baltimore, 1977) 139-40, and passim.

43. See Map 2 in the Appendixes (The Jews of Palestine before the Arab Conquest, 1000 BC-636 AD).

Chapter 7

1. See *Origins,* pt. 2, pp. 36-37, and *Resolutions,* pp. 49-54. For full titles and citations see supra, Introduction, n. 4.

2. *The Status of Jerusalem,* United Nations, N.Y.: 1979, stated to be "prepared for and under the guidance" of the committee, but disclosing no author. It will here be referred to as *"Jerusalem."* And see the earlier accounts in *Resolutions,* pp. 49-54, *Origins,* pt. 2, pp. 36 ff.

3. *Jerusalem,* p. 26 and passim.

4. See R. H. Pfaff, *Jerusalem: Keystone of an Arab-Israel Settlement* (Washington, D.C., 1969), pp. 24-26, 29-31, and documents there cited. This work will here be cited as "Pfaff."

5. Pfaff, p. 23. For the Draft Statute of April 21, 1948, see Trusteeship Council Official Records, 2d session, 3d para., Annex Doc.T/118/Rev. 2, Annex, 4-24, repr. 3 Norton Moore 425-45. Other drafts discussed included: U.N. Conciliation Commission Draft Instrument Establishing a Permanent Regime for the Jerusalem Area, Sept. 1, 1949, G.A.O.R. (IV) Ad Hoc Political Committee, Annex at 10-14, U.N. A/973 (1949), repr. 3 Norton Moore, 447-56, General Assembly (G.A.) Resol. 303(IV) Concerning an International Regime for Jerusalem . . . Dec. 9, 1949, G.A. Resol. 303(IV), Resols. Sept. 20-Dec. 10, 1949, at 25, repr. 3 Norton Moore, 458-59; Statute for Jerusalem Approved by Trusteeship Council, April 4, 1950, U.N. Doc.A/1286 (1950), repr. 3 Norton Moore 461-83.

6. On this movement away from the *corpus separatum,* see M. van Dusen, "Jerusalem, the Occupied Territories, and the Refugees," in M. Khadduri, ed., *Major Middle Eastern Problems in International Law* (Washington, D.C., 1972), 38 ff. He points out that as Arab attacks ceased, the General Assembly instructed the Conciliation Commission to "propose" an international regime for the Jerusalem area, and that the commission recommended (of course, inconsistently with the Partition Proposal) that Israel and Jordan administer the respective areas controlled by them, while a United Nations administration would control the holy places. This is substantially what we have here called a mere functional plan. The documents are cited ibid. Cf. S. S. Jones, "The Status of Jerusalem," *Law and Contemporary Problems* 33 (1968): 169-82, repr. 1 Norton Moore, pp. 915-28, esp. 923-25.

7. *Yearbook of the U.N.* (1948-49), p. 171.

8. *Jerusalem,* pp. 5-7.

9. Ibid., pp. 9-10.

10. See, e.g., pp. 16, 22.

11. At p. 10.

12. General Assembly Official Records (G.A.O.R.), 3d session, pt. 2, Ad Hoc Political Committee, 46th meeting, p. 254.

13. This characterization is from the committee's *Jerusalem* pamphlet itself, p. 12.

14. *Jerusalem,* p. 14.

15. Ibid., p. 13.

16. Ibid., p. 26.

17. See *Resolutions,* pp. 45-54, esp. at 50-51.

18. The lines are between pp. 49-50 and pp. 51-54 of *Resolutions.*

19. For the Jordanian parliament's Resolution of Annexation of April 24, 1950, see Keesing's *Contemporary Archives* 8 (1950-52): 10,812. For the Israeli rejection see Foreign Minister Sharrett's statement of April 25, 1950 (5 Divrei HaKnesset [Parliamentary Records]), p. 1282, col. 1 (transl. in Y. Z. Blum, "The Juridical Status of Jerusalem," in John M. Oesterreicher and A. Sinai, eds., *Jerusalem* [New York, 1974], p. 108). On the Arab League's rejection and other reactions, see the short account in Blum, ibid., pp. 116 ff., and documents in (1950-52) 8 Keesing 10,912. As others have well pointed out, on May 31, 1967, with the June War impending, the Jordanian representative in the Security Council, Mr. El-Farra, seemed to admit the legal ineffectiveness of the annexation when he said that the Armistice Agreement "did not pass judgment on rights. . . . Thus I know of no boundary; I know of a situation frozen by an Armistice Agreement." Security Council Official Records (S.C.O.R.) 22nd year, S/P V 1345, para. 84.

It may be added, for completeness, that the U.K., one of the two states that clearly recognized the annexation, did not do so as to East Jerusalem, and many states made reservations as to this. On the U.S. attitude see M. M. Whiteman, *Digest of International Law* 2 (Washington, D.C., 1963): 1163-68. On the Arab League's positions see H. A. Hassouna, *The League of Arab States . . .: A Study of Middle East Conflicts* (Dobbs Ferry, Oceana, 1975), p. 33. Jordan was admitted to the U.N. by Resol. 995(X) of Dec. 14, 1955. Further, the purported annexation flatly violated the status quo "freezing" effect of Art. 11(2) of the Israel-Jordan General Armistice Agreement. It also violated the rule that a *mere* belligerent occupant may not annex as long as the war continues: cf. J. Stone, *Legal Controls of International Conflict* (New York, 1954), p. 720; H. Kelsen, *Principles of International Law* (2d edition, ed. R. Tucker, New York, 1967), p. 139; G. von Glahn, *The Occupation of Enemy Territory* (Minneapolis, 1957), p. 390; E. Castrén, *Present Law of War and Neutrality* (Helsinki, 1954), pp. 215-16; M. Greenspan, *Modern Law of Land Warfare* (Berkeley, 1959), p. 390. Cf. the reservations as regards East Jerusalem on the admission of Jordan to the U.N. by Resol. 995(X).

For the relevant Armistice Agreements see Israel-Egypt, Feb. 24, 1949, 42 *United Nations Treaty Series* (*U.S.T.S.*) 251-70 (1949), 3 Norton Moore 381-89; Israel-Lebanon, March 23, 1949, 42 *U.N.T.S.* 287-98 (1949), 3 Norton Moore 391-96; Israel-Jordan, April 3, 1949, 43 *U.N.T.S.* 303-20 (1949), 3 Norton Moore, 398-406; Israel-Syria, July 20, 1949, 42 *U.N.T.S.* 327-40 (1949), 3 Norton Moore 408-15.

20. *Jerusalem,* p. 16. This is strangely at odds with the earlier flat assertion (p. 8) that the division of Jerusalem "had no effect on the Partition Resolution's provisions for the internationalisation of Jerusalem."

21. See *Jerusalem,* pp. 17-23, *Resolutions,* pp. 51-54. Ermette Pierotti, *Customs and Traditions of Palestine* (London: Cambridge, 1864, pp. 75 ff.), reported that as late as 1861 it was still customary "on the death of one Sultan and the succession of another" for the keys of Jerusalem to be formally surrendered to representatives of the Jewish community there. These then delivered the keys to the incoming Sultan for safe custody, "the Jews not having a garrison to defend the keys." Ermette Pierotti, who recounts this symbolization of the Jewish historic title to the city, was at the time in the service of the Arab governor of Jerusalem, Surraya Pasha.

22. *Jerusalem,* pp. 18-23. The *Jerusalem* pamphlet adds an argument as to references to withdrawal of Israel forces, or inadmissibility of acquisition of territory by conquest. I have already shown in Ch. 3, sects. 1, 3, and 4, that these phrases are directed to unlawful entry onto territory, and that Israel's entry and status were entirely lawful.

23. Cf. *Jerusalem,* p. 20; *Resolutions,* p. 51.

24. P. 20.

25. P. 51.

26. See Y. Z. Blum, "The Missing Reversioner: Reflections on the Status of Judea and Samaria," *Israel Law Review* 3 (1968): 279-302, revised and repr. in 2 Norton Moore 287-315. This article was written before Professor Blum entered Israel government service.

27. I.e., G.A. resols. 181(II), 194(III), or 303(IV).

28. *Resolutions,* p. 51.

29. The authors of *Resolutions,* at 52-53, in an effort to overcome this, argue that the Security Council has no power to limit the meaning of General Assembly resolutions. But the authors of *Resolutions* themselves have admitted that those resolutions will bear the meaning taken by the Security Council. And the present analysis has shown that the meaning they wish to attribute to them is far-fetched to the point of absurdity.

On 1979-1980 controversies concerning Jerusalem and related Security Council Resolutions 476 (1980) and 478 (1980), arising from Arab claims to sovereignty in Jerusalem, and the Israel Knesset's response by Basic Law: Jerusalem Capital of Israel, 5740-1980, see Discourse 2 infra at n. 10.

The terms of these resolutions reinforce the above legal analysis. Both call for the maintenance of the status of Jerusalem in terms of belligerent occupation and of Israel as "the occupying power," invoking also in this connection Geneva Convention IV of Aug. 12, 1949, Relative to . . . Civilian Persons in Time of War. One recital in Resolution 476 (1980) also speaks of "the specific status" of the city in terms of "the unique spiritual and religious dimension of the Holy Places," and particularizes its "physical character, demographic composition, institutional structure," but not the territorial *corpus separatum.* Resolution 478 (1980) resiles even from this ambiguous use of "specific status" to refer to the "religious dimension" substituting the nonlegal term "character."

On the strict nonapplicability of the above Geneva Convention IV to territories illegally held by Jordan from 1948-1962 see Discourse 2 in the Appendixes.

30. Elihu Lauterpacht, *Jerusalem and the Holy Places* (London, 1968), pp. 13-36, where relevant documentation is found.

31. *Resolutions,* at 53.

32. Ad Hoc Political Committee, G.A.O.R. 4th session, Annexes at 46 (A/AC.31/L.42). Cf. on Israel's steady willingness to accept such a functional international regime, the report of M. Roger Garreau, president of the Trusteeship Council, of April 4, 1950, G.A.O.R. 5th session, Supp. no. 9 (A/1286) Annex III (p. 28). And so recently also, in its reply of Nov. 15, 1971, to Security Council Resolution 298 (1971), Israel has reasserted its willingness in consultation with the religions concerned to give effect to the principle of "the universal character of the Holy Places." Israel there also affirmed that it did not wish to exercise "unilateral jurisdiction or exclusive jurisdiction or exclusive responsibility, in the Holy Places of Christianity and Islam." S.C.O.R., 26th year, Suppl. for Oct., Nov., Dec. 1971 (S/10392) at 37. And see Oesterreicher and Sinai, *Jerusalem,* p. 284. Cf. the Statement on Jerusalem and Israel of the Emergency Christian Leadership Conference, N.Y., of May 19, 1971, commending Israel's efforts towards a functional regime and rejecting both territorial internationalization and division as undesirable, and "regretting all interventions that fail to take into account the political rights and sovereignty of the state of Israel." The statement is reprinted in Oesterreicher and Sinai, *Jerusalem,* at 288. Cf. to the same effect the Statement by Evangelical Protestants, repr. in ibid., p. 292.

33. See G.A.O.R. 5th Session, Annexes, Agenda Item 20 (A/AC.38/L.63).

34. An amendment offered by the U.K., the U.S., and Uruguay to the Swedish plan shortened and simplified it and added a general principle requiring pledges from Israel and Jordan to "observe human rights in the Jerusalem Area." Ibid., (A/AC.38/L.73/Res.2).

35. See the details, including the renewed failure to adopt any proposal in 1952, and the U.N. inaction from 1952-1967, in E. Lauterpacht, *Jerusalem and the Holy Places* (London, 1968), Ch. 2, at 27-34, repr. 1 Norton Moore 929-1009.

36. The Arab states, before the 1948 War, opposed internationalization of Jerusalem; after Jordan and Israel were left in control of the respective parts of Jerusalem after 1948, the other Arab states reversed their positions and supported the idea of territorial internationalization. See Pfaff, p. 29; M. van Dusen, "Jerusalem," in M. Khadduri, ed., *Major Middle Eastern Problems in International Law* (1972), pp. 38-40. Clearly, the latter author's own focus, as his concluding "Policy Alternatives" on pp. 52-54 show, is on the politico-territorial issues rather than just the functions essential for meeting world concern for the holy places.

37. See, e.g., his speech to pilgrims at Mecca, reported in *Al-Hayat* (Beirut), Dec. 31, 1973. This may also, perhaps, though less patently, have been an objective of the Sudanese-Ethiopian-Lebanese mission to the Holy See, arranged at the Algiers Conference of Arab Heads of State in Nov. 1973. For representative Christian views rejecting Arab-Moslem territorial claims to the city in terms of either (1) predominant historical identification; or (2) comparative Israeli and Jordanian records of assurance of international functional concerns as to the holy places, see recently James Parkes, *Whose Land: A History of the Peoples of Palestine* (rev. Penguin ed., London, 1970, based on idem, *A History of Palestine from 135 A.D. to Modern Times* [London, 1949]), passim; Monseigneur John M. Oesterreicher, "Jerusalem the Free," in Oesterreicher and Sinai, *Jerusalem,* pp. 249 ff. (being an Open Letter to the Jordanian Ambassador of Dec. 1971); Statement of Evangelical Protestants of June 17, 1971, in Support of United Jerusalem as Capital of Israel, quoted in the latter work at 292.

The Christian population from 1948 to 1967, while Old Jerusalem was held by Jordan, fell from 25,000 to 12,646, and began to rise again after Israel assumed guardianship. See Oesterreicher and Sinai, *Jerusalem,* pp. 147, 157, 163. And see ibid., p. 163 on the generosity of Israel's war compensation to the religious institutions for war damage even when inflicted by the Jordanian attack.

And see Monseigneur Oesterreicher's article, cited above, at 252 ff. for a severe critique of Jordanian governance, covering also the origins of the Moslem custody of the keys of the Church of the Holy Sepulchre, and the importance of not confusing Mameluke and Turkish with Arab control, and "Arab" with "Moslem."

38. Especially since there was a sharp reaction to Jordan's action by the League of Arab States. See Hassouna, *The League of Arab States and Regional Disputes . . .,* cited supra n. 17 at pp. 33-40. See supra, Ch. 3, at n. 23.

39. S.C.O.R. 22d year, Suppl. for July, Aug., Sept, 1967 (S/8146/A6793) 232-33. Pfaff, pp. 40-41, does not mention this part of the Thalemann report in his section on it. The (principal legislative measures involved were the Law and Administration ordinance (Amendment [Am.] No. 11) Law, 1967; the Municipal Corporations Ordinance (Am. no. 6) Law, 1967; the Protection of the Holy Places Law, 1967, all in 21 *Laws of the State of Israel* (Jerusalem, 1966/67), pp. 75-76 and regulations thereunder.

40. 21 *Laws of the State of Israel,* pp. 75-76.

41. The first order is published in Kovetz HaTakkanot (Subsidiary Legislation) no. 2064 (June 28, 1967) at 2960 and the proclamation on enlarging the area of the municipality of Jerusalem, ibid., no. 2065 (June 28, 1967) at 2964. A translation of that proclamation is published in the *Jerusalem Post,* June 29, 1967, p. 2. A ban by the chief rabbinate on orthodox Jews entering the Temple Mount was published in the same newspaper earlier, on June 11, 1967, p. 6.

42. It is to be noted that the area of the enlarged Jerusalem Municipality under these regulations is less than the area proposed in 1947 for the *corpus separatum* of the city of Jerusalem.

43. *Records of the People's Council and Provisional Council of State,* May 14, 1948, 3d meeting, vol. 1, 19 (in Hebrew) transl. in Blum, "Juridical Status," pp. 111. See also the re-

cently published records of a so-called Minhelit Ha'am (predecessor of the Provisional Council of Government), on the drafting of the Declaration of Independence (Israel State Archives, 1979, meeting of May 13, 1948).

44. 1 *Laws of the State of Israel,* p. 64.

45. Cf. Ben-Gurion in the *Records of the . . . Provisional Council of State,* cited supra, n. 43, vol. 2, 26th meeting.

46. Divrei HaKnesset (Parliamentary Records), vol. 49, col. 2420, transl. in Blum, "Juridical Status," n. 43 at 195, text at n. 61.

47. See the report of the secretary-general's representative (Thalemann) cited supra, n. 39. Cf. the stern rebuttal by Msgr. John M. Oesterreicher of King Hussein's claim that such measures violated "the rights" of the Arab population of the Old City, in Oesterreicher and Sinai, *Jerusalem,* at 250.

For the official Israel account of these measures, see Foreign Minister Eban's Letter of July 10, 1967, to the secretary-general, Doc. S.8052, S.C.O.R. 22nd year, Supp. for July, Aug., Sept., 1967, p. 73, repr. ibid., 416-20. And see for a detailed testing of the question of "annexation" by reference to the actual facts of Israeli administration, M. van Dusen, "Jerusalem, the Occupied Territories, and the Refugees," in M. Khadduri, ed., *Middle Eastern Problems in International Law* (1972), pp. 42-44.

48. While the Temple Mount is the site of "the Holy of Holies" in Judaic history, both the government and the rabbinate in Israel have discouraged and even forbidden Jews to go and pray there—a singular display of self-restraint. See n. 41, this chapter.

49. Letter of Abba Eban to the Secretary-General, July 10, 1967. See Report of the Secretary-General, 22 S.C.O.R. Supp. for July-Sept. 1967, at 73, U.N.Doc.S/8052, repr. in 3 Norton Moore 958, at 959. See also the Israeli reply of Nov. 15, 1971, to Security Council Resolution 298 (1971) and Secretary-General U Thant's report, Doc. S/10392, cited in n. 30 above. The above reply interpreted "status" in the censuring resolutions to refer to *status quo ante* 1967, and after detailing the then conditions, said that a return to this was "inconceivable." It said (referring to Jordan's previous record) that "it is not the case that an internationally accepted or valid status for Jerusalem has been set aside" by Israel's actions since 1967.

50. See the short account in Pfaff, *Jerusalem,* pp. 27-28.

51. Parkes, in *Whose Land?,* p. 230, points out that Jews outnumbered both Christians and Moslems in Jerusalem as long ago as 1872, steadily increasing since then; e.g., 1899, 30,000 Jews as against 10,900 Christians and 7,700 Moslems; in 1948, 100,000 Jews as against 25,000 Christians and 45,000 Moslems; in 1967, 195,000 Jews as against 10,890 Christians and 54,900 Moslems; in 1970, 215,000 Jews as against 11,500 Christians and 61,000 Moslems.

52. Examined below, pp. 117-20.

53. Examined below, pp. 120-21.

54. For a summary with citations see Oppenheim-Lauterpacht, *International Law,* vol. 1, sects. 94 ff. (8th ed., London, 1955), p. 222. Cf. in the U.N. period, U.N. Deputy Secretary-General Kerno, addressing the International Court of Justice (I.C.J.) in the *International Status of S.W. Africa Case 1950,* who said as to this matter that "there exists no consensus, nor even a clearly discernible preponderance of opinion" (I.C.J. Reports 1950, p. 192).

55. See above, Ch. 1, under "Parallel Liberations: 'Arab Asia' and Jewish Palestine," as to the absence of reference in the mandate to political rights or standing of the inhabitants.

56. Whatever the future may prescribe for East Jerusalem, this cannot lawfully be restoration of a Jordanian occupation illegal in its origins, and in much of its administration. As will be shortly explained, international law does not attribute reversionary rights to a mere ousted occupant, but only to an ousted sovereign. Much less (if that were

possible) would it attribute them to an occupant whose original entry was unlawful. It is thus very strange that R. H. Pfaff, in his *Jerusalem,* p. 54, seems unaware of such problems in placing this solution very high among his six "policy alternatives."

57. Since the city was reestablished as the capital of the state in 1949, a number of states have established or retained their diplomatic representation in Jerusalem. Others, however, including the U.K., U.S., France, Turkey, and Australia, have not as of the date of writing. All states with missions in Jerusalem moved them under Arab state pressure in 1980.

58. Citing British official attitudes as to Formosa and the Pescadores on Feb. 4, 1955 536 *House of Commons Debates,* [H.C.D.] Written Answers, col. 159), and as to Gaza on March 14, 1957 (566 *H.C.D.,* col. 1320).

59. See L. M. Goodrich and E. Hambro, *Charter of the United Nations* (2d rev. ed., London, 1949), p. 105. The underlying principle is made explicit in Article 9 of the Organization of American States Charter signed at Bogotá in 1948 (119 *U.N.T.S.* 49, at 54): "The political existence of the State is independent of recognition by other States. Even before being recognized the State has the right to defend its integrity and independence, to provide for its preservation." And see discussions in W. Wengler, 2 *Völkerrecht,* vol. 2 (Berlin, 1964), p. 1388; A. Verdross, *Völkerrecht* (3d rev. ed., Vienna, 1955), pp. 514-15. Cf. with the present view D. W. Bowett, *Self-Defence in International Law* (1958), pp. 153-54; Q. Wright, "The Middle East Situation," repr. in 2 Norton Moore 107, at 115-16. And see other authorities cited in N. Feinberg, "Arab-Israel Conflict in International Law" (1970) quoted in 1 Norton Moore 386, at 451-57. Since the original "non-recognition" doctrine of the thirties was designed as a sanction against resort to force, its invocation as a means of enabling a state to grant to itself a license to use force against a selected target state, despite Article 2(4), may be grotesque in the extreme.

60. Elihu Lauterpacht, *Jerusalem and the Holy Places* (London, 1968), p. 47, points out that the provisions in Article 2 of the Armistice Agreement that "no military or political advantage should be gained under the truce ordered by the Security Council," and that the agreement should not "prejudice the rights, claims and positions of either Party . . . in the ultimate peaceful settlement of the Palestine question," barred any legal effects from the duration of Jordan's occupation or her purported annexation of the West Bank and Jerusalem in 1950.

61. For texts of this and other armistice agreements, see citations in n. 19 above. Art. 2(2) of the Israel-Jordan Agreement, which might otherwise have hindered acquisition by Israel, but which ceased to have effect on June 5, 1967, when the major Jordanian attack operated as a material breach of articles 1 and 3. On the effect of material breach on a bilateral treaty, and more particularly breach by repudiation, see also Article 60 of the Vienna Convention on the Law of Treaties, 1969. For first-hand accounts by Foreign Minister Eban and General Odd Bull of attempts to dissuade Jordan from this course, see G.A.O.R. 1526th Meeting, June 17, 1967, pp. 12-13, and General Bull's interview in the Oslo *Aftenpost,* of August 22, 1970. For King Hussein of Jordan's own account, see his *My War with Israel* (London, 1969), pp. 64-65.

On the "freezing" effect of the armistice agreements generally see S. Rosenne, *Israel's Armistice Agreements* (1951), pp. 24-32; H. S. Levie, "Nature and Scope of the Armistice Agreement," *Am. J. Int. L.* 50 (1956): 880; N. Feinberg, *The Legality of a State of War after the Cessation of Hostilities under the Charter of the United Nations and the Covenant of the League of Nations* (Jerusalem, 1961), reprinted in his *Studies in International Law With Special Reference to the Arab-Israel Conflict* (Jerusalem, 1979), p. 74.

62. He sees this as consistent with the provisions of the Armistice Agreement of 1949 that the lines there laid down shall not prejudice the future political settlement. Wherever Israel had lawfully asserted control prior to the agreements, her title had established itself in the sovereignty vaccum before these agreements came into effect. See Lauterpacht, *Jerusalem,* at 47-49.

63. Ironically, the Soviet Union added its own confirmation to the Israel side, at the opening of the very next General Assembly session after the one at which she had attempted to brand the defensive action of Israel as aggression. The Soviet Union solemnly claimed on October 5, 1968, that her invasion of Czechoslovakia in August 1968 was in "self-defence" against an attempt by western states to "snatch a link" from "the Socialist Commonwealth." This, of course, was before even any hostile mobilization began, let alone any such besieging of all frontiers by vastly superior forces, which faced Israel the year before. This Soviet claim, however extravagantly wrong it was for the Czechoslovak case, certainly shows that the Soviet Union recognizes that international law may, in extreme situations like that facing Israel, sanction self-defense against an enemy's armed attack, even before the enemy actually crosses the frontier.

64. Ukrainian Representative, Mr. Taresenko, S.C.O.R., 3d year, 306th meeting, May 27, 1948, p. 7.

65. U.S. Representative, Senator Austin, S.C.O.R., 3d year, 302d meeting, May 22, 1948, pp. 41-42.

66. Cf. Y. Z. Blum, "The Missing Reversioner: Reflections on the Status of Judea and Samaria" Israel L. Rev. (1968): 279-302, at 281-95.

67. See the statement of the representative of Jordan, Mr. El Farra cited n. 19.

68. Cf. von Glahn, The Occupation of Enemy Territory (Minneapolis, 1957), p. 245.

69. Cf. Y. Z. Blum, "The Missing Reversioner: Reflections on the Status of Judea and Samaria," Israel L. Rev. 3 (1968): 293.

70. I.C.J. Reports, 1953, p. 67. The International Court again relied on this principle in the Western Sahara Opinion, I.C.J. Reports 1975, 12 at 38. And see generally on the relative title doctrine D. P. O'Connell, International Law, vol. 1 (2d ed., London, 1970), p. 407; Y. Z. Blum, Historic Titles in International Law (The Hague, Nijhoff, 1965) 222-29, 335-36 (written before Ambassador Blum entered the service of the government of Israel).

71. On the Jordanian Agreement to the cease-fire, and on acceptance or not by other States, S.C.O.R. 22d year, Supp. for April, May, June 1967 (S/7985), pp. 250-52, and ibid., Supp. for Oct., Nov., Dec., 1967, esp. pp. 261 ff.

The point in the text applies with particular strength as against Jordan in the light of the binding force of the unconditional cease-fire agreement of 1967 replacing (or at least superimposed upon) the cease-fire ordered by the Security Council. (Cf. as to its binding force as an agreement the ruling of the Permanent Court of International Justice in the Lithuania-Poland Railway Traffic Case: Series A/B No. 42, at 116.) Such a binding agreement might establish a territorial standing going beyond "belligerent occupation." And see E. Feilchenfeld, The International Economic Law of Military Occupation (Washington, D.C., 1942, repr. 1971), p. 4.

72. S. Schwebel, "What Weight to Conquest?" Am. J. Int. L. 64 (1970): 344. The quotations in the text are respectively at pp. 345-46, 346-47, and 347. Cf. S. Schwebel, "The Middle East: Prospects for Peace" (1969) Papers of the 13th Hammarskjold Forum, 1969, pp. 70-74, repr. 2 Norton Moore 133-40; W. O'Brien, "International Law and the Outbreak of War in the Middle East" Orbis 11 (1968): 692-723, repr. 2 Norton Moore 75-106, esp. 105-6.

73. See E. V. Rostow, "'Palestinian Self-Determination': Possible Futures for the Unallocated Territories of the Palestine Mandate" Yale Studies in World Public Order, vol. 5, no. 2 (1979): 147-72. His point on 152-53 as to the meaning of "Palestinian" is an auxiliary one, but interesting and important. Cf. Rostow in the New York Times, June 21, 1979.

74. In the League Permanent Mandates Commission (P.M.C.) the Balfour Declaration was stated to be "the very soul of the Mandate" (P.M.C., Minutes of 27th session, 1935, p. 138, Spanish Member Palacios). Cf. in terms of "the primary purpose of the Mandate," the Peel Royal Commission Report (Command Paper 5479, 1937, p. 39). Even the so-called Churchill White Paper, June 3, 1922, Cmd. 1700, backtracking as it was, was concerned to

insist that Jews are in Palestine "as of right and not on sufferance" (3 Norton Moore 65, at 67). And see other citations in N. Feinberg, "Sovereignty over Palestine," repr. in 1 Norton Moore 224, at 238.

75. See Discourse 2 in the Appendixes section on Jewish settlements in Judea and Samaria, and Geneva Convention IV, Article 49(6).

Discourse 1

1. *Dweikat et al.* v. *Government of Israel et al.*, High Court of Justice (H.C.J.) 390/79, decided Oct. 22, 1979. The official translation into English by the Foreign Ministry of Israel is here cited as *"Elon Moreh* transl." We are not here concerned with the possible bearing of the decision on the disputed application of Article 49(6) to the settlements challenged by the litigation. On that matter see infra n. 11 and Discourse 2.

2. *Ayyub et al.* v. *Minister of Defence et al.*, H.C.J. 606/78, Judgment of March 15, 1979 (the case of *Malawa et al.* v. *Minister of Defence et al.*, H.C.J. 610/78 being joined therewith). The official translation into English by the Ministry of Justice of Israel is here referred to as *"Beit-El* transl."

3. Landau D.P. in *Elon Moreh* transl., pp. 15-16. Cf. Bekhor J. in *Elon Moreh* transl. at 45: "The very text of the order issued by the Military Commander has its foundation in the powers that international law vests in the Army holding territory of the State. Therefore *on this basis the decision must be handed down"* (emphasis supplied). Cf. Witkon J. in *Beit-El* (transl., pp. 4-5, 10). However, the argument of Justice Witkon that despite the fact that the court must not deal with political questions, it must deal with any case in which property rights are unlawfully impaired, is not convincing. (*Beit-El* transl., p. 15.) For it may, under other rules of customary law than those as to belligerent occupation determine whether the impairment is unlawful. So also with Justice Landau's argument in the *Beit-El* case in terms of an invocation of "non-justiciability of issues under negotiation." (*Beit-El,* transl., p. 22.)

It may be added as to the judgments of both Justice Landau and Justice Bekhor, that the argument that intended "permanence" of civilian settlements shows that they are not required for merely military needs, and makes them unlawful under customary international law, presupposes that the only part of such law that is relevant is that concerning belligerent occupation. If it is not so, the arguments from "permanence" fall. That they do fall seems clear from Justice Landau's answer in the *Beit-El* case (transl., p. 25) to the petitioners' argument that the permanence of a civilian settlement necessarily fell outside the authority to requisition for temporary use. He there observed that "this occupation can itself come to an end some day as a result of international negotiation, leading to a new arrangement which will take effect under international law and will determine the fate of this settlement as of other settlements in occupied territories." And cf. Justice Ben Porat, ibid. at 30. What is true for the contingency of a different rule from that of occupation law arising from a future negotiation, is also true for a different rule now offering under existing customary law that, in the matrix set by the pleadings in this case, this municipal court could not apply. And see infra n. 11.

4. We may here note the difficulties of clear statement both of the affiant Major-General Orly, and of the judges. What the former apparently meant is that he was not going into the international law of territorial acquisition ("the legal question"), on which depends the question whether the government's relations with the inhabitants involved merely that part of international law dealing with belligerent occupation.

5. The language of Justice Witkon in the *Beit-El* case (transl., pp. 4-5) that "the status of the respondents in respect of the occupied territory is that of an occupying power," is to be read in the context of his even more emphatic assertion in the same place that the court

must limit itself to what was contained in "the affidavits of the parties." In particular, he said, only statements of the authorities and those of the state's attorney "constitute for us an authoritative expression of the position of the Government."

6. It may be asked whether the words "all agree" include the Israel government, and if so, what was the ground for this deliberate self-denying ordinance by that government.

7. Cf. President Landau's reassertion in *HaEtzni* v. *State of Israel et al.* (H.C.J. no. 61/80) that "it is not what could have been done and what could have been proclaimed which decides the matter, . . . from the Israeli municipal law point of view, but what was and was not done in fact by the Government and the Knesset." (Transl. kindly provided by the Israel Ministry of Justice, p. 9.)

Here in *Elon Moreh* (transl., p. 16) there follows the rather jurisprudential point: ". . . the basic norm upon which Israeli rule in Judea and Samaria was based, and is until today, is the norm of a military administration, and not the application of Israeli law, which accompanies Israeli sovereignty." Yet, even if the military commander's proclamation no. 1 is (as the learned judge held) the source of decision, the military commander must be thought to draw his ultimate authority to issue it from Israel law (incorporating of course the customary international law rules as to belligerent occupation). Otherwise one has to say, following the other alternative left open by Kelsen, that not merely "the norm of military administration" but the entire legal order of Israel, and all other municipal orders, are but delegated orders from some supreme basic norm of international law. Unless the judge was adopting this latter extreme version of the monist position, it is submitted that the basic norm in the Kelsenite sense lies within Israel law, and it is only in the choice of subordinate norms applicable to the facts that problems arise. Justice Landau himself recognizes this (transl., p. 17) when he speaks of the commander's order being "issued in accordance with" municipal Israel law. When he adds that the military commander "derives his authority" from international law, this may be understood as referring to his view discussed in the text, that the action (and inaction) of the competent Israel law authorities had directed the court to decide the case as if the appropriate body of law was that part of the customary international law incorporated into Israel law that deals with belligerent occupation.

8. Conceivably, the court might have considered the effect of the absence of any state entitled to the reversion of sovereignty even within the matrix of occupation law. Justice Landau himself observed in the *Beit-El* case (transl., p. 23) that section 3 of the Hague Rules is headlined "Military Authority over Territory of Enemy State." Even in terms of occupation law the question might be raised whether rules so described are indeed applicable to territories like Judea and Samaria (the West Bank), which never in international law belonged to the "Enemy State" concerned—Jordan—or to Gaza, which never so belonged to Egypt. So far as this writer knows, however, this question has not been discussed by international law authorities, and it is understandable that the court did not direct its mind to the possibility.

9. The judge referred to his observation in the *Beit-El* case (transl., p. 127) that "we are not required to consider this problem in this petition and this demurrer joins therefore the group of demurrers of which I spoke in H.C.J. 302/72" (the *Hilu* case on which see infra n. 13). And see supra, n. 3.

10. This position under international law was not changed, despite current debates, by the Basic Law: Jerusalem, the Capital of Israel, 5740-1980, passed by the Knesset on July 30, 1980. This declared that "Jerusalem, complete and united, is the capital of Israel, the seat of the President, the Knesset, the government and the Supreme Court," and assured protection of, and access for, all faiths to its holy places, and special provisions and resources for its prosperity and development. This was essentially a declaratory measure asserting no change from the status quo, even as to the law that had been applicable in Jerusalem from 1967 onwards. Nevertheless, it was censured (the United

States abstaining) by Security Council resolutions of June 30, 1980 (S/Res.476[1980]) and of August 20, 1980 (S/Res.478[1980]), the latter of which also called on States to remove their diplomatic missions from the city.

The significance of these events is for political warfare, rather than for law. For instance, Egyptian "statements" of the Foreign Ministry (of February 26, 1980), and of the People's Assembly (of April 1, 1980), asserted "Arab sovereignty" over Jerusalem, the latter specifying that Jerusalem was "the capital of the Palestinians." These statements joined a stream of Arab State and Soviet initiatives that had already begun in 1979. On July 3, 1979, the Islamic Conference threatened sanctions against states establishing embassies in Jerusalem. The Jerusalem question was placed, at Syrian and P.L.O. initiative, on the agenda of the Islamabad Conference of Islamic Foreign Ministers in January 1980. On March 12, 1980, a committee of that Conference threatened severance of diplomatic relations with states already having missions in Jerusalem, and this was endorsed by the Council of the Arab League on March 26, 1980. The Eleventh Islamic Conference of May 17-21, 1980, adopted and elaborated these and other threats, and the Pakistani Chairman of the Islamic Conference then, by letter of May 28, 1980 (Doc.S/13966), brought the question to the Security Council, leading to Resolutions 476 (1980) and 478 (1980).

The political campaign on Jerusalem thus began long before the presentation in the Knesset of the private member's bill which later became the Basic Law: Jerusalem . . . , and many months before the first reading of the bill. It consisted of Arab initiatives that provoked the Israel parliament's declaratory measure, rather than were provoked by it. In view of this purely political import, it is not surprising that Security Council Resolutions 476 (1980) and 478 (1980) add nothing new to the legal issues of territorial entitlement. And this too comports with the fact that, according to United States Senate sources, Saudi Arabian threats concerning oil supplies induced the United States not to veto resolution 478, despite the Secretary of State's condemnation of it as "fundamentally flawed" (*Jerusalem Post Weekly*, Aug. 24-30, 1980, p. 1).

The legal import of the terms of Security Council Resolutions 476 (1980) and 478 (1980) for the major territorial issues is examined at the relevant point in Chapter 7, n. 29.

11. This was a central legal issue in the later case of *HaEtzni* v. *State of Israel (et al.)*, decided April 17, 1980, H.C.J. no. 61/80.

12. The question how "permanent" the settlement was intended to be was treated as relevant to how primarily it was related to military security. In *Beit-El* (transl., p. 25) the court accepted the submission of counsel for the authorities that though the settlers were to build their homes in the settlement, which thus were "permanent" in that sense, that "permanence" "can itself come to an end some day as a result of international negotiations which . . . will determine the fate of this settlement as of other settlements . . . in the occupied territories." In *Elon Moreh* (transl., p. 29) the court concluded from the evidence of the individual respondents (not contradicted by the authorities concerned) that the Israel authorities contemplated the "permanence" of the settlement going beyond the time when belligerent occupation came to an end. Its ground here again was not to deny that Israel might have bases of territorial title other than as a belligerent occupant, a question that we have seen it always reserved. It was that the contemplation of "permanence" in this latter sense contradicted the legal matrix set for the court by the authorities themselves—namely, that the court must decide as if the governing law were solely that of belligerent occupation. By the same token, on the court's reading of the facts, it showed that the dominant purpose of the requisition was not that of military security, as required by that law.

13. See also supra text preceding n. 4, and n. 9.

14. *Hilu et al.* v. *Government of Israel et al.* (1972) 27 *Piskei Din* 2. Excerpts from the judgments at 169 ff. have been translated into English by the Israel Ministry of Justice. Page references in the text are to this translation.

15. Witkon J. (*Elon Moreh* transl., pp. 43-44), whose opinion came closest to a consideration of the matter, stopped short of an answer, saying that "this abstention is not to

be interpreted as an agreement to the status of one or other of the parties." On the interpretation of Article 49(6) see Discourse 2, following.

16. The Geneva Convention, said Justice Witkon (*Beil-El* transl., pp. 42-44), was a part of "international conventional law," not applicable by the Court "unless it is accepted by national legislation." The question whether voluntary settlements in Judea and Samaria were within the prohibition of "transferring sections" of Israel's population to occupied territories, was "not an easy one." He refrained from answering it since the convention was not part of the law applicable in Israel courts. "But this abstention is not to be interpreted as an agreement to the status (i.e., position) of one or other of the parties (transl., p. 44). Cf. Justice Landau (*Elon Moreh* transl., p. 18): "Article 49(6) of the Geneva Convention was at the time not considered at all in the hearing, since it belongs to the area of consensual international law which is not in the nature of a law that binds an Israeli court."

17. The court, in the *Elon Moreh* case, also did not, of course, pass upon questions of the ultimate disposition of the territories in the course of peace negotiations with interested Arab states, for the additional reason that this was a "political" and not a "legal" question. For a critique of the case from the aspects of the relations of municipal and international law, and the meaning of "military" purposes in occupation law, see Julius Stone, "Aspects of the *Beit-El* and *Elon Moreh* Cases," *Israel Law Review,* October 1980, pp. 476-95.

18. He also pointed out that according to Halakha the passage in Numbers 33:53 was to be read subject to the possibility of its application under the secular law for the time being.

Discourse 2

1. *Ayyub et al.* v. *Minister of Defence et al.,* High Court of Justice (H.C.J.) 606/78, 610/78 (1979) 33 *Piskei Din* (2) 113, here cited as the *"Beit-El* case," with official translation into English by the Ministry of Justice of Israel, here cited as "transl."; *Dweikat et al.* v. *Government of Israel et al.,* H.C.J. 390/79, judgment of Oct. 22, 1979, here cited as the *"Elon Moreh* case", with official translation into English by the Foreign Ministry of Israel, here cited as "transl." This aspect is discussed in the preceding discourse.

2. The Geneva Convention 1949.was signed by Israel August 12, 1949, and ratified May 31, 1951. It came into force in general, Jan. 6, 1952, but whether it is by its terms applicable to the West Bank and Gaza under Israel control is a separate question. Thus, under Article 2 of that convention, the convention applies only to occupation by one state of territory belonging to another high contracting party. Insofar as Jordan has, by virtue of the principle *ex iniuria non oritur ius* no territorial rights in the territories concerned, the case would not fall within the convention. While taking this position as to her legal obligations, the state authorities of Israel have claimed that their administration has in fact conformed to the substance of the convention provisions. The present examination is directed to that claim.

3. See, e.g., *U.S.* v. *Milch* (1947) U.S. Military Tribunal, Nuremberg, 7 L.R.T.W.C. at 46.

4. Art. 6(b). A number of authorities suggest no other context or relevance of Article 49(6). See, e.g., M. Greenspan, *Modern Law of Land Warfare* (Berkeley, 1949), pp. 268 ff.; G. von Glahn, *Law Among Nations* (New York, 1965), p. 674; M. Sörensen, *Manual of Public International Law* (London and New York, 1968), p. 831.

5. Jean S. Pictet, *Commentary, IV Geneva Convention Relative to the Protection of Civilian Persons in Time of War* (1958), pp. 278-79.

6. Ibid., p. 283.

7. The ambiguity reflects the *travaux préparatoires.* The addition of the final paragraph of the present Article 49 (then Article 45) was proposed by Danish delegate Cohn at the Legal Commission of the 17th International Red Cross Conference (*Summary of Debates of the Sub-Commissions,* pp. 61-62) and adopted (ibid. pp. 77-78). The protection of the

indigenous inhabitants from "invasion" was there expressed as an objective, though M. Pillaud (C.I.C.R.) thought that the International Red Cross should rather be concerned to protect the nationals of a country than prescribing duties for occupying powers. At the Diplomatic Conference of Geneva of 1949, Final Record, vol. II-A, 759-760, the Rapporteur, in presenting the whole of Article 49, stated its object as being "to prohibit, once and for all, the abominable transfers of population which had taken place during the last war." The whole article, including paragraph 6, was adopted on this basis (ibid. p. 60).

8. J. Stone, *Legal Controls of International Conflict* (1954), pp. 704-5.

9. See E. V. Rostow, "'Palestinian Self-Determination': Possible Futures for the Unallocated Territories of the Palestine Mandate," *Yale Studies in World Public Order* 5 (1979): 147-72, esp. pp. 154-61, and in his brief "Of Israel's Future and American Folly," *Washington Star,* March 21, 1980, and earlier articles cited in Chapter 7, n. 73.

10. See 2 Lauterpacht-Oppenheim, *International Law* (7th ed., London, 1952), p. 447; Stone, *Legal Controls,* pp. 698-99.

Index

· · · · ·

Aggression. *See also* Force, use of; Self-Determination claims; Territorial rights; United Nations; United Nations Charter; Wars of liberation
of Arab States against Israel, 60, 69, 117-18, 127, 128, 139, 141, 143, 194 n.24
by armed bands, 46-51. *See also* Armed bands, incursions by
definition of, in 1974 (text in Appendixes, 161-63), 3-4, 22, 33, 39, 51. 130
  art.1, Explanatory Note (a), 85, 86-87, 161
  art.2, 55, 162
  art.3, 55, 162-63
  art.3(f), 85, 90-91, 163
  art.3(g), 85, 87-90, 164
  art.3(e), 198 n.31
  art.5(3), 55, 163
  art.7, 85, 88-90, 93, 163, 198 n.30
  Ferencz on, 88. *See also* Ferencz, B. B.
  interpretation of, 85
  main drafts before 1967 Committee, 194 n.23, 198 n.38
  political warfare and, 6-7, 55, 56, 86, 192 nn. 28, 29
  preamble, paras.6-8, 83
  Resolution 3236(XXIX) and, 71, 163
  response to. *See* Necessity, and self-defense
  Schwebel on, 88-89. *See also* Schwebel, S.
  and Security Council Resolution 242, 53-56
  Soviet proposals for, 88-89
  territorial acquisition and, 45-48, 55-56, 63-65, 117-21, 127-28
  Thirteen-Power Draft for, 192 n.28
economic, 2-4, 83-84
  and U.N. Charter, arts. 1 and 2, 38-39
  and U.N. Charter, art. 2(4), 38
  and U.N. Charter, art. 39, 38-39
  and U.N. Charter, art. 53, 28

Friendly Relations Declaration and, 39
as ground of self-defense, 3-4, 37
OAPEC states and, 37. *See also* Oil Weapon
oil pressure and, 1973, 2-5, 51, 74, 142-43. *See also* Oil Weapon, and Maps 7 and 8, at 142-43
Soviet proposal on, 36-37
as support for unlawful activities, 37-39
third states as targets, 37
Thirteen-Power Draft, 192 n.28
Western states and, 37
General Assembly and, 69
hosting armed bands, 46-51
by Israel, Security Council negation of, 63, 191-92 n.25
Jewish and Arab refugees and, 69
by Jordan, admissions as to, 63
Partition Resolution aborted by, 60
territorial rights, S.C. resol. 242 and, 191 n.24
territorial rights and, 10-18, 45-58, 115-23, 167-76, 177-78
Agreement of Understanding and Cooperation, 1919 (Feisal-Weizmann, 13-14
Al-Husseini, Haj Amin, 58
American Council of Judaism, 130
Annexation, 54, 120-21, 200 n.19
armistices and, 200 n.19. *See also* Jordan, Hashemite kingdom of
of West Bank by Jordan, 204 nn.59-61. *See also* Armistices; Jerusalem; Jordan, Hashemite kingdom of; Judea and Samaria; Territorial rights
Arab Asia. *See* Peel Commission; Self-Determination claims
Arab Asia (Arab State) and Jewish Palestine, 13-14, 125
Arab-Israel conflict. *See also* Aggression; Force, use of; Israel; Jerusalem; Judea and Samaria; Palestine; Self-De-

211

Arab-Israel conflict (*continued*)
    termination claims; Territorial rights;
    and other particular aspects
  intertemporal aspect of, 57-58
  legal issues in, 6-7
  1948, 46, 96, 139
  1967, 47, 96, 141
  1973, 47, 96
  oil weapon in, 2-5, 34-44, 74, 142, 143
  Soviet role in, 35-42
Arab League, 14
  annexation of, by Jordan 1948, 191 n.23,
    200 n.19
  and Iraq mediation, 1948, 191 n.23
  and Tunis Conference, 1979, 47
Arab Nation, 136. *See also* Arab States;
  Intertemporal law; Palestinians; P.L.O.;
  Self-Determination claims
Arab Refugees. *See* Refugees
Arab States. *See also* Aggression; Arab-Israel conflict; Jerusalem; Jordan, Hashemite kingdom of; Palestine; Self-
  Determination claims; Territorial
  rights; *and other particular topics or
  states*
  "Arab nation" and, 57-58, 136
  and "the Arab State," in Feisal-Weizmann
    Agreement, 14
  Area of Jurisdiction . . . Ordinance (Is-
    rael) 170. *See also* Jerusalem
  and attacks on Israel, 117-18, 139
  European oil dependence on, 142, 143
  international law and, 46-51. *See also* In-
    ternational law
  Jewish refugees from, 1948-1967, 140
  offensive operations
    1948, 46, 96
    1967, 47, 96, 141
    1973, 47, 96
Arafat, Yassir, 12, 20
Arangio-Ruiz, G., 40-51, 126, 186 n.23
  on effect of repeated resolutions, 41, 126
  on "soft" law, 41
Armed Bands, incursions by, 46-51, 87-90.
  See also Aggression; Self-Determina-
  tion claims; Wars of liberation
  abatement of, 47-51
  Caroline Affair and, 49
  Code of Offenses on, 49
  Consolidated Draft on, 89
  Declaration of Rights and Duties of States
    on, 49
  and delinquency of host state, 48-51, 87,
    90
  de Vattel on, 49
  García-Mora on, 48-51, 189-90 nn.8, 11,
    13, 17, 19, 21
  Kunz. J. L.. on, 49

Lauterpacht, H., on, 49
Palestinians in Lebanon and, 90
political warfare and, 89
proportionality in abatement of, 91
self-defense and, 90-91
Six-Power Draft on, 88-92
Soviet draft on, 88-92
state practice and, 48-49
Stone on, 190 n.21
Thirteen-Power Draft on, 88-92
and U.N. Charter, art. 51, 59
Armistices, 200 n.19, 209 n.4. *See also* Aggression; Annexation; Force, use of;
  Jordan, Hashemite kingdom of
  annexation and, 200 n.19
  "freezing" effect of, 204 n.61
Assad, President, 12
Ayyub et al. v. *Minister of Defence et al.,*
  206 n.2, 209 n.1

Balfour Declaration (1917), 7, 12, 14, 96, 153
  (text in Appendixes, 146). *See also*
  Israel; Mandate for Palestine; Pales-
  tine; Self-Determination claims
  Balfour's understanding of, 184-85 n.12
  historic basis of, 137
  McMahon letter, 146
  Palestine National Covenant and, 12
  pledges and border changes, 1917-23, 138
  and "soul of the mandate," 205 n.74
Baltic states, Soviet invasion of, 46
Beit-El case, 168-75. *See also Elon Moreh*
  case; Israel; Requisition
Belligerent occupation. *See* Occupation,
  belligerent
Bessou, M., 197 n.18
Broms, Bengt, 37
Bull, Odd, 204 n.61

Camara, Sette, 30
Camp David Accords, General Assembly
  on, 35
Capital punishment, 172
Caroline Affair, 49-51, 189 n.4
Cattan, Henry, 58, 130, 193 n.4
Cease-fires. *See also* Aggression; Arab-Is-
  rael conflict; Force, use of; Terri-
  torial rights; *and under particular
  states*
  Arab State violations of, 41-42, 46-48, 51,
    205 n.71
  resolutions, 189 n.5
  Security Council orders for, 154-56
Cisjordan. *See* Jordan, Hashemite kingdom
  of,
Concert of Europe, 34

Cristescu, Aureliu, 196 n.17
Cyprus, 96

Damascus, 10
David, kingdom of, 12, 14, 131. *See also* Israel; Palestine
Decolonization. *See* Aggression; Self-Determination claims; Soviet Union; Wars of liberation
Dusen, M. van, 199 n.6
Dweikat case. *See Elon Moreh* case

East Jerusalem. *See* Jerusalem
Economic aggression. *See* Aggression
Egypt, 28
   attacks of, on Israel, 1948, 1967, 139, 141, 194 n.24
   Gaza and, 55, 127
   Jewish refugees from, 140
Egypt-Israel Treaty of Peace, 35, 127, 133
Elias, Mr., 86
Elon Moreh case (*Dweikat* v. *Government of Israel*), 167-75. *See also* International law; Israel; Occupation, belligerent
   judicial achievements in, 175-76
   political warfare and, 169-70, 174-76
   territorial questions reserved in, 168-70, 173, 175-76

Feisal, Emir. *See* Feisal-Frankfurter exchange; Feisal-Weizmann agreement
Feisal-Frankfurter exchange, 13, 184 n.9
Feisal-Weizmann agreement, 1917 (text in Appendixes, 147), 13-14, 125. *See also* Intertemporal law; Self-Determination claims
   "Arab-Asia" and Jewish Palestine, 125
   concurrence of Jewish and Arab liberations, 7-18, 147
   Jewish-Arab cooperation and, 13-14, 147
Ferencz, B. B., 197 nn.18, 23, 27
Force, use of, 47-51, 53-56. *See also* Aggression; Armed Bands, incursions by; Self-Determination claims; Territorial rights; *Uti possidetis* rule; Wars of liberation
   Friendly Relations Declaration and, 52
   General Assembly and, 129-30
   General Assembly connivance at, against Israel, 42-44, 70-71
   General Assembly resolution 2131(XX), 1965, on, 82
   General Assembly resolution 2625 (XXV) on, 81-85
   idealist-restrictivist and realist-traditional

views, 50-51
   Iraq and use of, 47-48
   1974 Aggression definition on, 52, 81-93
   secretariat studies and, 129-31
   Security Council Resolution 242 and, 53-56
   self-determination and, 81-93, 129-30
   various instruments, 81-85
Friendly Relations Declaration. *See* General Assembly resolutions (particular)

García-Amador, V. F., 189 n.10
García-Mora, M. R., 47-51, 189 nn.8, 11, 13, 196 nn.17, 19, 21
Gaza, 132
General Assembly of United Nations. *See also* General Assembly resolutions (general); General Assembly resolutions (particular); General Assembly Resolution 181(II); Self-Determination claims; United Nations; United Nations Charter; Wars of liberation
   aggression definition, 1974 and, 52, 55
   connivance at force against Israel, 42-44, 71
   as "conscience of mankind," 2-3, 43-44
   as dismantler of states, 6-7, 76-87, 91-93
   double standards in, 33-34
   duress and, 34-36
   international law, "rewriting" by, 2-7, 53-56, 129-31
   magisterial power and, 2-8, 79, 126-27
   majorities, nature of, in, 2-5, 33-44, 76-79, 126-27
   membership, changes in, 1-4
   oil pressure and, 2-4, 74, 142-43
   self-determination and, 20-22, 80-85, 92-93, 125-27
   voting and abstention in, 3-4, 29, 43-44. *See also* majorities, nature of, *subrubric supra*
   wars of liberation and, 80-85, 92-93
General Assembly resolutions (general). *See also* General Assembly of United Nations; General Assembly resolutions (particular); International law; Palestinians; Refugees
   accumulation of, effect of, 5
   Arab refugees and, 27-29
   Arango-Ruiz, G., on, 40-41, 126, 186 n.23
   coercion in treaties and, 33, 36-40
   conditions of influence of, 33
   consensus and, 32-33
   economic aggression and, 36-40
   Fitzmaurice, Sir G., on, 29-30, 126
   international law context of, 45
   Israel Independence Declaration and, 62

General Assembly resolutions (*continued*)
Lauterpacht, H., on, 29, 126
lawmaking claims, 125, 129-31
legal effects of, 6-7, 29, 56, 126-29
limits on legal force of. 36-40
majorities in, 1, 3, 30, 35
oil pressure and, 36
political warfare and, 34-44, 92-97, 126-27
powers under art.10 in 1947, 60
right of return and, 67-68
role of, in 1947, 6
self-reversals in, 5
Sixth Committee debate on, 1974
Third World voting on, 126
title to Palestine and, 60
treaty adoption and, 30
Uncio Commission on, 29
usurpation of powers by, 129
voting, theories as to effect of, 32-33
General Assembly resolutions (particular).
See also General Assembly of United
Nations; General Assembly resolutions (general)
declarations, 1960, 95-96 (independence),
1970, 84-85 (security)
Resolution 181(II), Nov. 29, 1947 (Partition Resolution), 7, 28, 45, 57, 76,
98, 99, 101, 104
Resolution 194(III), 68, 98, 99, 101, 104,
125, 132
Resolution 273(III), May 31, 1949, 156-57
Resolution 303 (IV), 98, 99
Resolution 2253 (ES-V), July 4, 1967, 104,
106, 113
Resolution 2254(ES-V), July 14, 1967, 104,
106
Resolution 2535(XXIV), 68
Resolution 2625(XX), Oct. 24, 1970
(Friendly Relations Declaration), 21,
22, 52, 76, 77-78, 83-84, 186 n.25, 197
n.16
Resolution 2649(XV), Nov. 30, 1970, 27-28
Resolution 2672C(XV), Dec. 8, 1970, 28,
29, 74
Resolution 2963(XXVII), Dec. 13, 1972,
68
Resolution 3089D, Dec. 7, 1973, 28-39
Resolution 3236(XXIX), Nov. 22, 1974,
9, 28-29, 42-44, 67-68, 125, 196 n.12
Resolution 3314(XXIX), Dec. 14, 1974,
56, 81, 85-93. See text in Appendixes,
161-63, 189 n.32
Resolution 3379(XXX), Nov. 10, 1975, 34-36, 57
General Assembly Resolution 181(II) (Partition), 9, 59-66, 153, 193 n.11. See

also General Assembly resolutions
(general); General Assembly resolutions (particular); Jerusalem; Jerusalem, *corpus separatum* project
Arab armed force aborting, 58, 63, 125,
193 n.14
Arab claim of invalidity *ab initio,* 60
General Assembly disinterest in, 1950-1967, 102, 103
general principles of law and, 128
Israel, conditional attitude to, 62, 65
Jerusalem and, 131-32
Jewish Agency, conditional attitude to,
63
legal standing and effect of, 125, 127-28
Mallisons' view of, 60-64
nonlegislative character of, 60
operation, E. Lauterpacht on, 117
operation, failure to enter into, 60-61, 63-66, 194 n.23
pacta sunt servanda and, 60, 62
Palestine Conciliation Committee and,
99, 101
Palestinian Rights Committee view of, 98,
99, 100-106
recommendations of, 63
Security Council Resolution 465 and, 108
Shertok, Moshe, on, 193 n.11
as supposed "juridical" basis of Israel, 58
territorial title, E. Lauterpacht on, 117
territorial title, inchoateness for, 59, 60,
62, 99, 101, 102, 104
Trusteeship Council and, 99, 100, 102
U.S. legal adviser's view on, 65
General Syrian Congress, 1919, 10
Geneva Convention IV, 1949, Art.49(6). See
also Israel; Israel, law of; Judea and
Samaria (West Bank); Palestine
art.2 of Convention IV, 209 n.2
art.49, 167, 177-81
travaux préparatoires of, 178-79, 209
n.7
art.49(6)
dual aspect of, 179-81
basis of adoption, 210 n.7
Israel signature and ratification, 209 n.2
Israel voluntary compliance with, 209 n.2,
168, 171-73
Judea and Samaria (West Bank), application in, 179-81
judenrein designs and, 179-81
limits of applicability, 209 n.2
Pictet on, 178-79, 209 n.7
settlements and, 177-81, 190-91 n.22
Genocide, 130
Germany. See Nazi Germany
Greco-Turkish conflict, 1974, 96
Gromyko, Andrei (U.S.S.R.)

on Jewish liberation in Palestine, 93, 194
    n.24
Group of 77, 2, 35
Guney, Mr. (Turkey), 30
Gush Emunim, 170, 172

Hadrian, 11
HaEtzni v. *State of Israel,* 208 n.11
Hague Rules, art.43, 172, 181. *See also* Is-
    rael, law of; Occupation, belligerent;
    Requisition
Haj Amin al-Husseini. *See* Mufti of Jeru-
    salem
Halpern, B.
    on "anti-Zionist-phobia," 192-93 n.38
Herzl, Theodor, 153
Higgins, R.
    on General Assembly resolutions, 31-32
Hilu et al. v. *Government of Israel et al.,*
    208 n.14
Hitler, Adolf, 130
Holborn, L. W., 186-87 n.27
Holocaust, 153
Holy Land. *See* Palestine
Holy Places, protection of, 110-12, 132, 153-
    54. *See also* Israel; Jerusalem
    consultative body for, 133
    as peace settlement issue, 132
    Protection of Holy Places Law, 1967 (Is-
        rael), 133
    national law and, 133
    Security Council Resolution 465 (March
        1, 1980), 132
Hussein, King, 23-25, 203 n.47, 204 n.61
Hussein-McMahon exchange of letters, 13,
    23, 146-47

International Court of Justice, 132
    continuity of principle of self-determina-
        tion, 18-19
    Lithuania-Poland Railway Traffic Case
        (P.C.I.J.), 205 n.71
    Minquiers and Echrehos Case (U.K.-
        France), 119, 120
    on relative territorial title, 116-20, 205
        n.70
    Namibia, opinion on, 18
    self-determination and, 18-22, 121-23
    status of S.W. Africa, 1950, 121, 122, 185
        n.21, 203 n.52
    status of Western Sahara, opinion on,
        1975, 20, 185 nn.21-22, 205 n.70
    Statute, Article 38, 30-31, 33
International law. See also *Ex iniuria non
        oritur ius;* Occupation, belligerent;
        United Nations Charter; *Uti posside-*

tis rule; Wars of liberation; *and other
        particular aspects*
absence of community enforcement, 45-
    46
assault on, 2-7, 53-56, 80-81, 124-33
condonation of breach of, 42-44, 47, 71
consent basis of, 45
General Assembly, future of, 55-56, 126-
    30
General Assembly "rewriting" of, 5, 32-
    44, 53, 54-55, 76-77
imposed treaties of peace and, 47
ius cogens, 72-73, 195 n.16
municipal law and, 167-76
    as to customary law, 173-74
    as to treaty law, 173-74
non-recognition doctrine, 204 n.59
requiring peace negotiations, 52-53, 117-
    23, 127, 173-74
rights and duties of state under, 127
sociology of, 1-7
International order. See also Aggression;
        Force, use of; International law;
        Self-Determination claims; Terri-
        torial integrity of states
Soviet Union and, 20, 38-40, 92, 97, 127
threats to, sources of, 19-22, 76-93
International security organizations
escapes and evasions from, 1
magisterial and nonmagisterial power in,
    1-5
sovereignty and, 1, 3-8, 77-81, 84-87
veto and, 1-4
Intertemporal law, 7, 57-58, 71-72, 74-75,
    96-97, 125. See also Self-Determina-
    tion claims; Palestine; Palestinian
    Arabs
Iran. *See* Teheran
Iraq
    attacks on Israel 1948, 1967, 139, 141
    Jewish refugees from, 140
    National Charter of, 48
Islam, 11. *See also* Arab Nation; Arab States
Israel, 16, 28, 45. *See also* Aggression; Bal-
        four Declaration; Force, use of;
        General Assembly resolutions; Man-
        date for Palestine; Self-Determina-
        tion claims
    admission of, to U.N., 18, 46, 61, 68
    ancient kingdom of, 11, 12, 14
    Arab attempts to destroy, 76-79, 139, 141,
        143
    assurances on admission to U.N., 195 n.3
    boundaries of, 125, 129
    Declaration of Independence of, 61-63
        (text in Appendixes, 152-54)
    East Jerusalem, postwar measures in (1967),
        111-14

Israel (*continued*)
  Egypt, Peace Treaty with, 35, 127, 133
  General Assembly, collusion with force
    against, 42-44, 70-71
  Gromyko on, 93, 194 n.24
  and holy places, protection of, 100, 102,
    109, 111-13, 153-54, 201 n.32. *See
    also* Holy places, protection of; Is-
    rael; Jerusalem
  independence of, 46, 61
  international law and, 45-56
  Jerusalem and, 102, 105, 106. *See also*
    Jerusalem; Jerusalem, *corpus separa-
    tum* project
  law of. *See* Israel, law of
  Law of Return of, 26
  liberation basis, Gromyko on, 93, 202-3
    n.43
  negotiation and, 52-53, 117-23, 127, 173-
    74
  People's and Provisional Council, 202-3,
    n.43
  P.L.O. and, 19-20, 188 n.26. *See also* P.L.O.
  self-defense by, 53-56, 103, 116-18, 191-
    92 n.25. *See also* Territorial rights
  self-determination, based on, 18, 61-62,
    129. *See also* Self-Determination
    claims
  Sinai and, 52-53
  social and political rights in, 153
  Supreme Court, recent decisions as to
    settlements, 167-81
    government pleadings in, 169, 171, 173-
      74, 175
    limited import of, 168-69, 173-75, 176
  territorial rights of, 52-53, 61, 127. *See
    also* Territorial rights
  West Bank "occupation," legal basis of,
    52-56, 115-23, 127
  West Jerusalem, title in, 102. *See also*
    Jerusalem; Jerusalem, *corpus separa-
    tum* project
Israel, law of. *See also* Israel; Jerusalem;
    Occupation, belligerent; Palestine;
    Territorial rights; *and under particu-
    lar laws*
  Bible and, 170, 209 n.18
  common law and, 167-76
  Geneva Convention IV, 1949, and, 174,
    177-81, 209 n.16
  international law and, 167-76, 206 n.3, 207
    n.7
  "basic norm" approach to, 207 n.7
  "justiciability" problem, 209 n.17
  "political" and "legal" questions in, 209
    n.17

Japan, 51

Jerusalem
  alleged Jewish annexation, 111-15, 201
    n.39, 203 n.49, 207-8 n.10
  Arab political campaign on, 1979-1980,
    208 n.10
  Arab states' territorial demand, 110
  Basic Law, 201 n.29, 207-8 n.10
  Christian, Islamic and Jewish concerns
    in, 108-10, 131, 133
  Christian rejection of territorial change,
    1971, 202 n.37
  Church of Holy Sepulchre, 202 n.37
  controversies as to, 1979-1980, 201 n.29,
    207-8 n.10
  David, as City of, 12, 14, 131
  diplomatic missions in, 204 n.57
  division of, 98-115, 131-32, 200 n.20
  East Jerusalem, territorial title in, 115-23
  functional proposals on, 109-10
  General Assembly resolutions relating to.
    See also General Assembly resolu-
    tions (particular)
    181(II), 98-101, 104
    194(III), 98-101, 104
    303(IV), 99
    2253, 104, 106, 113
    2254, 104, 106
  holy places, Israel protection of, 110-12.
    See also Holy places, protection of
  internationalization of. *See* Jerusalem,
    corpus separatum project
  Jewish custody of keys of, 200 n.21
  Jordanian annexation not censured, 111
  Jordanian seizure of, 102, 103, 105, 110,
    118. *See also* Jordan, Hashemite
    kingdom of; Territorial rights
  Jordan not a "reversioner," 105, 106, 118,
    119-21. *See also* Jordan, Hashemite
    kingdom of; Territorial rights
  legal bases of Israel title in, 105-6, 116,
    117-20
    E. Lauterpacht on, 107, 117-18
    E. V. Rostow on, 121-23
    S. Schwebel on, 120-21
  municipality, and Old City of, 111-15, 202
    n.41
    area of, 202 n.42, 203-4 n.56
  oil pressure concerning, 110
  population statistics, 131, 202 n.37, 203
    n.51
  Security Council Resolution 465 (1980)
    and, 108
  self-determination principle and, 131. *See
    also* Self-Determination claims
  sovereignty in, 131. *See also* Territorial
    rights
  "status" of, 98, 99, 101, 104, 105, 106, 113
  Temple Mount, 202 n.41

ban on Jewish access to, 202 n.41, 203 n.49
Holy of Holies, 203 n.48
territorial and functional concerns distinguished, 98-99, 108-10
territorial title, reservations of, 115
Zion and. *See* Zionism
Jerusalem, *corpus separatum* project, 125, 131-33, 194 n.23, 199, 204. *See also* General Assembly resolutions; General Assembly Resolution 181(II); Israel; Jerusalem; Jordan, Hashemite kingdom of; Territorial rights
Arab states opposition to, 202 n.36
Ben Gurion, rejection by, 100
competing "functional" proposals for, 199 nn. 5, 6, 201 n.32, 202 n.37
General Assembly disinterested in, 1950-1967, 102, 103
"status of Jerusalem," meaning of, 98-101, 104, 106, 113
Trusteeship Council draft, 99, 100, 102
"validity," "coming into operation," and "effectuation," distinguished, 194 n.23
Jerusalem, Mufti of, 58
Jewish agency, 149
Jewish national home, 14-18. *See also* aggression; Force, use of; Israel; Jews; Jordan, Hashemite kingdom of; Self-Determination claims; Zionism
Balfour Declaration, 146. *See also* Balfour Declaration
Basle Programme for, 146
self-determination and, 16
Transjordan and, 22-25
Jews. *See also* Israel; Palestine; Self-Determination claims
continuity in Palestine, 14, 137
dispersion of, 14
distribution of Ottoman lands, 10-14, 17, 125
immigration of, to Palestine, 153
national rights of, 129
Palestine National Covenant and, 12
self-determination and, 9-26, 129, 152-53
Jordan, Hashemite kingdom of, 16, 17, 126. *See also* Aggression; Force, use of; Palestine, Self-Determination claims; Territorial rights
admitted to United Nations, 200 n.19
application of law of, 172
armed bands from, 47-51
armistice agreement, 200 n.19
as barring annexation, 204 n.60
attacks on Israel, 1948, 1967, 139, 141, 194 n.24. *See also* Aggression
Bedouin population of, 24
capital punishment by, 172

exclusion of Jews by, 181
ex iniuria principle and, 51-56
Jerusalem draft statute, rejected, 102. *See also* Israel; Jerusalem
Jewish refugees from, 140
Mandated Palestine, four-fifths of, 22-25, 43
nationality policies, 187 n.29
negotiation, refusal of, after 1967, 105
as Palestinian Arab state, 22-25, 187 n.29
Palestinian population of, 24, 43
peace process and, 133
Tunis Conference and, 47
unlawful occupation by, 51-56, 127, 187 n.28
no title from, 105, 106, 116-21
West Bank and, 23, 51-56, 127, 187 n.28
reactions to annexation by, 191 n.23, 200 n.19, 202 n.38
Judah, kingdom of, 11
Judaism, 131. *See also* Israel; Jews; Zionism
Judea and Samaria (West Bank), 132. *See also* Aggression; Annexation; Balfour Declaration; Force, use of; Jews; Jordan, Hashemite kingdom of; Self-Determination rights
annexation, legal liberty of, 120-21
Arabs in, 179. *See also* Palestinian Arabs
area of, 189 n.30
capital punishment suspended in, 172
Civilian Persons Convention 1949 and. *See* Geneva Convention IV, 1949
demographic balance in, 179-81
economic development in, 179
Geneva Convention IV, 1949, art.49(6) and, 167, 177-81, 190-91 n.22. *See also* Geneva Convention IV
Jewish settlements in, 1967, 181
legality of, 179-81, 190-91 n.22
Jews in, 177-81
law applied in, 172-73
legal bases of Israel title, 105-6, 116-20
sovereignty vacuum, 117-18
mandate, continuing obligations of, 121-23
S.W. Africa opinion on, 121
names not archaic, 188-89 n.29
sovereignty in, 45-56, 115-23
West Berlin analogy, 172-73

Kelsen, H., 200 n.19, 207 n.7
Kerno, Deputy Secretary-General, 203 n.54
Khadduri, M., 199 n.6
Khartoum Summit (Sept. 1, 1967), 190 n.22
King-Crane Commission, 14, 184 n.6, 185 n.13

Landau, Deputy President, 169-70, 173, 206
    n.3, 207 nn.7-9, 209 n.16
Lausanne, Treaty of, 157
    renunciation of territories, 115, 157
Lauterpacht, E., 117-18, 195 n.4, 201 nn.30,
    35, 204 nn.60, 62
Lauterpacht, Sir Hersch, 29, 126, 193 nn.7, 8
League of Nations, 1, 18. *See also* Balfour
    Declaration; International security
    organizations; Mandate for Palestine;
    Self-Determination claims; Territo-
    rial rights
    self-determination and, 18-21
League of Nations Palestine Mandate, 9,
    12. *See also* Mandate for Palestine
Lebanon, 10. *See also* Armed bands, incur-
    sions by
    armed bands from, 46-51
    attacks on Israel, 1948, 1967, 139-41
    P.L.O. and, 47, 90-91, 198 n.35
    Syrian force in, 94
Legitimate Defense
    against armed bands, 46, 51
    1967 Middle East War, 46, 47
Lewis, Bernard, 10-12
Liberation. *See* Aggression; Self-Determina-
    tion claims; Wars of liberation

McMahon, A. Henry, 146, 147
Mallison, W. T., and S. B., 5, 58, 102-3,
    106-7, 108, 124-25, 130, 184 n.11, 192-
    93 nn. 34-35, 38, 193-94 nn.14, 19,
    20. See also *Resolutions*
    and "anti-Zionist phobia," 192-93 n.38
Mandate for Palestine 60, 132-33, 153 (text
    in Appendixes, 148-51). *See also* Bal-
    four Declaration; International Court
    of Justice; Israel; Jordan, Hashemite
    kingdom of; League of Nations; Pal-
    estine; Self-Determination claims
    border changes 1917-23, 22-25, 43, 138,
    151
    civil and religious rights of non-Jews un-
    der, 9-10, 149-52
    General Assembly and, 1947, 60,
    territorial sovereignty in, 115, 121, 122
    International Court, and self-determina-
    tion in, 18
    Jordan, excision of, from, 22-25, 43, 138,
    151
    Permanent Mandates Commission on, 181
    provisions made not applicable to Jordan,
    150-51
    United Kingdom and, 1947, 60
Mayotte. *See* Self-Determination claims,
    Comoros case
Mufti of Jerusalem, 58, 130

Namibia Advisory Opinion. *See* Interna-
    tional Court of Justice
Nazi Germany, 178-81. *See also* Geneva
    Convention IV, 1949
Necessity. *See also* Aggression; Armed
    bands, incursions by; Force, use of;
    Self-determination claims
    armed bands and, 47-51
    Y. Z. Blum, D. W. Bowett, and R. A.
    Falk on, 198 n.35
    proportionality problem, 91, 198 n.35
    and self-defense, 46-48
Negotiation, role of, 51-56, 79, 117-23, 173-
    75
New World Economic Order, 2
Non-Recognition Doctrine, 48, 204 n.59
Nuremberg Trials, 178. *See also* Nazi Ger-
    many
    and crimes against humanity, 178-81

OAPEC, 2-3, 36, 37, 51, 126-27. *See also*
    Oil weapon
Occupation, belligerent, 51-56, 107, 114,
    118, 119
    East Jerusalem and, 101-5, 118, 131, 132
    international law of, 51-56, 167-81
    Israel courts on, 172-73
    law applied in, 172
    Minquiers and Echrehos case and, 119,
    120
    "missing reversioner," 105, 106, 115-21
    1974 aggression definition on, 87-90, 92
    rights of lawful occupant, 51-56, 167-81
    uti possidetis rule, 51-53, 127
    West Berlin analogy, 172-73
Oesterreicher, J.M., 201-3 nn. 32, 37, 47
Oil Weapon, 2-3, 34-44, 74. *See also* Gen-
    eral Assembly of United Nations;
    General Assembly resolutions; Treaty
    law
    European vulnerability to, 51, 142, 143
    Japan and, 51
    Third World and, 2-4, 143
    use of, 142, 143
Omar, Mr. (Libya), 90
Opinio iuris sive necessitatis, 31-32, 35, 126
Oppenheim-Lauterpacht
    on armed bands, 47, 49, 189 n.2, 203 n.54
Orly, Major-General, 169
Ottoman Empire, 10-12, 14, 16-17, 125, 157.
    See also Balfour Declaration; Jews;
    Palestine; Self-Determination claims
Palestine, 15, 22.
    See also Balfour Declaration; Inter-
    temporal law; Jordan, Hashemite
    kingdom of; League of Nations; Man-
    date for Palestine; Palestine National

Covenant; Self-Determination claims
Arab attacks on, 1948, 1967, 139, 141
Arab entry by conquest, 7, 11, 12, 96, 137
Arab "nation" and, 48, 136
border changes 1917-23, 138
Crusaders and, 11
excision of Jordan from, 22-25, 148-51,
   185 n.20
Feisal-Weizmann agreement on, 26-27
as historic-geographic entity before 1917,
   10, 43, 186 n.26
Bernard Lewis on, 10-11
as the Jewish state, 15, 26, 27
Jews of, before Arab conquest, 137
mandate for. *See* Mandate for Palestine
modern history of, 13-18
"national" rights in, 76-77
Ottoman Empire, part of, 10
Palestine Conference, Jericho, 1948, 184
   n.3, 187 n.28
Palestine National Covenant and. *See*
   Palestine National Covenant
"part of natural Syria," 11, 184 nn.3, 6
Southern Syria and, 10, 12
Palestine Conciliation Commission, 99, 101,
   102, 103, 132, 194 n.2
Palestine Higher Arab Committee, 130
Palestine Liberation Organization. *See* P.L.O.
Palestine National Charter. *See* Palestine
   National Covenant
Palestine National Covenant, 12, 17, 25, 42,
   76, 77 (text in Appendixes, 63-65)
   art.6, 164
   art.9, 165
   art.19, 164
   claim of Jewish "invasion," 14, 17
Palestinian Arabs, 9, 10, 16, 18. *See also*
   Intertemporal law; Jordan, Hashe-
   mite kingdom of; P.L.O.; Refugees;
   Self-Determination claims
"Arab Nation" and, 28-29, 48, 57-58, 136
civil and religious rights protected under
   Mandate, 149-52, 184 n.12
Jordan as state of, 22-25, 125-26
Mallisons on. *See* Mallison, W. T. and
   S. B.
as nation, late appearance of, 12, 27-29,
   90, 125, 129
   General Assembly vote on, 28
   oil pressure concerning, 28-29
P.L.O., 11, 20, 24-25, 188 n.26
"right of return," 28, 67-69, 125, 128
Security Council Resolution 242 and, 28.
   See also Security Council
Syrian identification of, 10-11, 184 nn.3, 6
Palestinians, Committee on . . . Rights of,
   5-6, 9, 15, 17, 30-31, 56, 76, 79-81,
   91-93, 97, 100-101, 103, 107-8, 124-

25, 129, 130-32, 195 n.16, 196 n.10.
   See also other Palestine *entries*
anonymity of studies by, 5, 7
biased positions of, 56-58, 124-25, 130-
   31, 192-93 n.98
central theses of, 7-8, 38, 44, 125
consultants of, 58. *See also* Mallison,
   W. T., and S. B.
disregard of General Assembly Resolution 3314(XXIX), 80-81, 87-90
on General Assembly Resolution 181(II),
   98, 99, 100-106
on General Assembly resolutions, 126-
   27. *See also* General Assembly resolutions
Jerusalem pamphlet by, 199-200 nn.2, 3,
   nn.8-10, nn.14-16, nn.21-23
law and history, attempted rewriting by,
   33-44, 124-25, 130-31
Parkes, James, 202 n.37, 203 n.51
Partition Resolution. *See* General Assembly
   Resolution 181(II)
Peel Commission (on Palestine), 15, 16, 125,
   185 nn.18, 20
Peoples. *See also* Aggression; Force, use
   of; Self-Determination claims
as agents or targets of aggression, 83, 84,
   86-87
in non-self-governing territories, 84
Permanent Mandates Commission, 9, 15
Pfaff, R. H., 199 nn.4-5, 203 n.50, 203-4 n.6
Pictet, Jean, 179-80
Pierotti, E., 200 n.21
P.L.O. (Palestine Liberation Organization).
   See also Arab States; General Assembly of United Nations; General
   Assembly resolutions; Jordan, Hashemite kingdom of; Palestine National
   Covenant; Palestinians, Committee
   on . . . Rights of; Self-Determination
   claims
attacks on aircraft by, 188 n.26
attacks on civilians by, 188 n.26
attacks on nationals of 40 states by, 188
   n.26
destruction of Israel as goal, 20
Palestinian identity, disavowal of special,
   11
Palestinians, Jordan and, 22-25
Prieto, Mr. (Chile), 30

Rabat Conference, 24
Rao, R., 195-96 nn. 10, 27, 199 n.39
Rasoloko, Mr. (Byelorussia), 30
Refugees, 23-26, 126, 128. *See also* General
   Assembly resolutions; Palestinian
   Arabs; Return, "right" of

Refugees (*continued*)
  aftermath of Arab armed aggression, 69,
    128
  Arab and Jewish, 57-58, 128
  duties toward, 25-26, 128-29, 186-87 n.27
  Europe, management of problem in, 128,
    186-87 n.27
  General Assembly resolutions on, 68
  Jewish, from Arab States, 23-26, 126, 128,
    140
  Law of Return (Israel), 26
  Palestinian Arab, 23-26
  "right of return" of, 67, 69, 128, 186-87
    n.27
  Security Council Resolution 242 on, 28,
    69. *See also* Security Council
Requisition. *See also* Israel, law of; Occupa-
    tion, belligerent
  Geneva Convention IV, 1949, art.49(6)
    and, 167-76, 181
  limits on, 167-76
  military and civilian roles in, 175-76
  military commanders, source of authority
    of, 207 n.7
  "military requirements," test of, 167-76,
    206 n.3, 209 n.17
  relevance of "permanence" to, 206 n.3,
    208 n.12
Res nullius modo juridico, 132
Resolutions. *See under particular body, e.g.,*
    General Assembly
Resolutions (study by Mallisons), 45, 124,
    130-31, 132. *See also* General As-
    sembly of United Nations; Mallison,
    W. T., and S. B.; Palestinians, Com-
    mittee on . . . Rights of
  on General Assembly's powers over states,
    76-79
  on General Assembly resolutions, 31-33,
    45
  inaccuracies in, 62
  intertemporality and, 57-58
  Jewish refugees ignored in, 69, 128
  methods of argument in, 56-57, 62, 130
  on partition resolution (181[II]), 60, 64,
    65-66, 67
  Security Council Resolution 242 and, 69
  self-determination "law" and, 70, 72, 74,
    79-81, 93-97
Return, Law of (Israel), 26
Return, "right" of, 67-69, 125, 128. *See also*
    Israel; Jews; Palestinian Arabs; Refu-
    gees
Rosenne, S., 204 n.61
Rosenstock, Mr. (U.S.), 30, 197 nn. 16, 18
Rostow, E. V., 121-23, 205 n.73, 210 n.9

Sadat, Anwar, 46

Safed, 10
Samaria. *See* Judea and Samaria (West
    Bank)
Schreuer, C., 188 nn.13, 14
Schwarzenberger, G., 195 n.16
Schwebel, S., 21-22, 120-21, 185-86 nn.23,
    25, 197-98 nn.14, 28, 205 n.72
Security Council, 1, 26. *See also* United Na-
    tions; United Nations Charter
  magisterial powers of, 2-4
  partition resolution and, 58
  resolution 49 (1948), May 22, 1948, 154-55
  resolution 54 (1948), July 15, 1948, 155
  resolution 73 (1949), Aug. 11, 1949, 155-56
  resolution 95 (1951), Sept. 1, 1951, 157-58
  resolution 242 (1967), Nov. 22, 1967, 127,
    128, 165-66
    and refugee question, 22
    and Palestine Mandate, 22
    and territorial acquisition, 53-56, 127,
      191 n.24
  resolution 338 (1973), 188 n.24
  resolutions 242 and 338, 28, 29, 41, 42,
    51, 53-56, 79
  resolution 465 (1980), March 1, 1980, 108,
    132
  resolution 476 (1980), 192 n.27
  resolution 478 (1980), 192 n.27
Self-Determination claims, 9-26. *See also*
    Aggression; Force, use of; Wars of
    liberation; *and particular territories
    of claimant peoples*
  aggression definition and, 70-71. *See also*
    Aggression
  Arab and Jewish liberation movements,
    concurrence of, 9, 12, 13, 25-26, 57-
    58, 125-27, 129
  "Arab Asia," and Arab "State," and Jewish
    "Palestine," 13, 57-58, 129, 136
  "Arab Nation" and, 13-26, 57-58, 136
  Balfour Declaration, text, 146. *See also*
    Balfour Declaration
  Baltic peoples and, 93
  Comoros case, 94-96
  context of World War I distribution, 9-26
  Cristescu, A., on, 73
  decolonization and, 1, 10-11, 14-21
  Declaration on Friendly Relations on, 70,
    83-84
  doctrine as to, 10
    legal rule or policy?, 7, 70-74, 79-81,
      93-97
    Rao, R., on, 70, 195 n.6, 196 n.27, 199
      n.39
  Hungary and, 93
  International Court of Justice and, 18-22,
    121-23
  international law and, 7, 70-74, 86-97, 128-
    29

intertemporal dimension, 7, 57-58, 71-72, 74-75, 96-97
Israel and, 13-18, 57-58, 126-27, 129
ius cogens and, 73
Jewish, Basle Programme for, text, 146
Jordan, a Palestinian Arab State, 71, 72
Katanga and Biafra and, 94
Palestine Mandate, text, 145-51
Palestinian, against Arab States, 23-26, 71
political warfare and, 38-40, 53-56, 92-97, 126-27
problematics of, 7, 93-97
"racist," "colonialist," "imperialist" oppression and, 93-97
Resolution 2672C(XXV), Dec. 8, 1970 on, 74. *See also* General Assembly resolutions
rival national claims, 94-97
"self" in, 93-97
"struggle" for, 80-93. *See also* Aggression; Force, use of
Walloons and, 94
Western Sahara Case on, 18-21, 75
Wilson's Fourteen Points on, 11-12, 18, 57-58
Shakri, Aziz, 198 n.39
Sharrett, M., 200 n.19
Sinai, A., 201 n.32
Sórensen, M., 209 n.4
Southern Syria. *See* Palestine
South West Africa Voting Opinion, 1955, 29, 31
Soviet Union. *See also* Aggression; Force, use of; Self-Determination claims; Wars of liberation
Arab-Israel conflict, role in, 35-36
Baltic peoples in, 93
"police" action within, 86, 92
view on response proportionality, 91
General Assembly, role in, 38-40, 92-97, 127
Spain, in Western Sahara case, 20-21
Stone, Julius
Aggression and World Order (1958), 6, 183 n.3, 190 n.17, 197 n.26
Conflict Through Consensus (1977), 4, 6, 188 n.17, 192 n.28, 198 n.36, 199 n.42
Of Law and Nations (1974), 188 n.15
Legal Controls of International Conflict (1954), 6, 179, 183 n.2, 190 n.17, 200 n.19, 210 nn.8, 10
Problems Confronting Sociological Inquiries Concerning International Law (1956), 6
publications on Middle East legal problems, 183 n.5, 188 n.25, 191 n.24, 192 nn.25, 33
Suez Canal, 157-58

Syria, 133, 139, 140, 141. *See also* General Syrian Congress, 1919; Palestine

Tanaka, Judge, 31-32
Teheran, seizure of embassy and diplomats in, 37-38
Territorial integrity of states, 21-22. *See also* Aggression; Armed bands, incursions by; International law
Friendly Relations Resolution, 1970, on, 77-78, 83, 84
1974 aggression definition on, 92-93
threat to, from General Assembly usurpation, 77-81, 129
Territorial rights. *See also* Aggression; *Ex iniuria non oritur ius;* General Assembly of United Nations; General Assembly resolutions; Jerusalem (*and other particular territories*); Judea and Samaria (West Bank); Mandate for Palestine; *Uti possidetis* rule
annexation, right of. *See* Annexation
Charter, Article 2(4). *See* United Nations Charter
effect on, of Arab attacks on Israel, 45-48, 55, 63-65, 117-21, 127-28
Elon Moreh case and, 167-76, 177
Hague Rules, 207 n.8. *See also* Occupation, belligerent
international law and, 45-56, 75, 127, 171-73
legal bases of Israel title, 46-56, 105-7, 116-20, 168, 171-73
Mandates, sovereignty in, 115, 121-23
Mandate for Palestine, continuing obligations of, 121-23
"relative title" principle, 116, 117, 118-20, 205 n.70
Minquiers and Echrehos case (U.K.-France), 119-20
reversioner, "missing," and occupation law, 105, 106, 118-21, 207 n.8
S. Schwebel on, 120
Security Council Resolution 242, "inadmissibility" recital in, 53-56
sovereignty vacuum principle, 117-18
Turkey, territorial renunciation, 1923, 114
Terrorism. *See also* Aggression; Armed bands, incursions by; Force, use of; General Assembly resolutions; P.L.O.; Self-Determination claims
General Assembly Resolution 3236 and, 42, 43
Third World. *See also* Aggression; General Assembly of United Nations; OAPEC; Oil Weapon
oil dependence of, 2-4, 34, 41, 126-27, 142, 143

Third World (*continued*)
Thirlway, H.W.A., 29-30
Transjordan. *See* Jordan
Treaty law. *See also* Aggression; Force, use
    of; International law
  on coercion-induced treaties, 36-41
  material breach, effects of, 204 nn.60-61
  1969 Convention on, 36, 204 n.61
  pacta sunt servanda, as cease-fire basis,
    205 n.71
  travaux préparatoires and, 56-57
  travaux préparatoires and Security Coun-
    cil Resolution 242, 56-57
Treaty of Lausanne, 1923, 114-15
Trusteeship system. *See* Self-Determination
    claims; United Nations
Turkey, 57-58, 114-15. *See also* Ottoman
    Empire

Ulyanova, Mrs. (Ukraine), 30
United Kingdom. *See also* Balfour Declara-
    tion; Mandate for Palestine; Peel
    Commission
  commission of inquiry (Palestine), 9
  Palestine Mandate and, 60, 63
  recognition of annexation by Jordan, 191
    n.23
  view on response-proportionality, 91
United Nations. *See also* Aggression; Force,
    use of; General Assembly of United
    Nations; General Assembly resolu-
    tions; International security organi-
    zations; Palestinians. Committee on
    . . . Rights of; Security Council; Self-
    Determination claims; Territorial
    rights; United Nations Charter
  anonymous "studies" on Arab-Israel con-
    flict, 124-33
  blocs in, 1-4, 33-36, 43-44, 76-79, 126-27
  Charter of, and self-determination, 18.
    See also Self-Determination claims
  Conciliation Commission for Palestine,
    99, 101, 102, 103, 194 n.2, 132
  international stability and. *See also* Inter-
    national law; International order
  Israel, admission to membership, 156-57.
    See also Israel
  law of nations and, 3-6, 41-44, 77-81, 124-
    33
  Mediator for Palestine, 155-56
  membership in, 1-3, 19, 35
  membership in, 1-3, 19, 35
    imbalance in, 30
  Palestinian rights and, 10
    Unit on, 124-25, 130-31. *See also* Pal-
      estinians, Committee on . . . Rights
    of; Return, "Right" of

trusteeship system, 18-22
United Nations Charter. *See also* Aggres-
    sion; Force, use of; General Assembly
    of United Nations; General Assembly
    resolutions; International security
    organizations; Palestinians, Com-
    mittee on . . . Rights of; Security
    Council; Self-Determination claims;
    United Nations
  article 1, 158-59
  article 2, 7, 47, 159
  article 2(1), 42
  article 2(2), 48
  article 2(3), 48, 50
  article 2(4), 42, 48, 50, 117, 127
  article 4(2), 29, 157
  article 10, 60
  articles 12-14, 32
  article 17(2), 29, 32
  article 25, 32
  article 27, 79
  articles 33-38, 32
  article 39, 58, 117, 155, 159
  article 40, 155, 156, 159
  article 51, 50, 84, 85, 161
  chapter 7, 79, 155, 159-60
  ex iniuria principle and, 7, 40-56, 127
  ex iniuria principle, and Security Coun-
    cil Resolution 242, preamble, 53-56,
    127
  obligations under, to unrecognized state,
    48, 117, 204 n.59
United Nations Relief Works Agency
    (UNRWA), 12. *See also* Refugees
United States
  view of proportionality in response, 91
U.S. v. *Milch,* 209 n.3
Uniting for Peace System, 1
Unit on Palestinian Rights. *See* Palestinians,
    Committee on . . . Rights of
Uti possidetis rule, 78, 127

Vance, Cyrus, 190 n.22
Versailles, Peace Conference, 13, 125, 147-
    48

Wars of liberation, 21, 195 n.16. *See also*
    Aggression; Force, use of; Self-De-
    termination claims
  M. Gromyko on Jewish liberation strug-
    gle, 1948, 63-64
  selective use of, 39
  "softening" publicist doctrine on, 39-40
  Soviet, Arab, and Third World support,
    39-44

Webster, Secretary of State, 47-51
Weizmann, Chaim, 13, 147
West Bank. *See* Israel; Jordan, Hashemite
    kingdom of; Judea and Samaria; Oc-
    upation, belligerent; Palestine; Ter-
    ritorial rights
Western Sahara Advisory Opinion, 20-21.
    See also General Assembly of United
    Nations; International Court of Jus-
    tice; Intertemporal law; Self-Deter-
    mination claims
Western states
    General Assembly resolutions and, 3-4,
        34, 39-40
    dangers from, 78-81
    exposure to Arab oil pressure, 51, 142,
        143
Wilson, Woodrow, 11, 15, 18, 184-85 n.12.
    See also Self-Determination claims
Witkon, Justice, 169-70, 173, 206 nn.3, 5,
    208-9 nn.15, 16

"World Community Processes," 51, 190 n.21
Wright, Q., 189 n.7, 197 n.14

Yokota, Mr. (Japan), 30
Younger, Minister of State, 191 n.23

Zionism, 13, 125, 153. *See also* General As-
    sembly of United Nations; Intertem-
    poral law; Israel; Jerusalem; Jews;
    Self-Determination claims
Basle programme, text, 146
cooperation with "Arab" State proposed,
    13-14, 148
General Assembly resolution 3379(XXX)
    on, 35, 57
Iraq on, 40
and Israel, 48, 57
self-determination movement, preceding
    first Zionist Congress (1897), 125

MEH   O/R11OCT

STONE